For Scott,

Sixteenth Century North America

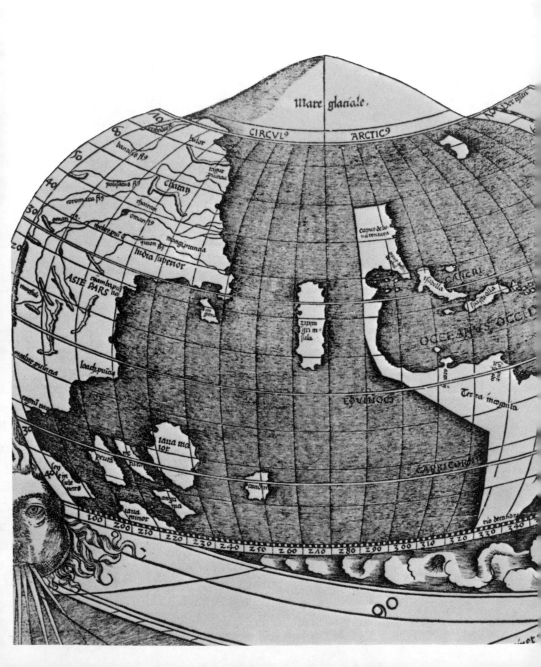

Sixteenth Century North America

The Land and the People as Seen by the Europeans

UNIVERSITY OF CALIFORNIA PRESS

BERKELEY   LOS ANGELES   LONDON

UNIVERSITY OF CALIFORNIA PRESS
BERKELEY AND LOS ANGELES, CALIFORNIA
UNIVERSITY OF CALIFORNIA PRESS, LTD.
LONDON, ENGLAND
COPYRIGHT © 1971 BY
THE REGENTS OF THE UNIVERSITY OF CALIFORNIA
FIRST PAPERBACK EDITION 1975
ISBN: 0-520-02777-9
LIBRARY OF CONGRESS CATALOG CARD NUMBER: 75-138635
DESIGNED BY W. H. SNYDER

Contents

v

Figures and Maps

Foreword

Map makers by old custom have delimited the two New World
continents at their narrowest connection, the Isthmus of Panama. Maps being of rectangular form, it was convenient to
draw the islands of the West Indies at the southeast of the
map of North America and to include them under its name.
This convention assigns to the northern continent the islands
at the southeast, and Central America and Mexico at the
southwest. This nominal allocation has little to recommend it
in land, climate, biota, or human society. Geographers have
therefore made use of a third division, Middle America, between North and South America, in part intermediate in
character but also a center of cultural origins and dispersals.
Thus reduced, North America is the continental United
States and Canada and is so considered here. It is also the
common usage of the countries to our south.

The sixteenth century is a major span of time in the historical geography of North America. European discovery began on its northeastern shores by cod fishers before Columbus
sailed on the discovery of the Indies. John Cabot landed on
the northern mainland in 1497 to claim possession for England, a year before Columbus saw the mainland of South
America. The brothers Corte Real, licensed by the King of
Portugal, explored shores about Newfoundland in 1501 and
1502. In the course of the century the Atlantic coast was
largely discovered, from the Gulf of Mexico north into Baffin
Bay, the Pacific coast as far as northern California. The interior
was explored to Tennessee, Arkansas, and Kansas. Permanent
European settlement, however, did not begin until the seven-

teenth century except for the small Spanish post at St. Augustine in Florida, a garrison rather than a colony.

The first knowledge of the nature and the people of the northern continent was taken to Europe in numerous accounts, some as official reports and some by individuals who told in books or tracts what they had seen and experienced. Some were interviewed by historians, for example by Peter Martyr, Gómara, and above all Oviedo for Spanish accounts. At mid-century Ramusio made the first great collection of voyages in Italian, in some cases only thus known. Towards the end of the century Hakluyt published the *Principal Navigations,* also the sole record of some voyages. Many reports were filed in archives to remain undisclosed until the nineteenth century or later, Spanish archives being especially rich in such documents. Spanish, French, English, Portuguese, and Italian sources hold a great deal of information on sixteenth-century North America.

Land and life as observed by these early reporters provide various and mutually supporting data to reconstruct the conditions before Europeans came to stay. They also tell of the beginnings of change by European contacts. For such an overview of what this country was I have made large use of quotations, from other languages by my translations, in English in modern spelling.

Flora and fauna of the eastern woodlands were recognized as like those in Europe. Deciduous hardwoods and pines were properly named, but not other conifers. As we still call trees red and white cedar and cypress that are not such, there was like but recognizable error. Strange plant or animal forms were so well described that we can know them as *Yucca,* pecan, persimmon, prickly pear *Opuntia,* great auk, whooping crane, turkey, opossum, walrus. The grassy buffalo plains and their hunters were portrayed true to life.

We are well informed of what was planted in the fields, how it was done, how the harvest was stored and prepared. Grapes, plums, and nuts were so carefully described that in some cases we know the particular species. Kinds of houses were described as to exterior and interior plan, their clustering, and the nature of their sites.

The composite of observations is sufficient to outline the geography as it was when the Europeans came. Mainly it appeared a land favored by nature and well inhabited by natives, differing in their usages but of good habits and presence, and hospitable.

To know the context of nature and culture it is necessary to know the routes taken by the explorations. For some, in particular those by sea, there are journals of a kind. For most there are enough data of calendar, topography, and vegetation to plot their course in fair detail. Such reconstructions have been made from time to time, with high fidelity for the Cartier, De Soto, and Cabrillo expeditions. I have used whatever I remember having seen of terrain and plant cover as I checked the excellent topographic maps that air photography has made possible. Small-scale sketch maps accompany the text or general orientation; these maps were drawn by Mrs. A. D. Morgan, cartographer of the Department of Geography at the University of California, at Berkeley.

Except for the fisheries round about Newfoundland, the European activities were motivated and carried out as parts of the greater game of power politics of that century. Four states of Atlantic Europe became engaged in a contest for world power. Northern America was involved primarily because it was thought to have a sea passage that would lead to the coveted lands of the Far East of Asia. Portugal dropped out after gaining her own route around Africa to the Indies. Spain found unknown lands of treasure in Mexico and Peru and thereby an intermediate base from which to sail across the Pacific. France sought a passage at the north and harrassed Spanish shipping to the south, as did England. The chancelleries kept themselves informed of what other states were doing; such intelligence provided important records of the progress of discovery. The expeditions were moves in the game of geopolitics, of determined objective and sequence.

France served its strategy against Spain by sending Protestants, thinking thereby to relieve as well the internal religious confrontation that led to civil war. The English venture at Roanoke also had a strategic purpose against Spain as well as the expectation of a trading and planting colony and therefore was begun by a reconnaissance of local resources.

The Spanish operations by Luna and Menéndez were countermoves against France. The earlier Spanish ones were internal contests, those of Garay and Narváez of legitimists against the self-assumed authority of Cortés, that of De Soto to restrict the domain of the Viceroyalty of New Spain.

It thus appears proper to introduce in broad outline the political background that explains where and why and in what order the explorations were undertaken.

The volunteer help of Franco Ferrario and of Sharon Vannucci is acknowledged with gratitude as is the free access to the Bancroft Library.

Part I

The Atlantic Coast as Known

to Midcentury

1
Antecedents

THE ROUND EARTH

Cosmographers taught that the earth is a globe. Idea and proof had passed from Classical Greece to western centers of learning along with knowledge of its approximate size. The world was held to be arranged in parallel belts of climatic zones from Equator to Pole. The world ocean, strewn with islands, was thought to surround the world continent of Europe, Africa, and Asia, the latter being the greatest, its southern and eastern parts known as the Indies, divided into the Near and Far Indies by the River Ganges.[1]

When the trade routes overland between Italy and India were blocked in the fifteenth century Prince Henry the Navigator set Portugal on the course of discovering a sea route to the Indies. He tried both options, that of going east by detouring around Africa and that of going west across the ocean. He colonized the Azores Islands midway across the Atlantic, taking time to stock them with domestic animals before settlers were brought from Portugal. At midcentury shiploads of Flemish colonists were introduced, with their horses and cattle, to the Azores from a distance about twice as great as that from Portugal. The Azores were occupied before the

1. The substance of this chapter is presented in different form and context in my *Northern Mists* (Berkeley, University of California Press, 1968) and *The Early Spanish Main* (Berkeley, University of California Press, 1966).

death of Prince Henry in 1460; the larger islands were by then well populated and prosperous.

Azorians were able seafarers who traded to the mainland and ranged also north and west into the ocean. Columbus heard from one of a voyage a hundred and forty leagues west of the Azores in search of the Island of Seven Cities, during which he had come in sight of Cape Clear in Ireland (1457 the inferred date). This mid-Atlantic base was the earliest outpost of exploration of the western ocean, as Portuguese scholars have maintained. Cosmographical knowledge of the time supported discovery to the west of the Azores.

Alfonso V carried on the work of his uncle Henry, though he was continually short of funds. The discoveries along the African coast passed beyond the eastward-tending Guinea coast and made a discouraging turn south. Unable to pay for western exploration from the Azores, the king gave licenses to persons of means to discover and possess at their own expense, with indifferent results. Alfonso bethought himself of the old friendship with the rich royal house of Denmark and asked King Christian I to send ships west across the northern ocean, for which he would send along a gentleman of his household, João Vaz Corte Real. Christian did so, giving command to his captains Pining and Pothorst, with Corte Real as companion. The voyage has been interpreted as going to Greenland, a neglected but not unknown part of the Danish realm. Sophus Larsen, Royal Librarian at Copenhagen, made a strong case that it reached eastern North America (*The Discovery of North America Twenty Years Before Columbus,* 1924). Corte Real after his return was appointed governor of the Island of Terceira in the Azores in April 1474, the date being secure. Twenty-six years later his sons took up exploration in the direction their father had taken.

Prince Henry had gathered the most knowledgeable mathematicians and cosmographers of the time for his instruction and advice. King Alfonso later asked an outside opinion of Paolo Toscanelli in Florence about sailing westward to the Indies. The Toscanelli letter was sent in June 1474 with assurance and arguments that the route west was preferable to the one around Africa. Toscanelli had a prestigious name, but his knowledge of the size of the earth was greatly in error and must have been thus noted by the scholars in Lisbon. His gross shrinkage of our globe was bad cosmography, as was his pretended location of an Island of Seven Cities sought by Portuguese nagivators. Portuguese ships continued their slow progress south along the coast of Africa, finding fair profit in trade. In 1488 Bartolomeu Días returned to Lisbon with the news that he had rounded the southern end of that continent and thereby ended the interest of the Portuguese Crown in an alternate western route.

Columbus spent years in Portuguese ports collecting items and tales of what lay in or beyond the western sea. There are large blanks in his life before 1484 and 1485 when he was heard at Lisbon by King João II about the plan to sail west to the Indies. What he presented was in substance what Toscanelli had written ten years before to the Portuguese crown, in particular the erroneous reduction of the size of the earth and the place geography of Marco Polo.[2] He was listened to courteously as he proposed again a plan that had been examined and found unacceptable. Columbus then took his project to Spain and in the end gained its acceptance by Queen Isabela in 1492, returning at Easter 1493 to announce the discovery of the Indies. A second voyage added the discovery of the Leeward Islands, Puerto Rico, and Jamaica (1493–1494).

JOHN CABOT AND BRISTOL MEN
CROSS THE NORTHERN ATLANTIC

The familiar account of John Cabot's landing in North America in 1497, the year before Columbus dropped anchor in the South American Gulf of Paria, has lately been greatly revised to give major and earlier credit to seafarers from Bristol.[3] John Cabot, like Columbus a Genoese, had engaged in Venetian trade with the Near East, perhaps visiting Mecca. He

2. Angel de Altolaguirre, *Cristobal Colón y Pablo del Pozzo Toscanelli* (Madrid, 1908), a calm and learned study of a subject that still is emotionally laden.

3. The principal revision is by finding a misfiled secret document, a 1497–98 report to the Grand Admiral of Spain by John Day, an English agent in Spain, published by L. H. Vigneras in the *Hispanic-American Historical Review*, 1956 (pp. 503–509), and translated in my *Northern Mists*. James A. Williamson, *The Cabot Voyages and Bristol Discovery*, exhaustively documented, takes the place of the prior Cabot literature. Professor David Quinn presented the "Argument for the English Discovery of America between 1480 and 1494" in the *Geographical Journal* of September 1961.

may have lived in Spain at Cartagena before moving to England around 1495. In middle age and of small means, he brought a world map and a solid globe of his own making to promote his project of a sea route from England to the Spice Islands. The Portuguese at the time were in the Indian Ocean but had not yet reached India. The islands discovered by Columbus were not those of the splendor of the Orient. England was prosperous, had good ships, experienced seamen, and merchants trading abroad. Cabot proposed to them and to King Henry VII another trade route, west from England to northern Asia and thence southwest to the lands of spices and other precious goods.

The plan was not a shot in the dark. Cabot came to England with his family and possessions to settle at Bristol, the English port long established in commerce to Madeira and Iceland, and of best knowledge of the western sea. Bristol provided ship and crew for his first two voyages, made in 1496 and 1497. Cabot had no experience of Atlantic waters, but Bristol ships had been going west, perhaps since 1480, fishing across the sea, and had discovered "the island of Brasil," the Irish legendary name of a western land. The John Day letter saying that the Brasil "found in other times" was in fact mainland is supplemented by other items (Williamson and Quinn). Bristol seamen took Cabot on the first unsuccessful voyage in 1496, and again in May 1497 in a bark with a score of men that made the crossing in five weeks.

The Cabot voyage of 1497 took possession of the discovered land for the Crown of England at the first sighting of land (about June 24) and then turned east and north without further landing, continuing thus for about a month, before leaving the coast from the "cape nearest Ireland" for a fast return in fifteen days to British shores. The landing and act of possession thus would have been on the coast of northern New England, the return crossing from Cape Race. At the place of their landing "they found large trees from which masts were made" and evidence that the land was inhabited, but had no sight of people. Later they saw two persons running on land and found the water "full of stockfish [cod] such as are taken in Iceland" (Day). Cabot gave the name Seven Cities to the new country, for the legendary island of the western sea in the me..ieval lore of Spain and Portugal.

On his return Cabot was received with acclaim at court and by the merchants of Bristol and London. Soncino, the Milanese ambassador, reported in December 1497: "Messer Zoane [John Cabot] has his mind set upon even greater things, because he proposes to keep [west] along the coast from the place at which he landed, more and more to the [Far] East, until he reaches an island which he calls Cipango [Japan], situated in the equinoctial region, where he believes that all the spices of the world have their origin as well as the jewels. . . . He tells all this in such a way, and makes everything so plain, that I also feel compelled to believe him," adding that the King of England had thus gained a part of Asia without a stroke of the sword. Cabot's eloquence persuaded London that a western coast to which Bristol ships had been going for some time would lead to the Indies of spices and treasure. The word was sent to Italy by several channels and the Spanish Admiralty secured a detailed report from John Day. It was thought that Cabot had found a northeastern extension of Asia, from which the coast could be followed southwest to the tropical spice lands. Like Columbus, Cabot was unaware that he had come to the New World.

Cabot sailed anew from Bristol in May 1498 with five good ships, well manned and laden with goods of London and Bristol merchants to be traded for precious articles from the Orient. One storm-battered ship got back to an Irish port, the others were not heard of again. With the disappearance of Cabot, followed shortly by the death of Henry VII, English interest in gaining its own route to the Far East lapsed. The Bristol seamen who had taken Cabot to a North American coast continued to visit it yearly in the codfish trade, but the records are silent.

THE MAP OF JUAN DE LA COSA (1500)

Juan de la Cosa, most experienced of Spanish navigators, was commissioned in 1500 to draw a world map for official use. This earliest outline of the western shores of the as yet unidentified Atlantic Ocean was made in the summer and fall of 1500 at Puerto de Santa Maria on the Bay of Cádiz (fig. 1). The affairs of the Indies, discovered and governed by Columbus, had gone badly; Bobadilla had been named to take charge there in 1499, the removal and arrest of Columbus taking place in August 1500. The Cosa map was information needed for the redirection of Spanish colonial plans.

Juan de la Cosa had rented his ship, *Santa Maria,* for the discovery voyage of Columbus and went along as shipmaster. He accompanied the second voyage as chart maker, in which he signed the avowal demanded by Columbus that Cuba was part of the Asiatic mainland. His 1500 map, however, showed Cuba as an island, in pretty fair outline, the first such representation. The islands of the West Indies are reasonably well located by its own observations.

Four voyages of discovery were licensed in 1499 as moves against the large rights that had been given Columbus. All four were sent to explore the inferred southern mainland on which Columbus had touched briefly in 1498. Cosa was chief pilot of the Hojeda expedition that coasted the northern shores of South America from Guiana (Guayana) west to the peninsula of Goajira (Guajira in Colombia) and mapped that long stretch of coast. Other parties sailed hundreds of miles to the southeast beyond the Equator and the mouth of the Amazon River. All were back in Spain by the summer of 1500 with proof of a southern continent and of great rivers, another *tierra firme,* henceforth thus called. One of the ship captains, Amerigo Vespucci of the Florentine intelligentsia, made celestial observations of longitude that were close to reality. On the Cosa map the eastern tip of the continent (the shoulder of Brazil) is shown as being on the meridian of the Azores, only four degrees off true position. In one year these so-called "minor voyages" had established the existence and position of South America, though that name was given later.

Juan de la Cosa also drew the outlines of a northern mainland west of the British Isles, marked by the standards of England as of its possession, the sea adjacent named *mar descubierto por yngleses,* and a score of place names entered along the coast, the westernmost entry *cabo descubierto,* the most eastern *cabo de ynglatierra.* It was not known until the John Day letter was found that the Cabot discovery, landing, and act of possession took place at the west nor that Cabot had then turned east along the coast to Cape Race from which he returned to the British Isles. Earlier versions of the Cabot voyage, such as that of Henry Harrisse, missed the meaning of these two entries of capes on the Cosa map, and reversed the

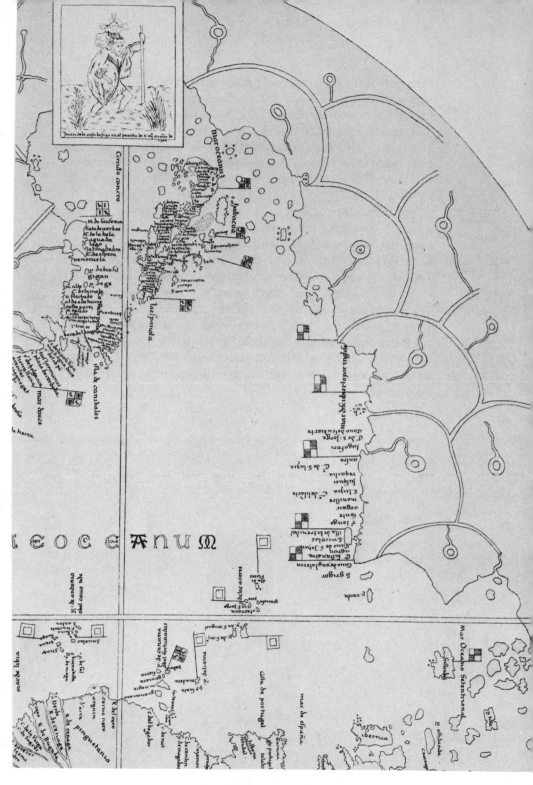

FIG. 1. The northern Atlantic of Juan de la Cosa (1500). From the atlas *Die Entdecklung Amerika* by Konrad Kretschmer, 1892.

direction of the Cabot coastal exploration. The John Day letter was written before Cabot left on his last voyage in the spring of 1498, was in possession of the Spanish Admiralty by then, and served Juan de la Cosa for the design of his map in 1500. It explains also the instructions Hojeda received to proceed west beyond the known coast (eastern Colombia) in order to block English advance from the north, the Cabot expedition that was lost.

The Cosa map did not commit itself as to whether the southern and northern mainlands were joined. That this was surmised is suggested by the instructions given to Hojeda. Cosa drew a continuous coastline southwest from the sea of English discovery to a narrow passage of the ocean sea between Cuba and the mainland that resembles the Bahama Channel. Farther west a framed vignette of St. Christopher occupied the place of the Gulf of Mexico, suggesting that if it were removed northern and southern mainland might be seen to meet. The map was made for official and secret use, and did not come to public attention until the nineteenth century, when Humboldt studied it.

2
Early
Sixteenth Century
(1501-1518)

Fishermen left few records. Few could write and they had little about which to write, not being given to lawsuits or to asking for privileges. The agreement by which they associated themselves at sea was by custom, as was their sharing of fishing grounds. The seas were free to all to fish, fishermen of different nationalities mingling amicably in pursuit of their trade. Territorial rights of nation states were not exercised beyond land, and fishermen at sea were little concerned with national rivalries.

The earlier commercial fisheries of the northern Atlantic waters were mainly of herring and mackerel, taken by nets in the North and Norwegian seas and marketed abroad by Hansard merchants. The origins of the trade in salt cod, known as stockfish or *bacalao,* are obscure. Cod and its relatives are game fish of cold waters, and were taken by hook and line as they moved in great schools to feeding grounds in shoal waters. Bristol entered into competition with the Hanse for fish taken off Iceland early in the fifteenth century and thereby became a market of some importance for stockfish as well as for herring. In the latter part of the century, as has been noted, Bristol ships visited, perhaps annually, the greatly productive cold waters off northern American shores, the mainland first known by the Irish name of Brasil. By present information Bristol fishermen discovered these greatest cod waters.

Breton traditions have claimed an earlier discovery, unproven and suspect because it was advanced by the French crown. Breton cod fishers did take part early and actively in American cod fishing. Philip I of Spain became concerned that Portuguese, namely the Corte Real brothers, might be trespassing to the west of the Tordesillas line of demarcation into territory reserved to Spain. The concern was about land rights, not about fishing. Philip I therefore licensed a Spanish expedition (undated; Philip died in 1506) to one Juan de Agramonte to check on the location of this new land. He was to go to Brittany to get pilots who knew the way there.

In 1506 the Portuguese Crown imposed a tax in its northern ports on cod brought from Terra Nova, the name used for the land found by the Corte Real voyages of 1501 and 1502. It does not follow that the Portuguese commerce in cod resulted from these later voyages, which did not sail from nor return to those north Portuguese ports. Fishing in Portuguese home waters was a simple matter of small boats and nets, going out overnight, as anchovies and tunny still are fished. Cod are found in waters distant from Portugal, those of Iceland being of early fame. The *bacalhao* fishery, as it is known in Portugal, required cargo ships that stayed at sea for months, carried small rowboats for fishing by hook and line, and had room where the catch could be dressed, salted, and stored. This mode of fishing is still characteristic of the Portuguese ports named in 1506. It is unlikely that such a different kind of fishing, gear, and ship, the necessary working capital, and the establishment of a market could have taken place in the short time after the Corte Real voyages.[1]

During the course of the century fishing fleets from Brittany, Normandy, Biscayan ports of France and Spain, and Portugal sailed annually to American waters of the "new land," as it continued to be called; English participation was perhaps minimal until midcentury. The fleets landed for water, wood, rest, and to dry fish, not to lay claim to land. Bacalao became a major staple of commerce throughout the Mediterranean countries, being less expensive than meat, and preferred to other fish. The demand was large, as more than a third of the

1. Reference in *Northern Mists,* chapters 3 and 4.

days in Catholic lands were meatless. Salt cod was the one great product of extratropical North America, but since it had nothing to do with national rivalries and very little with exploration of the New World, it received little attention.

THE LAND OF CORTE REAL
AND THE LAND OF LABRADOR

The sons of João Vaz Corte Real took up the northern route of the Danish voyage on which their father had gone. They were young, rich, privileged members of the royal household, and surely knew stories of the north from fishermen of the Azores. The record begins with the license to Gaspar in 1500. The King acknowledged that Gaspar in the past had sought islands and mainland at his own large expense and at the danger of his person and therefore approved that he continue. There is no explanation of this prior endeavor; it may have been a venture from the Azores. Gaspar sailed north in the spring of 1500, got into ice floes, sighted mountains, probably the east coast of Greenland, and turned back.

In 1501 he and his brother Miguel took three ships northwest and explored the coast of Newfoundland, perhaps also that of Nova Scotia.[2] Miguel was sent back with two ships, Gaspar remaining for further exploration. The two ships that returned to Lisbon were visited by the Italians Alberto Cantino and Pietro Pasqualigo, whose reports tell most of what is known. The ships brought back several score of natives, male and female, described in attentive detail. They were Indians, not Eskimos, and are thought to have been Beothuks, inhabitants of Newfoundland. The Italian letters told of a coasting of land for six hundred miles, the sighting of many large rivers, and abundance of pine timber suited for masts and spars, indicating that the coast was explored well to the south of Newfoundland. In 1502 Cantino had a Portuguese map copied on which *Terra del Rey de Portuguall* is shown as a great northern island covered with fantastically tall trees.[3]

2. Biggar, *Precursors;* also *Northern Mists.*
3. The map has been reproduced many times, as in part in the Paullin-Wright *Atlas of the Historical Geography of the United States* (1932). The Corte Real discovery is misplaced to midocean so as to put it on the east (Portuguese) side of the Tordesillas meridian of demarcation, which is clearly drawn. Perhaps this explains why Philip I wanted to send a Spanish expedition to find out its true location. See Isa Adonias, *A*

Pasqualigo surmised that the coast extended south to the newly discovered parrot land (Cabral's landing in Brazil), an early adumbration of the New World north and south. King Manuel was pleased by the prospect of another source of slaves and ship timber.

Gaspar and his ship failing to return, Miguel went in search in 1502 with three ships. He sent two ships back, remained to continue the search, and also failed to return. A third brother wanted to take up the search in 1503 but was restrained by the King, who dispatched two armed ships that found no trace of the lost ships. Biggar, who examined the records closely, thought the separation of the ships took place in Placentia Bay of southern Newfoundland, and that both Corte Real brothers might have gone into the Gulf of St. Lawrence.

From the time of Prince Henry, the Portuguese paid attention to the western sea and were interested in what lay beyond. The brothers Corte Real were almost the last of that tradition. Each sent back two ships while he kept on into the unknown. Both sailed northwest, as their father had, into high latitudes. Awareness of a northwestern mainland, vague and unnamed, was emerging. As their father and others had sought a western passage to the Orient, so would they. Such, I think, is the meaning of their repeated voyages. Vasco da Gama returned from India to Lisbon in September 1499, Cabral in 1502, giving King Manuel the long sought seaway around Africa to India. Cabral also had taken nominal possession of the land of Santa Cruz, later called Brazil, which might bring profit of tropical goods. There was nothing to be gained by putting further effort into the bleak seas to the northwest.

The Isle of Brasil or the Seven Cities of John Cabot became the New Land, the land of Bacalao or of Corte Real to cartographers who placed it below Labrador in latitude—a first approximation of Newfoundland, Nova Scotia, and part of New England.

The name Labrador began to appear on maps around 1502 as the most northerly part of the mainland.[4] An Azorian, João

Cartografia da Região Amazonica (Rio de Janeiro, 1963), pp. 5–20, for a late study and bibliography, utilizing a publication by Jaime Cortesão (Rio de Janeiro, 1945), which I have not seen. The Government of Portugal published in 1960 *Portugaliae Monumenta Cartographica* in six volumes by Armando Cortesão and Avelimo Teixeira da Mota, with the best informed text and reproductions, including the Cantino Planisphere (referred to as *Port. Mon. Cart.*).

4. Fuller statement in *Northern Mists*, pp. 43–46.

Fernandes, with the by-name *Lavrador,* had moved to Bristol in 1500. He was a person of substance in the Azores, had asked and received license from King Manuel for a voyage of discovery, but instead emigrated to England. The reason suggested is that the Corte Real brothers, who were favorites at court and wealthy, were engaging in a similar venture with which an islander of lesser means and status could not compete. Portuguese scholars have presented data in support of a prior long voyage of exploration by Fernandes, thought to have begun in 1492, which others have strongly denied. At any rate Fernandes had knowledge and plans which he took to Bristol.

In March 1501 King Henry VII gave letters patent for discovery to six men of Bristol, three of whom were "Esquires of the islands of the Azores," one being John Fernandes. They were given authority to go to any sea thus far unknown to Christians, including the Arctic. The Newfoundland region being well known to Bristol and continental fishing crews, a direction of exploration to the north of Newfoundland is indicated. Two voyages appear to have been made promptly, one bringing falcons, the arctic falcons having a high price, the other returning with three savages, presumably Eskimos. Additional letters by King Henry were given at the end of 1502 which included two of the Azorians previously named but not Fernandes, of whom there is no further mention. A partnership, including Fernandes and perhaps by his initiative, had been formed at Bristol to carry on exploration along the coast called Labrador. That the land came to be known by his nickname after 1502 suggests that he may have been lost there at that time. Labrador is the oldest geographic name north of the West Indies that has persisted.[5] The cold, bleak, and fog-ridden coast of Labrador would hardly have attracted merchant capital of Bristol. Was the objective again the western passage, sought by Fernandes to the north at the same time that the Corte Real search was made to the south?

THE NEW WORLD CALLED AMERICA

In 1507 a group of scholars at St. Dié in the Vosges Mountains brought out a new geography. The humanists there

5. Cape Breton and a number of coastal names of southeast Newfoundland have been proposed as deriving from earlier fishing or from Corte Real.

associated as the Gymnasium Vosagense were occupied in fashioning a system of geography that would take into account the newly available knowledge of the world. The Duke of Lorraine was their patron, and his canon, Walter Ludd, was the organizer and administrator of the institute, which consisted of scholars, draftsmen, wood engravers, and printers. The best-known member of its staff was Martin Waldseemüller (Hylacomylus) who had studied at the University of Freiburg and was largely concerned with printing and publishing, which was a main objective of the association.

The three publications of 1507 were a large map of the world usually known as the "Waldseemüller," a small globe, and the volume *Cosmographiae Introductio,* of which there were two editions in that year, each of the three a notable contribution. The world map (sections in figs. 2, 3, and 4) was printed from twelve wood blocks and measured eight by four and a half feet, a coniform projection framed in a decorative border with insets of an eastern and a western hemisphere. A monumental achievement of the art of woodcut and printing, it is memorable also in its use of projections. By using a grid of meridians and of parallels of latitude the cartographers committed themselves to assigning a coordinate position to every place entered. Their information was slight. The earth being divided into 360 degrees of circumference, the data plotted left only about twenty degrees of longitude between Africa and the newly known continent to the west (fig. 2). This was getting close to the reality of longitude, east-west distance, and implied that the mainland of Spanish discovery was removed by half the circumference of the globe from the true Indies and so was a new continent in the western hemisphere. A thousand or more copies of the great map were made; only one is known to have been preserved.[6]

The three St. Dié maps—the great map, its hemisphere inserts, and the gores of the globe—differ in many particulars, having been designed and drawn by various hands. Only the globe carried the name AMERICA and it was entered only on the southern continent. All three maps show two continents west of Europe and Africa and far to the east of Asia, the

6. It was found by Joseph Fischer at Burg Wolfegg in Württemberg. He and Franz von Wieser published a facsimile with a memoir on the St. Dié school of map makers (Innsbruck, 1903). On occasion of its fourth centenary in 1907 the United States Catholic Historical Society issued a facsimile with introductory text by Fischer and Wieser.

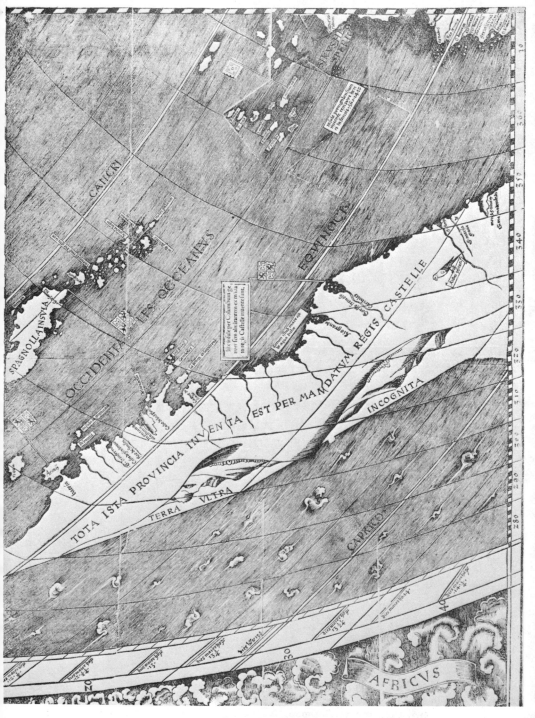

FIG. 2. Excerpt from the St. Dié map of 1507 by Martin Waldsee-müller showing the narrow ocean between Africa and the New World (Josef Fischer and Franz v. Wieser, *Die älteste Karte mit dem Namen Amerika aus dem Jahre 1507*, Innsbruck, 1903).

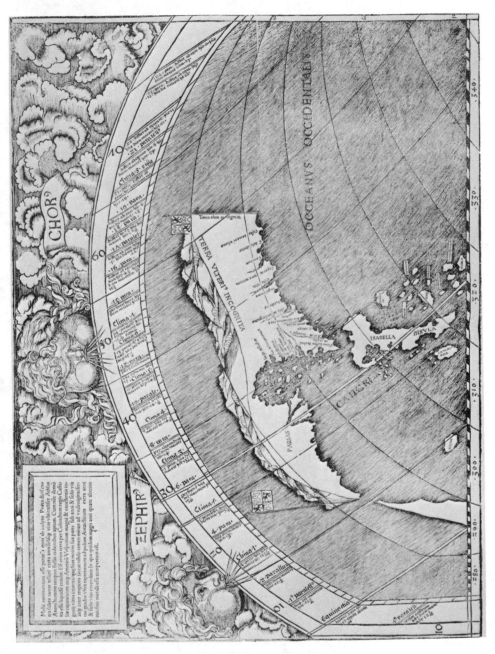

FIG. 3. Excerpt from the St. Dié map (1507) of the northern part of the New World.

Fig. 4. Inset from the St. Dié map showing the New World as a continuous mainland from 50°N to 40°S latitude.

southern one of known long coastline and the northern one as but little known. Their western limits being wholly unknown, a more or less meridional line was drawn at the west that narrowed both continents greatly, especially the northern one. On the large map (fig. 3) and on the globe the two mainlands are separated by a strait; on the vignette of the western hemisphere (fig. 4) they are connected. The question was asked, the answer was left open.

To the northern continent a large peninsula was attached north of the island of Isabela (Cuba), indicating some early knowledge of Florida, and also of the gulf to the west (Gulf of Mexico) (figs. 3, 4). The east coast was continued to 50° N. latitude, with names of capes and coasts of unknown Spanish origin at the south and perhaps of Portuguese derivation at the north. At 50° N. the continent was truncated by a transverse line with the label *terra ultra incognita* to signify the northern limit of known land. On the great map the standard of Castile and León was planted at the northwest extremity and again at the southern tip of the inferred northern continent, at the putative strait between the two continents. The anonymous map maker thus was awarding North America to Spain at a time when the Spanish Crown admitted ignorance of the north. The source of the misinformation is not known. Possibly there was none, the assignment of the northern continent to Spain made because it was west of the Tordesillas line of demarcation.

All three maps agreed on a girdle of ocean all about the north. On the large map it is shown as open water north to the Arctic Circle, beyond it a frozen *mar glaciale* to the pole. A sea passage west from Europe to the Far East was thus inferred to the north of 50° N. latitude. The universal ocean was accepted, shown as continuous about the North Pole and divided to the south by the newly known mainland. The New World was given a fair location and preliminary outline within a hemisphere west of Europe and Africa and east of Asia.

The appendix to the widely circulated cosmography is an account of four voyages of Vespucci to the New World, the first two for King Ferdinand of Spain, the other two for King Manuel of Portugal, ranging from 1497 to 1503 or 1504. This account made Vespucci the principal discoverer. In it Vespucci boasted of having been the discoverer in 1497 of a tropical mainland far to the west, with a coast that would have extended to the far side of the Gulf of Mexico. The geographers of St. Dié credited Columbus on the large map with the discovery of the West Indies, Vespucci being the other discoverer of great and excellent ingenuity. Since Columbus insisted to the last that he had found the true Indies whereas Vespucci did know better and had made voyages of discovery along the new mainland, the scholars at St. Dié thought it fitting to name the new continent America. In their Vosges town, remote from the centers of information, they had been taken in by a spurious account.

The discoveries of strange lands overseas were of great interest to the literate public in western Europe. The young craft of printing was quick to provide such reading matter, in Latin for the learned, in the native language for the public. A letter of Columbus was printed in 1493 in several places and languages. Ten years later letters of Vespucci came into the hands of Italian printers, to pass from one to another in a score of editions and spread his fame through Italy, the German empire, France, and beyond. Printers published without permission of the author, his knowledge, or credit of his name in the text. Peter Martyr thus complained that private letters of his had been printed and dispersed throughout Christendom in the so-called Libretto printed in Venice in 1504, a literary piracy against which there was no defense. The same thing happened to Vespucci's letters.

Vespucci represented a Florentine firm in Sevilla that provided one or more ships to the Hojeda expedition of 1499–1500, in which he took part. In 1501 he made an exploration for Portugal south along the coast that later was called Brazil. On the Spanish voyage he carried out astronomical observations that gave a near approximation of longitude. The Portuguese voyage was made to find out what land lay on their side of the Line of Demarcation. Vespucci wrote about both voyages to his friend Lorenzo di Pier Francesco de Medici in Florence. Probably after the death of the latter the letters came into the hands of a printer and were published in numerous versions (1503 and later). They are important documents, including the first serious consideration of longitude.

In the fall of 1504 a long letter was printed in Italy purportedly by Vespucci to Soderini, then gonfalonier of Florence. It added two more voyages. The first was claimed as having been made for Spain in 1497, extending far west along coasts verdant and tropical, populated by naked and friendly savages skilled in the use of bow and arrow. (By the distances given it would have run out the south coast of the Caribbean Sea to its western end and continued greatly beyond.) The voyage described is impossible as to direction, distance, vegetation, and native cultures. It comprised the major part of the letter, florid in style and incidents. The second and third voyages were in substance those related to his Medici friend and previously printed. The fourth was another voyage for Portugal farther south along the coast of Brazil, which did take place. The Soderini letter, in French translation, reached the St. Dié group, was accepted and incorporated into their cosmography, and gave the idea of naming the New World America.

The protest began with Las Casas, who was angered by what he thought was an attempt by Vespucci to rob Columbus of credit and therefore charged Vespucci with fraud. He was followed by Herrera, the earlier part of whose history was little more than a copy of Las Casas. Later historians—Charlevoix, Robertson, Fernández de Navarrete—regarded Vespucci as a fraudulent pretender. There were early scholars, such as Hondius, Cluverius, and Léry, who thought otherwise. In the early nineteenth century Humboldt, knowing Vespucci's competence as navigator and his service as the first Pilot Major of Spain, held him guiltless of fraud. Later Henry Harrisse concluded after long study that there was "not a particle of evidence, direct or indirect, implicating Amerigo Vespucci in an attempt to foist his name on the continent."

This is also the judgment of later inquiries.[7] The Soderini letter that damaged Vespucci's reputation is held to have been concocted by a printer and written in language not used by a well-educated Florentine. Printers (and map makers) took whatever liberties they wished. Invented or legendary islands decorated the seas; the names of known explorers sold books. Vespucci left off seafaring, was made a citizen of Spain in 1505, a consultant in marine matters, appointed to the office in charge of navigation in 1508, and worked quietly thus to his death in 1512. He sought no publicity, had been a friend of Columbus (who died in 1506), and could do nothing about

7. Alberto Magnaghi, *Amerigo Vespucci, Studio Critico* (1926); Frederick Pohl, *Amerigo Vespucci, Pilot Major* (1944); Robert Levillier, *America la Bien Llamada* (1948).

the publications attributed to himself, if indeed he knew about them.

Ten years after the disappearance of John Cabot his son Sebastian promoted another try for a western passage to the Orient. This was to be in the manner shown by the maps and cosmography of St. Dié, by an open sea to the north of 50° and south of the Arctic Circle. Whether Sebastian knew the works of the St. Dié school is not of record. The notion held by his father that the mainland west of Britain was Asia was outdated. In its stead awareness of a northern large mainland indicated that the sea passage should be sought to its north, farther north than the Corte Real brothers and *el Labrador* had gone.

No English documents are known authorizing or reporting the voyage, which was made in 1508 or 1509 and reported in later years, at second or third hand, when Sebastian's reputation for frankness, truthfulness, or recall was questionable. James Williamson, in *The Cabot Voyages,* has collected the data and done the critical synthesis.

An undated map by Cabot was reported as existing in England in 1577, which showed a strait between 61° and 64° N. latitude as continuing west for about ten degrees of longitude.[8] This has been construed as the discovery and probably the passage of Hudson Strait, forgotten until Hendrik Hudson sailed through it in 1610.

Sebastian left England in 1512 to enter Spanish services, and did not return to England until 1548, dying about 1557. Peter Martyr knew him in Spain and wrote what he had been told by Sebastian in his *Third Decade* in 1515, and again in the *Seventh Decade* in 1524. The account was that Cabot, having crossed to the western land, met such drift of ice in July as to oblige him to turn from a northern to a western course. (At that time of year icebergs in great number ride the Labrador Current south out of Davis Strait. The ships were inferred to have gotten through or around them into the open water of Hudson Strait.) Nothing was said of the nature of land or life until the ships were on their return, when great numbers of

8. Hakluyt Society, 2nd Series, vol. 120.

cod were encountered, being fished by bears. Peter Martyr was told that Sebastian had discovered the land Bacalaos and thus named it, because the fish was so called by the natives. Thus a double whopper; the land of the great cod fishery was well known and the name given the fish was European. Peter Martyr was told further that Cabot followed the coast south almost to the latitude of Gibraltar (which is that of Chesapeake Bay). No mention was made of anything seen. It is doubtful that Cabot made such a coasting of Atlantic shores.

López de Gómara gave much the same story in his *Historia General de las Indias,* published in 1552. The section entitled *Bacallaos* is as follows:

There is a great stretch of land and coast which they call Bacallaos, extending to forty eight and a half degrees [N. latitude]. Those living there call a large fish bacallao, of which there are so many that they impede the ships in sailing. Bears go into the sea to fish and eat them. The person who is best informed about this land is Sebastian Cabot, a Venetian. He equipped two ships in England, where he lived from childhood at the costs of King Henry VII, who was desirous of trading with the spice lands as the King of Portugal was doing. Others say that he, Cabot, did so at his own cost and promised King Henry to go by way of the north to Cathay and bring spices thence in less time than the Portuguese did by the south; he went also to find out the disposition of the Indies for settlement. He took three hundred men and went by way of Iceland to the cape of Labrador and so on to fifty-eight degrees although he says much farther [north], relating how there was such cold and masses of ice in the month of July that he dared not go on. Also that the days were extremely long and almost without night, and the nights very clear. It is certain that at sixty degrees there are days of eighteen hours. Thereupon Cabot seeing the coldness and strangeness of the land, turned about to the west. Making repairs in the Bacallaos, he followed the coast to thirty-eight degrees and returned thence to England.

Both Peter Martyr and Gómara had about the same story from Sebastian, repeated over a span of thirty years. The few recognizable details may perhaps be fitted into an exploration of Hudson Strait. He did try to find a sea passage to the Far East in 1526, when he took Spanish ships to the La Plata estuary. After his return to England he was a sponsor of a search for a northeast passage that led to the formation of the Muscovy Company. Notorious for seeking publicity in his own interest, it is strange that there are no English records of exploration by him of a northwest passage, in which King Henry VII was said to have been concerned.

THE SPANISH INDIES (1502–1517)

Early Notice of Florida

From the founding of Isabela by Columbus in 1493 through 1508 Spanish settlement was limited to Española (the island of Haiti). Ships came from Spain by the southern route, following the trade winds by way of the Canary and Leeward Islands, and returned bearing north to have the benefit of westerly winds. On the north coasts of Haiti and Cuba they encountered a very strong westward set of current and wind, in crossing which they were borne to west of their intended northerly course. That this did happen is suggested by maps that give early notice of the mainland (Florida).[9]

Alberto Cantino, the Italian agent who reported the return of the Corte Real ships to Lisbon (1501), procured a copy of a Portuguese map (1502), which is known by his name. It is less well informed about the West Indies islands than the map of Juan de la Cosa but better as to the mainland northwest of Cuba (fig. 5), which is drawn as a wedge-shaped peninsula pointing toward Cuba, confirming the Cosa map that Cuba was known to be an island. The Cantino map is the earliest known representation of Florida and Florida Strait. A dozen place names, mostly of capes and rivers, are entered about the peninsula. They are Spanish, with errors in copying. From west to east there is a *rio de las palmas, cabo de martires, rio de las almadias,* and *rio de lagartos.* This is the first record of the Florida Keys, known in Spanish as *Los Martires. Lagarto* was the early Spanish name for any crocodilian; it is retained as alligator in English. *Almadia,* a Spanish-Arabic word, was used at first for the dugout boats of the island natives, but was soon replaced by the native name *canoa.* Some lost Spanish map gave information about Florida to the map office at Lisbon, where an Italian agent secured a copy of the secret document.

9. The 1511 first edition of Peter Martyr's *Decades* has a crude woodcut map with the two peninsulas (Yucatán and Florida, unnamed) and the earliest named representation of Bermuda.

R. A. Skelton on maps of the period, with reproductions, Appendix to Williamson's *Cabot.*

Expansion from Española

In 1509 Spanish occupation was extended from Española to Puerto Rico, Jamaica, and the Gulf of Darién. The gold placers that had supported Española were in decline, in part because they worked out, largely because the forced native labor was about used up. The formerly greatly populous island was far advanced toward the extinction of its natives, which took another decade. To replenish the failing labor force King Ferdinand gave orders in 1509 that as many Indians as could be taken could be brought from the "useless islands," meaning such as lacked gold or did not provide food. The Carib islands, to the south, that were inhabited by stout fighters were passed up by slave hunters, while the peaceful Arawak islanders were harried from the Bahamas to Barbados, Curaçao, and Aruba. The Arawaks of the Bahamas, called Lucayos, lived on many small islands without interior place of refuge and were almost wholly removed by 1513, the emptied islands being of no further interest. Velázquez went from Española to occupy Cuba in 1511 and, finding profitable gold placers there, used up most of its natives in ten years.

Ponce de León to Florida

Juan Ponce de León was a leading citizen of Higuey, the fertile limestone country of eastern Española, productive of food but lacking gold, which was found in mountain streams of the interior. His Indians told him that the stuff so prized by the white men was to be found also in streams of the neighbor island, Boriquen, first known as San Juan (Puerto Rico). He went to see, found it true, and got himself appointed to govern the island of San Juan in 1509. The new placers were handsomely productive and made Ponce de León one of the rich men of the Indies by 1512. By that time placers and natives were in sharp decline in Puerto Rico and Ponce was ready to look for wealth elsewhere. Velázquez, meanwhile, had struck it rich in Cuba; Jamaica was under Spanish occupation; he would try in or beyond the islands to the north from which Indians had been brought to Puerto Rico. King Ferdinand granted the license readily. At his own expense Ponce de León was given the right (1512) for three years "to discover and settle the island of Bimini." Ponce had not been to the northern islands, but he would find unappropriated territory in that direction. The name Bimini had been heard from the far side of the northern islands. The small keys of that name, lying at the margin of the Bahama channel, were not his objective. A legend of a spring at Bimini continually flowing, and of marvelous virtue, was first reported by Peter Martyr. Oviedo had heard of such a fountain of Bimini that restored youth and thought it an idle tale. If Arawaks of the Bahamas did tell such a story it would have been of limestone springs in Florida, unknown on the Bahama Islands. Spanish tradition perhaps added the legend of a fountain of youth, a legend old and widespread in Europe. Las Casas, who had soldiered with Ponce in Higuey, said Ponce's purpose in going north was to take slaves. Herrera thought his main end was to gain new lands. Ponce, in vigorous middle age, was not spending his wealth in search of a fountain of youth, nor did his conduct in Florida support the romantic story that is still told in school books.

The ships sailed from San Germán at the west of Puerto Rico in March 1513. Their course was by the Mona Passage northwest along the Atlantic side of the Bahama Islands, naming Caicos, Mayaguana, and Guanahani. Their route probably was that used by ships returning to Spain. Having passed the Bahamas they held the same direction for three hundred miles north to the coast of Florida near St. Augustine, reached Easter week (*pascua florida*) and therefore thus named. The beeline taken indicates that they were confident of land ahead in that direction.

Upon entering an Indian village they had a sharp fight (April 20), and again as they landed in a river to take on water and wood. From the vicinity of St. Augustine they turned south, keeping close to the coast, thereby skirting the northward sweep of the Gulf Stream. Shoals and islands were noted to the southern tip of Florida—Los Martires, as named earlier on the Cantino map. They then followed up the west coast as far as San Carlos Bay. Here they had another clash with the natives. Thence they doubled back south, across open water to the low keys (Dry Tortugas), where they took a hundred and seventy turtles, fourteen seals, and sea birds and eggs. Ponce de León got back to Puerto Rico August 21 after a voyage of about six months.[10]

10. The log was used by Herrera, *Historia General,* Decade I, Libro IX, chaps. 10–12.

Florida historians are in general agreement as to the voyage, thus T. Frederick Davis in *Fla. Hist. Soc.,* vol. 15 (1936) and Edward W. Lawson, *The Discovery of Florida* (1945).

Ponce's voyage is the first record of Europeans being met with hostility on arrival. Indians either welcomed strangers as guests or held off warily or timidly. Even the redoubtable Caribs of the south did not start the fights for which they were known. The cause of the conflict near St. Augustine was not declared. At the southwest the ships entered the bay called San Carlos, intending to careen one of the vessels, according to Herrera. Indians swarmed out in canoes to welcome the strangers; the Castilians, thinking one of the ships was about to be taken, pursued the natives onto the land, breaking up their canoes and capturing women. The account continued: "At other times when the Indians came there was no rupture, since they saw no occasion for one, but they traded hides and pieces of guanín." Later on there was more fighting which became serious enough as "to cause the Castilians to retire." [11]

The Indians of northeast Florida were Timucuas, by later identification, those of the southwest were Calusas—both populous tribes of Muskogean affiliation. Like the island Indians they used dugout canoes and built round houses (*bohios*). Unlike the Arawaks of the islands they used bows and arrows, and wore penis shields. The Lucayo Indians of the Bahamas called the land across the straits *Cautio* "because the people there wear their secret parts covered with palm leaves woven in a manner of plaiting."

Ponce got a new contract in September 1514 to occupy and govern "the islands Bimini and Florida," which makes little sense. After coasting Florida for five hundred miles he still thought it an island? He was given title to a long stretch of coast and an unlimited country inland. Nothing of profit had been found. The natives would be tough to capture or control. His grant could wait. In 1515 he undertook an expedition from Puerto Rico to take the Carib island of Guadeloupe and was soundly trounced.

11. Herrera mixed in events of later time. It is unlikely that guanín was traded. This alloy of copper and gold was familiar to Spaniards on the mainland south coast of the Caribbean, the product of advanced metallurgy, based in Colombia. Its manufacture was unknown to Florida natives or those of any part of the United States. Later, when Spanish treasure ships coming from Mexico and Panama were wrecked on the Florida coast, Indians salvaged the remains. Herrera wrote that Ponce awaited the coming of cacique Carlos who was reputed to be rich in gold. The high chief of that name, however, was a major figure of the De Soto expedition who lived a generation later.

The Pilot Alaminos and the Gulf Stream

The history of the Spanish Indies is written in terms of the men who led soldiers. The pilots, who took the captains to parts unknown, remain obscure.

Antón de Alaminos was the chief discoverer of the Gulf Stream, and thereby of the lifeline of Spanish empire. He piloted the ships that found the way to Florida, Yucatán, and Mexico. He was a native of Palos, the Andalusian port that with its neighbor Moguer provided the pilots and crew that made possible the discovery by Columbus. Alaminos may have taken part in the second voyage of Columbus, and he was one of the pilots on Columbus' last voyage when the mainland from the Gulf of Honduras to eastern Panama was discovered. Voyaging between Spain and Caribbean places, he knew and charted the coasts, currents, and winds to the end of the known waters.

He kept Ponce's ships east of the shoals of the Bahamas on a northwest course. After passing the Bahamas he held a northwest direction not known to have been followed earlier. This was a diagonal crossing of the wide Gulf Stream flowing at sixty miles a day, easily ridden to the landfall at St. Augustine —an impressive and remembered lesson of the greatest ocean current, bearing its waters northward. After the landing in northern Florida they turned south, keeping close to shore to have the benefit of a southward coastal drift. This took careful and slow sailing to keep from running aground in the shallow waters. Having passed the broad sandy cape built by the meeting of contrary seas and winds, Cape Canaveral, they made slower headway against the Gulf Stream, none on some days. It took six weeks to work their way south along the Florida coast, twice as long as it had taken to get to St. Augustine from Puerto Rico. Having passed west by the Florida Keys, they turned north into the quiet and almost tideless waters of the Gulf of Mexico, as yet nameless. On their way back they observed, south of the Dry Tortugas, the great drift eastward of waters from the West (Gulf of Mexico) and from the south (Caribbean Sea), the outflow mingling to form the beginning of the Gulf Stream. Alaminos had learned the circulation of sea and air from Panama to northern Florida and would soon apply his knowledge to pioneering the

Carrera de las Indias, the regular route of sail from the Indies
to Spain.

The Expedition of Hernández de Córdoba (1517)

Gold placers in the mountains of Cuba had attracted
Spaniards, made some of them rich, left many poor, and destroyed the natives. Las Casas had come to Cuba to take a
grant of Indians, was sickened by the exploitation of the natives, renounced his grant, and began a life devoted to the protection of Indians. Shortly, Velázquez was sending ships to
capture slaves elsewhere. These ranged as far as the Bay
Islands of the Gulf of Honduras, the southern part of Maya
land.

In February 1517 three ships under the command of
Hernández de Córdoba and piloted by Alaminos sailed west
from Cuba. Bernal Díaz del Castillo began his *True Account,* a
classic of the conquest of New Spain, with his part in this voyage. The party was well armed and ready for trade or capture.
It crossed from the western cape of Cuba, San Antonio, to
Cape Catoche in Yucatán, delayed by a storm, perhaps a
norther common to that season. The assurance of direction
suggests that Alaminos knew where he was headed. The
Spaniards were well received on landing but then were am-
bushed as they were on their way to the Mayan town that they
called Gran Cairo, because of the temple pyramids. Driven
back to the ships, they sailed west along the north shore of
the peninsula, being attacked wherever they attempted to
land. Half their number were killed, most of the rest wounded.
That the Mayas, not a bellicose people, acted like angry hor-
nets means that they had been injured by other people who
had come in ships. Perhaps this had happened to their kinsmen on the Gulf of Honduras. Perhaps, and this may be likelier, slave hunters from Cuba had raided Yucatán before.

Unable to land and get fresh water, the survivors were
forced to use the brackish water of a lagoon. Alaminos proposed that they seek safety and good water to the north where
he had been with Ponce de León. He underestimated the dis-
stance but took the ships on good course to the desired bay
(probably San Carlos). While digging pits in the beach for the
badly needed drinking water Indians came swarming upon
them, some from land, others in canoes. "They had very large
bows and good arrows and lances and a sort of sword, and

were dressed in deerskins. They were of large stature and came straight at us, discharging their arrows." Thus Bernal recalled the attack by the Florida Indians. These Indians had thrown out the raiders of Ponce de León and wanted no return of their kind. The Hernández party was driven to their ships, took brief respite at the Florida Keys, and then went to the nearest harbor on Cuba, soon to become the town of Havana. Here Hernández and a number of men died of the wounds received in Florida.

Alaminos had been with Columbus at the Bay Islands of Honduras in 1502 when the admiral failed to appreciate the significance of the great Indian trading vessel from the north bringing a cargo of products of an unknown civilization. In Yucatán Alaminos came in 1517 to Gran Cairo. In 1518 he piloted the Grijalva expedition from Cuba along the coast of Vera Cruz to the northern extremity of Mesoamerican high culture, to be followed in 1519 by his guiding Cortés to the conquest of Mexico.

3

Spaniards
on the Northern Gulf Coast
(1519–1528)

The Grijalva expedition brought news of a land of oriental splendor and riches, to gain which Governor Velázquez sent a fleet in charge of Hernán Cortés. After arriving on the coast of Vera Cruz (1519) the participants declared their loyalty to the Spanish crown, denied allegiance to Velázquez, and elected Cortés as their chief. They seceded from Spanish island authority while affirming loyalty to the king and promising great increase to the Spanish realm. Thereby Cortés and his adherents were held to be traitors by the island officials and were suspect in Spain.

Francisco de Garay was the first to challenge Cortés. Garay had made one of the largest fortunes in the islands, beginning with the greatest gold nugget found in Española. In 1515 he succeeded to the government of Jamaica, which lacked gold and was by that time largely depopulated, its Indian fields beginning to be replaced by stock ranches. Garay fitted out four ships in 1519 in charge of Alvarez Pineda to sail to Pánuco, which the fleet of Grijalva coming up the coast from the south had reached the year before.

Most of what is known of this voyage is in a royal cédula

of 1521 that granted Garay the government of the new discovery he had made at his own expense.[1] In condensed form
it said that the ships were well armed and hoped to discover
a gulf or strait through the mainland, were gone eight to nine
months, and never found such a passage. Along with other low
and sterile land that they discovered they came to the country
of Florida which Ponce had found. Land dead ahead to the
east and a contrary wind obliged them to turn about and to
follow the coast west, taking careful notice of land, harbors,
rivers, natives, and everything that was to be observed. They
went on thus until they met Cortés and his men (in Pánuco).
Here they set up markers to show the limit of their discovery,
which was of more than three hundred leagues, and they
took possession in the name of the King.

Having done this they turned back with their ships and entered a
very great river they found, which carried much water, at the mouth
of which they said they found a large pueblo. They stayed there
more than forty days during which they careened the ships. The people of that land were most friendly to the Spaniards of the fleet,
trading and giving whatever they had. The ships went up the river
for six leagues, finding forty pueblos on one side and the other.

Reference was made to a map drawn by the pilots and submitted by Garay. The newly discovered coast was known pro-
visionally as the Province of Amichel, a blank space left in the
text for the name to be given.

It is a very good country, peaceable, healthful, and of many provisions and fruits and other things edible and in it there are many
rivers carrying fine gold, as the Indians demonstrated by certain
samples, and also they wore many gold jewels in their noses and
ears and on other parts of their bodies. They are very amiable people . . . in some parts they are ten to eleven *palmos* [almost seven
feet] tall, others are short, and there are still other very short people
of five to six palms.

This is the earliest account of the Gulf Coast of the United
States west of the peninsula of Florida. It tells little and much
of that wrong, such as the stature of the Indians, their gold
adornments, and the gold-bearing rivers. The river with a
large pueblo at its mouth and forty more within six leagues up

1. CDI, vol. 39, pp. 514–525; also Navarrete, vol. 3, pp. 160–165.

river could not have been the Mississippi but may have been Mobile Bay and River. That such a voyage was made was confirmed by Cortés who met the party in Pánuco.

The cédula is a decree accepting a petition by Garay to be given the government of all the Gulf coast between Florida and Pánuco. A map drawn by the pilots was accepted, "by which it appears that the Adelantado Diego Velázquez and Juan Ponce de León and you have discovered that all is mainland and coast thereof." As Ponce's title was still considered valid, the ships sent by Garay turned west from the land discovered by Ponce. The cédula acknowledged Velázquez as discoverer of the mainland south of Pánuco. Velázquez, who stayed in Cuba, had sent Grijalva and Cortés. The cédula, issued in 1521 when Cortés was in control in Mexico, was in effect a disavowal of Cortés. It being impossible to set the limits of the mainland governments from Spain, it continued, an inspector living in the Indies was appointed to determine them. The decree was a move by a faction at court to outlaw Cortés and his men.[2]

In 1523 Garay went into action against Cortés by way of Pánuco. Thus far he had seen no part of his titular government nor would he stop for inspection but go to confront Cortés. Again the bias of official document: "The Adelantado Francisco de Garay left the Island of Santiago [Jamaica] with a fleet of sixteen ships, large and small, and with six hundred men, a hundred and fifty of them horsemen, to go to settle the Rio Pánuco and the other lands which he discovered in our name."[3] This was a larger force than Cortés had at his landing in Vera Cruz. It would strike the latter's weak northern flank. Garay brought the majority of the Spaniards of Jamaica, the horsemen with remounts. Instead of attacking the troops of

2. The person sent was Cristóbal de Tapia, who had been inspector of mines in Española. He presented his commission at Cempoala in Veracruz in December 1521, the writ declaring the authority of Velázquez over New Spain. The Spaniards before whom it was delivered rejected it as incompetent, citing among their refusal that the commission was not signed by the proper authorities of the Crown (CDI, vol. 24, pp. 30–58). The Tapia commission and the Garay cédula were both given over the same signatures, which were not those of the royal secretariat. Partisans of Velázquez, of whom Garay was one, were attempting to eliminate Cortés before the King and his Council might resolve their uncertainty in his favor.

3. December 1523 (CDI, vol. 13, p. 497).

Cortés, those of Garay went over en masse to Cortés' side. Garay was captured and shortly died in custody. His men joined Cortés in the further campaigns in New Spain and were given third ranking in the hierarchy of conquerors to whom the *encomiendas* were allotted. With his death and the desertion of his men such title as he had to the north side of the Gulf was vacant. Pineda's ships had shown the mainland to be continuous from Florida to Pánuco and therefore joined with South America.

THE RETURN OF PONCE DE LEÓN

Ponce de León made no use of his title to Florida after the failure of 1513 until 1521, when news of the wealth of Mexico was stirring Spaniards throughout the islands. Once again he equipped a party and sailed from Puerto Rico. There were two hundred men, fifty horses, other livestock, and diverse seeds for planting, according to Oviedo, also friars and a priest. The party was well armed and also was provided with the means to establish a pastoral and farming community.

Ponce's choice of a location in southwest Florida made sense. The Gulf was where the action was, Cortés on the southwest and Garay on the northwest. Ponce would go to the lagoons he had known eight years before (San Carlos Bay and Charlotte Harbor). Here there would be good harbors and land for planting. Ships leaving or entering the Gulf would have their nearest mainland port here.

He failed to take into account his previous defeat by the natives and that of Hernández de Córdoba. "The natives of the country were a very rough and savage and warlike and fierce and indomitable people, unaccustomed to quietude or to yield their freedom readily to the will of others," Oviedo wrote, in contrast to the Island Arawaks.[4] Shortly after landing there was a fight with the Indians in which the Spaniards were drubbed and driven out; Ponce was wounded by an arrow and died after he got to Havana. With his death, followed shortly by that of Garay, Spanish titles to government along the American Gulf coast were in abeyance, and the name Florida came to be used for an undefined stretch from the peninsula of Florida to the west.

4. Part 2, Libro XXXVI, chap. 1.

THE EXPEDITION OF NARVÁEZ (1527)

Pánfilo de Narváez was the last of the rich islanders to make a bid for power on the mainland. The fortune he had made in Española had been increased in Jamaica, whence he went to Cuba as second in command to Velázquez. Velázquez gave Narváez the main job of overrunning the island, which he did quickly and brutally. When Cortés defected with the Velázquez fleet and men, Narváez was sent to Vera Cruz to capture and dispose of Cortés (1520). He landed at Vera Cruz with twice the force Cortés had, and with better arms. How he was outwitted by Cortés, was captured, and his troops joined the other side is high drama of the conquest of Mexico. On his release the next year, Narváez went to Spain to press charges against Cortés. These charges found willing ears at court, Velázquez and Narváez being legitimate officials, Cortés the usurper.

Meanwhile Cortés and his lieutenants were extending their control to the Pacific coast and south into Central America. They made no further advance at the north, the Rio Pánuco remaining the frontier. Narváez, supported by Velázquez and partisans, promoted a plan that would include the northern periphery of the Gulf, from Río de las Palmas (on the coast of Tamaulipas in northern Mexico) on the west to the Gulf coast of Florida peninsula at the east. In December 1526 Narváez was named governor, captain general, high constable, and adelantado of a vast principality, without interior limits. The rights were given in perpetuity. He was to carry out the possession at his own expenses, but was given a salary, would have a share of the revenues, and was to select as his own property a tract ten leagues square.[5] What was known of the Gulf is shown in the so-called Weimar map of 1527 (fig. 6 below).

No one since Columbus had been given such grants and privileges. Cortés, who had won a realm greater than Spain, was still unacknowledged by the Crown, yet Narváez, although he had failed miserably against Cortés, was given power over a territory from which Cortés could be threatened.

What befell the expedition is known mainly by the relation of Álvar Núñez Cabeza de Vaca, principal participant. First printed in 1542, it has been a familiar classic of adventure

5. CDI, vol. 22, pp. 225–245.

mishap. Oviedo watched the preparations of the venture and tried dissuasion. López de Gómara, chaplain to Cortés, added items in his *Historia de las Indias* under the brief geographic sections named Florida, Río de las Palmas, and Pánuco.[6]

Narváez sailed from Spain with a fleet of five ships in June 1527 with six hundred men of high and low degree who were attracted by the prospect of profit and adventure and were unselected as to experience or skills. A leisurely stop at Santo Domingo gave opportunity to load more horses; also about a hundred and forty men chose to stay there. Another stop was made at Santiago de Cuba to visit with Governor Velázquez. The ships then continued along the south coast of Cuba to overwinter at Xaragua (Cienfuegos). Here they picked up more supplies and persons, including a pilot Miruelos who was said to know all the mainland coast to the north. (Apparently he had traded beyond the part where Ponce de León had come to grief.) They had committed themselves to indifferent hands and were stranded on shoals as they started from Xaragua, requiring fifteen days to get clear. The final departure was February 22, 1528 (Oviedo) with four hundred persons and a hundred and eighty horses (Cabeza de Vaca). Driven about by storms, they did not reach Florida until April 2, 1528, about ten months after leaving Spain.

The landing was made at the mouth of a bay with an Indian village at its far end. John R. Swanton, who was best informed on the Indians of our Southeast, thought this a Timucua village at the head of Tampa Bay.[7] The ships had kept out to sea until they were past the coast where Ponce and Hernández had been roughly handled by another Indian tribe, the Calusas as identified by Swanton. The Indians of Tampa Bay brought food including deer meat, but then slipped away overnight. The Spaniards examined the vacated village and found it to consist of small houses and a large *bohío* that would hold three hundred persons. (The use of the Island Arawak name suggested that it was a round ceremonial structure.) In rummaging about they found fishing nets and also a

6. Oviedo's Libro XXXV narrates the expedition. For Cabeza de Vaca and Gómara, I have used the texts in Enrique de Vedia, ed., *Historiadores primitivos de Indias*. Cyclone Covey, *Cabeza de Vaca Adventures* (Collier Paperback Series, 1961), is a competent translation and introduction.

7. Swanton's *The Indians of the Southeastern United States*, Bureau Am. Ethnology, Bull. 137, is the standard reference on the historical Indian tribes of the southeastern United States.

small "gold drum" that raised hopes of treasure. (Whatever it was, Florida natives did not make articles of gold.) After Narváez had taken formal possession, natives drifted back warily to observe the strangers and to indicate by signs that they wanted them to move out.

The party landed in Tampa Bay travel-worn and short of food. Carelessly they had left Cuba without adequate supplies. The horses had fared worst; of the one hundred eighty with which they started from Xaragua there were only forty-two left at landing. Two weeks were spent exploring the bay and making excursions inland. They saw fields of maize in an early stage of growth, reported many *vasos* (wooden mortars?) for grinding, but no ripe grain. On showing the natives samples of gold they were given to understand that there was none locally but that they would find a great deal to the north at a place called Apalachen. Oviedo commented, "everything they showed these Indians, whatever seemed to them to be something the Christians valued, they said that there was a lot of it in Apalachen." The natives remained inoffensive though the Spaniards gave offense, as when they came upon a burial place where they burned the chests containing the cadavers (looking for gold ornaments?). There was neither food nor treasure to be had on Tampa Bay and so they would get out in a hurry.

Narváez made the fateful decision to divide his party, sending the ships ahead to a port known to the pilot while the main body went north by land, taking the route to Apalachen, where there would be gold. Cabeza de Vaca wrote in later years that he had been overruled when he objected that the pilots were ignorant of where they were, that instead they should wait to bring supplies from Cuba, that the country was poor and thinly settled, and that their first business was to find a port where they could make a settlement. Gómara saw the division as the doom of the expedition: "He [Narváez] sent the ships to seek the Río de las Palmas north of Pánuco, in search of which nearly all the men and horses were lost; which happened because he failed to make a settlement where he had landed with his men, or because he landed where it was not proper to settle (*poblar*). Whoever does not settle will not make a good conquest and without it the natives will not be converted; the maxim of any conquest must be to make a settlement." Gómara was thinking as Cortéz did. Narváez was not concerned with making Christians of the natives, nor do we know what he had in mind other than finding gold and getting to Pánuco. He expected to make a rendezvous with the ships, but nothing was said as to how this would be arranged along a coast unknown except perhaps to the pilot Miruelos, who may have been there previously. The ships sailed out of Tampa Bay and were not seen or heard of again.

Narváez started north with an advance party of forty horsemen and two hundred afoot (fig. 5). They carried provisions of biscuit and bacon to last for fifteen days, during which

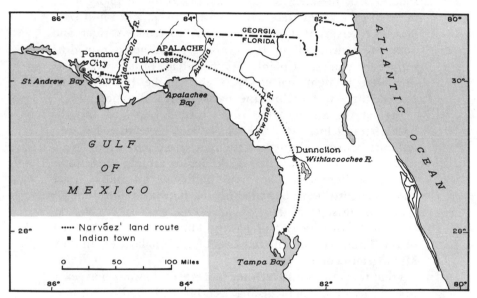

FIG. 5. Route of Narváez in Florida, constructed from the documents.

time they found nothing to eat other than shoots of palmettos, little palms like those of Andalusia. Their rate of progress was about eight miles a day. After fifteen days they came to a river which took them a day to cross, identified by Swanton as the Withlacoochee. In that distance they saw no villages, houses, or Indians, indicating that they were traveling north on the sandy coast plain close to the Gulf. After crossing the river they were met by a company of Indians who took them to their village (vicinity of Dunellon?). Here they found maize ready to harvest, for which Cabeza de Vaca gave thanks to God. (In this subtropical land, a first maize crop perhaps was mature by June.) Cabeza de Vaca took a party west to the sea, here a very shallow and wide bay (Withlacoochee Bay). They waded far out to *placeles* of oysters that cut their feet (Withlacoochee Reefs). Another party went on to look for a harbor and found only knee-deep water. A half-dozen dugout canoes were seen that displayed plumes.

The next leg of the journey was even slower, across a plain of which no features were reported. On June 17 they were met by another Indian party, a reception committee headed by a chief dressed in painted buckskin and carried on the shoulders of his men, to the accompaniment of many flutes made of cane. They were led to a wide, deep, and rapid river (Suwanee River) that required a day to cross. A rider and horse were drowned in the crossing, "the horse providing supper for many that night." At the village on the west bank they were brought maize. Overnight all the Indians disappeared, thereafter trailing the party from a distance.

Beyond the Suwanee the route turned westward and the pace of travel increased. Cabeza de Vaca remembered it as a toilsome journey through stands of marvelously tall trees, some fallen so that they needed to detour around them, some scarred by lightning. They were following an Indian trace and apparently were out of the pine flatwoods. On June 25 they came in sight of their objective, the town of Apalachen, at or in the vicinity of Tallahassee. They had left the country of the Timucuas and entered that of the Apalachees, another Muskogean people.

From the Suwanee River they had traveled as much as seven to eight leagues without seeing a cornfield. It had taken more than two months to come the two hundred miles from Tampa to Tallahassee. Here there was great quantity of maize ready to harvest in the fields and much old corn stored in cribs (*encerrado*) and many *vasos* for grinding (vertical log mortars in which the grain was pounded). There was sufficient food for the first time, and plenty of water; and there were straw-covered houses that the Indians had evacuated. Shortly the Indians returned to set fire to houses occupied by the Spaniards. Cabeza de Vaca remembered that they found many deerskins in the houses and some cloth made of thread, small pieces of indifferent quality, used by the women to cover themselves. If his memory served him rightly that there was woven cloth, the fibers may have been of native *Yucca* or *Apocynum*, cotton being unknown to the South. Gómara wrote that the place abounded in many things but lacked the gold they had come to seek. At any rate it was better country than they had seen and it was time to take a rest.

Cabeza de Vaca summed up the nature of the western Florida through which they had come:

For the most part the land is flat from where we disembarked to this pueblo and the country of Apalache, the soil being sandy in parts and in others of firm ground; throughout it are very great trees or open woods. There are *nogales* [the Spanish name applied both to walnuts and hickories], laurels [aromatic trees and shrubs, some related to the Mediterranean laurel], others called liquid ambar [the sweet gum, botanical name *Liquidambar*], cedars [the juniper we know as red cedar], *sabinos* [*Taxodium,* bald cypress], *encinos* [live oaks] pines and *robles* [deciduous oaks], and low palmettos such as grow in Castile. There are lakes in all parts, large and small, some difficult to cross, partly because they are deep, in part because of the many trees fallen into them. Their bottoms are sandy and those we found in the region of Apalache are much larger than those seen before. In the latter province there are many fields of maize and the houses are dispersed as among the Gelves [Arab name for Negroes]. The animals we saw there are deer of three kinds [white tailed deer and others?], rabbits and hares, bears and lions [pumas] and other wild animals, among which we saw one [opossum] that carries its young in a pouch in its belly and as long as they are small they are thus carried until they know how to search for food; if they are out searching and people come, the mother does not flee until she has gathered the young into her pouch. The country is [not] very cold; it has very good pasture for cattle; there are birds of many kinds, geese in great number [there follows a list of Spanish names for ducks and other water fowl, hawks, falcons, and their kindred, and others].

This is pretty fair description by a newcomer to the New World. Tree names he used are still thus used in both Spanish and English. He noted the diversity and abundance of birds, including the presence in summer of a lot of waterfowl that breed in northern latitudes. Until after the expedition crossed the Suwanee River they appear to have kept to the sandy coast plain. As they neared Tallahassee the country changed in appearance, the lakes (limestone solution features) being much larger and the land well peopled and cultivated. In this part settlement was dispersed, unlike Spain and uncommon for the

Indians of the Southeast. The note of very good pasture for cattle suggests grassy tracts, the result of Indian burning.

The village of Apalachen was occupied for about a month into late July. Three parties were sent to scout the interior and reported that the country was sparsely settled, indicating that they had ranged into the piney woods of southern Georgia. Meanwhile the dispossessed Indians prowled about Apalachen picking off an occasional Spaniard or a horse being taken to water. An Aztec "lord from Texcoco" was thus killed, without explanation how he came to be in Spanish company. Sniping continued, food was running short, there was no gold; it was time to move out and try a western direction.

They had heard of an Indian town called Aute as having an abundance of maize, beans, and squash, the first mention of the triple Indian crop complex. Also the location was near the sea and there were fish aplenty. Here they could live at ease and hope to make contact with their ships. They held to a westerly course, mainly through pine-forested sand plain, for eight or nine days, crossing a very great river somewhat more than midway (Apalachicola River). The distance to Aute was less than a hundred miles, a march of about twelve miles a day including the river crossing. They were trailed by Apalachee Indians until the Indians ran out of arrows, according to Cabeza de Vaca. He recalled an arrow driven six inches into a poplar tree and others that passed through oaks of the size of a man's leg. "All the Indians from Florida to here are bowmen and being tall of body and naked they look at a distance like giants. They are people of marvelous physique, very lean, and of great strength and speed. The bows they use are thick as an arm, ten to eleven palms long [about seven feet] and used with such accuracy as not to miss at two hundred *pasos* [paces]." The march had become a retreat.

Arriving at Aute they found the Indians gone and the houses burned, but the fields filled with much maize, beans, and squash, ready for harvest. Going on to a lagoon that opened to the Gulf they found many oysters, which were greatly appreciated. There is no mention of fishing or hunting. A party sent to reconnoiter the coast reported many embayments, the open sea at a distance. They had come to St. Andrew Bay, many-branched and opening to the Gulf by a sound hemmed in by a spit at the west. The swamps about the bay indicate that Aute and its fields were on higher land either to the northeast or east of Panama City.

They had parted company with the ships more than three months ago and had given up hope of meeting them again. Aute was a refuge that would support them for a while and hold off harassment by its displaced Indians. They could not go on by land. The remaining hope was to find safety in Pánuco by water, keeping close to shore. They knew that the Gulf coast extended from Florida to Pánuco, that it had in general an east-west direction, but they did not know the distance. The expedition to take possession of a new government had become a flight to survive.

Building the boats began August 5 and was completed September 20. "We did not know how to build them, nor did we have tools or iron or forge or oakum or pitch or tackle" (Cabeza de Vaca). One man had experience as a carpenter, and a Greek knew how to make pitch. Longleaf pine was at hand for making pitch; it and other yellow pines were convenient for felling and splitting into rough planks. Oars were made of bald cypress. Palmetto leaves served for calking and were used along with horsehair to make ropes. Shirts were pieced together for sails. The last of the horses were eaten, the hide of the legs providing *botas* (leather water bags). Four hundred *fanegas* of maize were gathered at Aute, about three bushels per man. Five rude boats were thus made, each about thirty feet long when loaded, with about six inches of freeboard.

The forlorn flotilla set out with about two hundred fifty persons September 22 from the bay remembered as the bay of horses because the last were eaten there. They followed the coast for seven days and came to an island or bar where there were some huts by the side of which five dugouts were beached. These they split into lengths thus adding a hand's breadth to their freeboard. Here they found many *lisas* (mullet) and dry eggs (turtle?). A bar outside of Pensacola or Choctowhatchee Bay is indicated.

Cabeza de Vaca remembered little of the nature of the coast until they came near the delta of the Mississippi. A low string of narrow islands, low sand ridges piled up on a bar parallel to the mainland, lies west of Mobile Bay a half-dozen miles out in the Gulf. Their troubles began with lack of water to drink. The botas of horses' legs had rotted and they had no

other containers. A storm held them for six days in the
shelter of an island, during which five men died from drinking
salt water. After the storm they sighted a canoe which they
followed to a village of mat-covered houses, where there were
large earthen jars full of fresh water and a lot of dressed fish.
The hospitable reception turned into a fracas in which the
visitors broke up thirty canoes. The incident may have occurred
on an island or spit at the entrance to Mobile Bay where a
fishing village was supplied with fresh water from pits dug in
the sand or brought from the mainland.

They then went on to a swampy land in which there were
many water courses, an indication that they had entered the
sound west of Mobile Bay and followed its sheltered waters to
Pascagoula. The Pascagoula River discharges through numerous branches, flowing through extensive swamps, and is
the only one that does so. They had come to the mainland
inhabited by Choctaws or their near-kinsmen. Many canoes
came and several chiefs dressed in fine fur mantles and wearing their hair long and flowing, noted by Swanton as a Choctaw
trait. The Greek and a Negro went inland with Indians and
did not return. (The De Soto expedition heard years later
north of Mobile Bay that the two had been killed.) Again a
fight broke out and the Spaniards took to their boats. From
Tampa Bay to here the Indians belonged to various Muskogean tribes and had welcomed the strangers except where
forewarned.

Ahead of them the delta of the Mississippi River protruded
into the Gulf with tongues of land and a scatter of marshy
islands. Cabeza de Vaca told how he took his bark to discover
a point of land on the other side of which "there was seen a
very great river and I landed at a small island formed at the
point to await the rest. The Governor stopped at a bay close
by where there were many islets. We took sweet water from
the sea, because the river entered the sea in flood. Landing to
roast some maize that we had, we could find no wood and
therefore went on to the river a league distant behind the
point." The current of the river and wind from the north
carried them out to sea where they sounded and found no
bottom at thirty fathoms. They had entered one of the
"passes," one of the arms by which the river discharges its
water and sediment into the Gulf, and were swept to sea on
its current. On sounding when they were no longer current-

borne, they found themselves in deep water. Where the flow of fresh water into the Gulf stopped they were beyond sounding depth. They had been carried out over steeply dipping foreset beds of one of the main distributaries, where it deposits its load of sediment in the Gulf. This rapid change in depth of water is found only at the passes. Which pass they entered is not known nor what changes have since occurred in the configuration of the delta.

The five boats continued west, circling the delta and coming to open waters of the Gulf, without shelter of islands. The intervals are obscure. They had started from the bay of horses September 22, and it was near the end of October when they reached the Mississippi River pass. Thereafter their rate of travel speeded up. A westward current may have added ten miles a day at that season, but they moved a lot faster than by such aid. One evening they saw many smokes on a distant shore. During the night the boats drifted apart; three of the five rejoined the next day, the other two were not heard of again. Narváez had the stoutest crew and the best boat. The hope of the three boats was to reach the coast to the north where they might find help from natives. Cabeza de Vaca asked the aid of a line from Narváez and was answered that it was too late for mutual help, "that each should do what seemed best, which was to save his own life, which is what he intended to do. And saying thus, he pulled away in his boat, and as I could not keep up with him I got to the other boat which was low in the water and so we navigated in company for four days." Narváez and his crew were lost somewhere off the southwest coast of Louisiana. Oviedo contrasted the faithless answer of Narváez with the conduct of good captains at time of crisis.

The two remaining boats stayed together, sped by seas that were perhaps the aftermath of a distant hurricane.[8] Of the morning of November 6 Cabeza de Vaca remembered "that before dawn it seemed to me that I heard the breakers of the sea, which sounded strongly since the coast was low." Shortly a great wave tossed the boat "a horseshoe's throw" out of the water onto the beach, a sandbar off Galveston Bay. The survivors found puddles of water to drink, gathered wood, and

8. This was suggested by Cleve Hallenbeck, *Cabeza de Vaca*, p. 11. Hallenbeck was an observer in the U.S. Weather Bureau, of long experience in the southwest.

made a fire against the freezing cold. Not far away the other craft was stranded in similar manner. About ninety men made it to the Texas coast, and were not to be heard of for eight years.

The loss of the Narváez expedition ended ventures from the Spanish islands. They had been of a pattern—ambition to gain wealth and status without the qualities of leadership that would have attended to provision, secured intelligence, and organized operations. All but Cortés. Oviedo called their roll and told their failure: Diego de Nicuesa panicked in setting up his government of Castilla del Oro, the later Panama. Hernández de Córdoba lost his fortune and life fighting Indians in Yucatán and Florida. Francisco de Garay went against Cortés, was outmaneuvered, and died in captivity. Ponce de León made a second attempt to take Florida and was killed. Vázquez de Ayllón (of whom more later) failed and died in Georgia. Pánfilo de Narváez came to the most ignoble end of all, Oviedo concluded. The island captains took to their mainland adventures a large, in some cases the greater, part of the Spaniards from Cuba, Jamaica, and Puerto Rico, few of whom survived or thrived except those who joined Cortés in Mexico.

4
The
Atlantic Coast
(1520–1526)

Portugal was doing very well in Africa and India and had in prospect the exploitation of Brazil. Portuguese fishermen were making yearly voyages to take cod off the shores of the land overseas, known to them as Terra de Bacalhaos, Terra Nova, or Terra de Corte Reales. The fishermen were natives of the ports of northern Portugal and of the Azores. Some had been with the Corte Real brothers, and they knew harbors and places to get water and wood and somewhat about the Indians of the coast. The cod fishery at the time, it is inferred, was still mainly in coastal waters of Newfoundland and the mainland. The fishermen of the several nationalities had not as yet set themselves apart at particular stretches of coast.[1]

Viana do Castelo in north Portugal enjoyed prosperity in procuring bacalhao for market in Portugal and to ships in the Africa-India trade. Viana was the base also of the last Portuguese attempt to take possession in North America. João Alvares Fagundes, a gentleman of the royal household, came to Viana in May 1521 to present letters patent given him by

1. Charles de la Morandière, *Histoire de la pêche française de la morue* (Paris, 1962), p. 220, found the Portuguese bases later on the southeast coast of Newfoundland.

King Manuel. These letters authorized him to carry out discovery between the land at the south, where Spain had rights,
and that at the north which the brothers Corte Real had discovered—in other words, to respect the Spanish claim to
Florida and the Corte Real title to Newfoundland.[2]

The patent was given to colonize a country which it said
that Fagundes had discovered, and named a number of islands
and bays he had found. Such a voyage can have taken place
no later than 1520. The designated list of places was beyond
the limits of Corte Real discovery. Fagundes asked for and
was given rights to occupy a coast on the side toward Florida,
held unknown prior to his discovery. The patent declared that
Fagundes "at his own cost and expenses discovered the said
lands and expended thereon large sums," which is not quite
the same as saying that Fagundes himself had been there. The
places listed as discovered are the key to what was found, in
this order: first a bay where they took on water as perforce
they would after crossing the sea; next four places given saints'
names; then the archipelago of S. Panteliom and the isle of
Pitiguoem; then the archipelago of the eleven thousand virgins; finally the "island of Santa Cruz at the foot of the bank."

The one native name was the island of Pitiguoem, associated
with an archipelago. This was the name of the Penobscot
region of coastal Maine as used in French toponymy. Nicholas
Denys, an early resident of Acadia, introduced his *Description*
of that French colony with the "River of Pentagouet, so named
by the Savages, adjoins New England." Champlain wrote
"Pemetegoiy" and "Peimtegouet." The French fort built
about 1613 in the Penobscot country was named Fort Pentagouet. The Indian name was given French and Portuguese
speech sounds and in the patent was placed in an archipelago,
which applies to Penobscot. The next patent entry was of the
isles of the eleven thousand virgins, appropriate for the
island-strewn coast east to Mount Desert.

The last entry on the patent was the island of Santa Cruz,
identified as being "at foot of the bank." This was an early

2. Later consideration by Marcel Trudel, *Histoire de la Nouvelle
France*, vol. I especially pp. 28–29; Ch. André Julien, *Histoire de l'expansion et de la colonization françaises*, vol. I (Paris, 1948). Ernesto Coto, *Os
Corte Reales* (Punta Delgada, 1883) reproduced documents, including the
letter patent; also E. A. Bettencourt. *Descobrimientos* (Lisbon, 1881–82).
The 1570 Azorian account by Francisco Sousa, *Tractado das Ilhas Novas*,
was not published until 1877.

name for Sable Island, the lone sandbar above water near the edge of the Continental Shelf. It is at the foot of the hundred mile long Sable Island Bank, a hundred and fifty miles east of Nova Scotia. Knowledge of the nature of the sea floor about the island must have come from bank fishers for cod. Insofar as I know, this is the earliest record of the name bank *(banco)* for shoals off the northeastern part of North America. By implication banks fishing as against along-shore fishing was an established practice by that time. The party did not discover the island; they recognized it and knew its name as Santa Cruz. The Reverend George Patterson read a paper before the Royal Society of Canada in May 1890, *Portuguese on the Northeast Coast of America,* which identified Santa Cruz as Sable Island. This was followed by his *Sable Island,* showing that the Reinal Map (1505) placed the island of Santa Cruz in solitary location far out to the south of Newfoundland.[3] Sable Island was known to Portuguese cod fishers early, before King Manuel imposed the tax in 1506 on the catch brought back to Viana and other ports.[4]

The voyage on which the Fagundes patent of 1521 was based should, I think, be reconstructed somewhat differently than has been its interpretation, as along the coasts of south Newfoundland, Cape Breton Island, and Nova Scotia, much of which was known. If the localities named in the patent are in the order of their visit, the discovery began with the shores of Maine and ended up with Sable Island. The two archipelagos are in proper location and the Indian place name on the Penobscot coast.

The patent was read at Viana to drum up participants. According to Francisco de Sousa, some of the local gentry joined to settle the new land in the seignorial manner by which the Azores had been occupied. Viana supplied a crew that knew how to cross the sea and where to go afterward. The colony would set up the first factory in North America, oddly a soap works to make white and black soap. How this was to

3. *Proc. Roy. Soc. Canada,* 8 (1891), Sec. II, 127–173; 12 (1894), 3–49.
4. The name Santa Cruz was replaced for a time by that of Joan Estevez (João Esteves). Thus the 1541 Islario of Alonso de Santa Cruz: "To the south of this land of Bacalaos and St. Mary's Bay [southeast Newfoundland, still thus called] at fifty leagues is an island called Joan Estevez, which was thus named after a pilot of that name who discovered it while fishing." Esteves is a common Portuguese surname. Whether he was the original discoverer is not known.

be done was not said. Lye of course would be made from wood ashes, and pines supplied resin used for the dark soap. Fat was available from fish or from seals and waterfowl. The colony was to be in the pattern of the Azores—tilling the soil, raising livestock, and fishing. Its aim was to live in peace—a civilian, not a military, venture.

Sousa, writing decades later in the Azores, told how the colony was established. In the Sousa account the voyage appears to have crossed by the farthest northern route used by the cod fishers. Accompanied by several gentlemen of Viana do Castelo they sailed

. . . in a large ship and caravel and finding the land to which they were bound very cold they followed the coast from east to west until it turned from northeast to southwest and there they settled and because they lost their ships there was no further notice of them except from some Basques who continued to seek and barter on that coast the many things to be had there, these bringing information [to the Azores] and saying that they [the colonists] ask that we here be told how they were and that priests should be brought, for the natives are gentle and the land very fertile and good, as I have been informed in more detail and as is known to men who sail into those parts; and these are at the beginning of the coast that turns north in a fine bay, where there is a large [native] population; and there are in that country things of great price, also nuts, chestnuts, grapes, and other fruits, by which it appears to be a good land; also there went in that company married couples from the Azores Islands.

The report brought by Basque traders to the Azores found the colony in good condition and at peace with a friendly and numerous Indian population, their only request being for priests. No date is given. The colony was established southwest of the coasts visited by the cod fishers. Having lost its ships, it was living in isolation until the Basque traders came by on a ship ranging beyond the fishing coasts for barter, which meant pelts. The Portuguese colony was described as at the beginning of a fine bay extending north, and of fertile land where there were grapes, nut and chestnut trees. Bay and vegetation suggest the Annapolis lowland on the Bay of Fundy. Fertile soil and the mildest climate of the Canadian maritime provinces here support mesophytic hardwoods elsewhere found only farther south. Later it was a land of orchards. The name Bay of Fundy is the Portuguese *baia fonda,* a deep bay in the sense of extending far into the land.[5] Nothing further is known of the Fagundes colony, which was established at the same time that Ponce de León was repulsed in south Florida. It was the first European settlement north of Cuba; it was made without armed support, and it may have lasted a number of years, longer than any other until St. Augustine was founded in 1565.

FRENCH MERCHANTS AND CORSAIRS

Norman ports, especially Dieppe, Honfleur, and Rouen, partly because they were most convenient to Paris, were principal shipping places of the early century, dried cod brought from Newfoundland by Breton and Norman fishers being a staple of their commerce. Merchants also on occasion sent their own ships to the fishing grounds. Thus there is record in 1508 of a ship belonging to Jean Ango of Dieppe bringing seven savages with their canoes, arms, and belongings.[6] They are considered to have been Beothuks of Newfoundland. Being taken with their canoes indicates however that they were perhaps Algonquians traveling at sea.

Of the three major Norman ports Rouen was the principal seat of merchant bankers from Paris and Italian cities, especially Florence. Dieppe was first in ownership and operation of ships, a field dominated by the Ango family who had moved there from Honfleur.[7]

Merchantmen were armed and trained for fighting, the peaceful trader on occasion becoming a corsair. When the opportunity to capture a good prize appeared it mattered little whether the ship belonged to a nation at war or at peace. Thus Columbus on his third voyage took refuge in the Madeira Islands until the alarm had passed that French corsairs were about, although France was at peace with Spain. Portugal, having great success in establishing profitable sea routes, suffered most at first from French corsairs. These

5. Thus identified by Patterson in 1890 (*Proc. Roy. Soc. Canada,* 8, Sec. II, 150). He appended (p. 173) a list of Canadian maritime place names of Portuguese derivation.

6. Julien, p. 336.

7. See Guénin, *Ango et ses pilotes,* with a collection of documents; Charles de la Roncière, *La Florida française.*

corsairs prowled about the Portuguese islands in the Atlantic, followed around Africa to India, and visited Brazil. Captains and crews of the predatory ships were mainly Normans.

When Spain struck it rich in the New World the attention of the corsairs shifted to the capture of Spanish treasure. Jacques Ango, later Viscount of Dieppe, sent his most redoubtable captain, Jean Fleury of Honfleur, to capture the ships on which Cortés sent the treasurers of Moctezuma to the emperor.[8] This was in 1522. Francis I, crowned King of France in 1515, had aspired to the throne of the Holy Roman Empire, as did Henry VIII of England. The Hapsburg succession was maintained by the election in 1519 of the teen-age King Charles I of Spain as Emperor Charles V. Francis saw himself hemmed in by Charles on all sides, from Flanders to Burgundy, Italy and Spain. Claiming title to Milan and some other parts of Italy, Francis moved into conflict with Charles. The war begun in 1521 had far-reaching consequences in Europe, ultimately to an alliance of France with Turkey and the Protestant German princes. In the first conflict, which was in Italy, Francis was defeated and captured at the Battle of Pavia (1525). The contest for power in Europe had its counterpart in the seas, Francis saying that he wanted to see the testament of Adam that divided the world between Spain and Portugal.

VERRAZZANO EXPLORES THE COAST
OF NORTH AMERICA (1524)

Giovanni Verrazzano, a resident of Rouen of good Florentine family, was associated with Italian merchants, largely of Florence, who were resident in Lyon, Paris, and Rouen. These merchants took part in commerce under the French flag. The survivors of Magellan's circumnavigation returned to Spain in the fall of 1522 with discouraging word of the far southern extension of the New World continent. Spanish pilots had shown its continuity north to Florida. North thereof the coast was uncertainly known as far as the coast of the cod fishery. In

8. Fleury was for years the great menace to Spanish ships and also to those of Portugal. He was captured off Cape Finisterre in 1527 by Basque ships and taken to Cádiz. The Basques refused the large ransom he offered. Fleury and his principal lieutenants were executed. Others were sentenced to slavery in galleys and some, who were land-owning gentry, were held for ransom (Guénin, chap. 2).

this stretch might there be a short sea passage to Cathay and the Spice Islands that Magellan had reached by a vast circuit? If this were found by France it would give France superior access to the Far East, the recurrent theme of the geopolitics of the century. Such a plan was proposed by Verrazzano and backed by his Italian associates. Ango's participation was secured at Dieppe, and the Admiral of France gave his authorization.[9]

France at the time was at war with Spain. A start with four ships was made from Rouen in the spring of 1523. A great storm caused them to go for refuge and repairs to a harbor in Brittany, after which two ships went on to raid the Spanish coast. According to the Ramusio version, Verrazzano wrote Francis "Your Majesty will have been appraised of the profit we made thereby." [10]

The voyage overseas was made by the ship *Dauphine,* of a hundred tons and a crew of fifty, provided with food for eight months; the record began January 17, 1524, at the uninhabited Ilhas Desertas southeast of Madeira. Land was sighted March 7, near Cape Fear, the latitude given as 34 degrees.[11] The ship turned southwest along a very long strand (the strand of Long Sound of South Carolina, Myrtle Beach being midway). Finding no harbor and not wishing to run the risk of meeting Spanish ships it turned north. While following the coast northeast a longboat was sent to take an occasional look at the land beyond the strand and dunes. At the farthest south they saw a land of cedars (bald cypress?), more to the north a laurel woodland (perhaps so named from the aromatic sweet and red bay trees). Contact was made with natives on the beach, to be noted below.

As they continued northeast open water was seen behind the strand. Verrazzano wrote that it was an isthmus a mile wide

9. Jacques Habert, *Vie et Voyages de Jean de Verrazane* (Ottawa, 1964), with large documentation.

10. The original report written by Verrazzano for the king at his return is not known, but four Italian versions have been preserved. The only one known for years was the one printed by Ramusio in 1555 in his collection of voyages. In 1909 Professor Alessandro Bacchiani published the Cellere manuscript (also called Roman Codex), with notation of differences, mostly minor, in the four versions. *Bol. Soc. Geogr. Ital.*, ser. IV, vol. II, pp. 1274–1323. English translation in XVth Ann. Rep., *Am. Scenic and Hist. Preservation Soc.* (Albany, 1910).

11. Verrazzano's report ended with a brief treatise on mathematical geography. It showed fair competence in determining latitude, not for longitude.

and two hundred miles long, across which one could see from shipboard "the oriental sea between west and north, which is without doubt the one that borders on India, China, and Cathay. We navigated along that isthmus in the continued hope to find some strait or true promontory where the land came to an end at the north and where we might penetrate to those happy shores of Cathay." They were coasting the outer banks about Cape Hatteras, extending for about two hundred miles, and enclosing the broad sounds of Pamlico and Albemarle. The ostensible mission of the *Dauphine* was to find a passage to Cathay. If it was possible to see from the crow's nest across the dunes to water beyond, why did they fail to enter "the oriental sea"? The passage of a ship of a hundred tons might be thought inadvisable, but there were inlets through the banks by which a longboat could have been taken readily. The astonishing error was incorporated into the map of Visconte Maggiolo in 1527, repeated in that of Girolamo Verrazzano in 1529, and continued to appear on later Italian maps. Thereby the Hatteras banks, known as the Isthmus of Verrazzano, were thought to separate the Ocean Sea of the east from the Indian Ocean, to connect Florida by a long narrow causeway with the mainland to the north, claimed for France as *Francesca*.

"Following always the shore, which turned somewhat toward north, we came in a distance of fifty leagues to another land that appeared much more beautiful and was full of great woods," green and of various kinds of trees, but not aromatic like those of the south. Grapevines climbed the trees which, it was thought, might give excellent wine under cultivation. Fifty leagues were somewhat more than the distance from Hatteras to the Eastern Shore of Chesapeake Bay, the crossing of which was not mentioned. Verrazzano called it Arcadia "for the beauty of the trees." This deciduous woodland would have appeared most attractive in its new spring leaf. The attraction was increased by seeing great grapevines climbing high into the trees, a sight unfamiliar to Europeans who know the vine only as something planted and tended with care in selected locations. As the Vikings had marveled at wild grapevines in North America, Verrazzano and Europeans who came later to the Eastern woodlands were most impressed by the presence and luxuriance of such vines.

They went on, sailing by day and dropping anchor at night,

taking a course between north and east along a coast that was very green of woods but had few harbors. (This is true of the coast plain, which they did not leave until they passed Sandy Hook at the entrance to the Outer Bay of New York.) Delaware Bay was crossed without mention as Chesapeake Bay had been, strange omission for a ship that was supposed to be seeking a western passage. Attention sharpened as they came to Lower New York Bay:

At the end of a hundred leagues [from Hatteras?] we found a very attractive site between two small prominent hills, in between which a very great river flowed to the sea, deep at its mouth, and from sea to the place where it merged any loaded ship could go on a rising tide, which we found to be eight feet. Having anchored off shore in a sheltered place we did not wish to venture farther without knowing the nature of the river mouth. We took the longboat from river to the land, which we found greatly inhabited. The people were about the same as we had met before, dressed with bird feathers of different colors, and came toward us happily, giving loud shouts of admiration, and showed us where we could take the boat safely. We entered the river into the land for about half a league, where we saw that it formed a very beautiful lake about three leagues in circuit, on which about thirty of their barks were going from one side to the other, carrying an infinite number of people coming from different parts to see us. Suddenly, as befalls in navigating, there rose a strong contrary wind from the sea which forced us to return to the ship and, greatly to our regret, to leave that land, so hospitable and attractive and, we think, not without things of value, all the hills showing minerals.

The sheltered place in the Lower New York Bay where the ship anchored may have been Gravesend Bay in back of Coney Island. The two prominent hills were Staten Island and Brooklyn, the deep water between, the Narrows. The longboat was taken through the Narrows to enjoy briefly the Upper Bay and the welcoming canoe loads of natives. Sudden wind cut short the visit, which may not have gone as far as Manhattan Island or Hudson River. The visit to New York took part of a day in mid-April.

Leaving Lower New York Bay they sailed east along the south shore of Long Island: "Having raised anchor, sailing east with the trend of the land, and having gone eighty leagues [fifty by the Ramusio version] always in sight of the land, we discovered an island of triangular form, ten leagues from the mainland, about of the size of Rhodes [a large exaggeration], the hills covered with trees, and well populated, judging by the fires we saw all along the shore." This was Block Island, which they passed without landing.

"Fifteen leagues beyond the island, we came to another land where we found a most beautiful harbor and as soon as we entered we saw about twenty boats of people who gathered about the ship with various cries of astonishment." They had come to Newport Bay where they made their one leisurely stop and got acquainted with the country and people of Rhode Island, Refugio as named by Verrazzano. The latitude was given as that of Rome (41⅔ degrees in the Ramusio version, a degree less in the Cellere one).

The coast there runs west-east. The mouth of the port faces south and is half a league wide. From the entry it extends for twelve leagues between west and north and widens to form an ample bay, about twenty leagues in circuit. Within it are five small islands, very fertile and attractive, full of tall and spreading trees. A fleet of any size could stay here in security without fear of tempest or other hazard of fortune. To the south of the entrance are pleasant hills with many brooks, discharging their clear waters from on high into the sea. In the middle of the entry is a living rock [bedrock].

Such is the first description of Narragansett Bay. Fifteen days were spent here from late April into May, the high experience of the voyage.

Beyond Rhode Island distances and time are given passing notice. They may have gone another hundred and fifty leagues and taken three weeks or less before heading home. "We left said port the sixth of May, following the shore, never losing sight of land. We navigated a hundred and fifty leagues, finding the land of the same nature or somewhat higher, with some mountains and everywhere showing minerals. We did not stop because the good weather aided us in getting along the coast." An obscure division into three stretches of fifty leagues follows. In the first were great and dangerous shoals, perhaps the passage of Cape Cod and Massachusetts Bay. In the second, "holding more to the north, we found a high land filled with very dense forest, the trees being firs, cypresses, and the like that grow in cold lands." This was the land of *mala gente* and "of no account whatever except for the very great forests." This stretch may be considered the coast of Maine. In the third sector the coast turned northeast and "we found it more beautiful, open, and free of forest, with high mountains inland, diminishing toward the coast. In fifty leagues we found thirty-two islands, all near the mainland, small and of pleasing aspect, high, following the curve of the coast, and between them beautiful harbors and channels like the Adriatic in Illyria and Dalmatia." Perhaps this was the coast of southern Nova Scotia. "After a hundred and fifty leagues we found ourselves near the land discovered in the past by Bretons . . . and having used up our naval supplies and victuals and discovered six hundred leagues and more of new land, supplying ourselves with wood and water, we decided to return to France."

Verrazzano had passed along the coast from Carolina to Nova Scotia in about eleven weeks, two of which were spent in Narragansett Bay. South of New York the coast was low, without a stone; to the north it was rock and showed minerals (metamorphic and igneous bedrock). South of Hatteras were aromatic woods, in the middle stretch hardwoods and grapevines, at the north conifers of cold climate. Verrazzano had an eye for the pattern of vegetation. In the south the higher land back of the beach showed many beautiful *campagne* (champaigns) and great woods, in part open and in part dense, the trees of various hues of gracious and delightful appearance. The middle coast named Arcadia was of special interest because of the grapevines that climbed the trees. Here some of the woods were open (*selve rare*).

The stay in Rhode Island gave time to see somewhat of the interior. "In it are champaigns twenty-five to thirty leagues in extent, open and without any impediment of trees, of such fertility that whatever be sown will give great return. Entering thence into the woods, all of which can be traversed in any direction by any army, the trees are oaks and cypresses and others unknown in our Europe. We found Lucullan apples [in the margin "or cherries"], plums and hazelnuts, and many kinds of fruit differing from ours." Game of various kinds was abundant.

They were in the most fertile part of New England, well peopled by sedentary Indians. The vegetation described by Verrazzano largely had been patterned by man. The treeless champaigns, which we would call prairies, and exaggerated as to dimension in the account, later impressed the English colonists. The woods were open in all directions so that an army could march through them, and an army moved by marching in rank and file—a picturesque overstatement that stressed the open nature of the woods. The "cypresses" were probably *Juniperus virginiana* (which we misname "red cedar"), secondary growth on old fields and retreating woodland margins. Such also are crab apples, hazelnuts, wild cherries, and plums. What Verrazzano described was a land well altered in plant cover by human occupation, partly by clearing for planting, largely by the seasonal practice of setting fires.

INDIAN NOTES BY VERRAZZANO

The *Dauphine* made six stops of record and was met at each by natives; thus Verrazzano gave the first account of Indians of our Atlantic coast. The first meeting was south of Cape Fear, probably with a tribe known by the name of that cape, affiliated with the Catawabas and of Siouan speech.[12] Fires had been seen along shore at the first approach. After the *Dauphine* turned about to start north a boat was sent to the beach, the waiting natives being shy. "Assured by various signs, some came near, showing great pleasure at seeing us, marveling at our dress, features, and whiteness; they showed us where to draw up the boat and offered us food." They were described as of medium stature, well proportioned, some of broad faces, others of sharp features, in complexion almost as dark as Ethiopians, with thick black hair tied in a pony tail. Some wore a headband of birds' feathers; all were naked except for a loincloth. Here, as later, Verrazzano was most interested in the appearance of the Indians.

Again as they were sailing along the Hatteras banks fires on shore signaled their course. A young sailor who had been sent to make contact was washed ashore half drowned, picked up, and carried to a fire. To his surprise and that of his shipmates, instead of being barbecued he was given good care. The Hatteras natives differed from those seen before in being of more delicate build and of sharper features and having very shiny skin (greased?). They had come to their first Algonquian tribe and would meet others of that speech in the course of their landings.

12. J. R. Swanton, "Indian Tribes of North America," Bureau Am. Ethnology, Bull. 125 (1952). He does not refer to Verrazzano.

In Arcadia they spent three days on land and learned about the wild grapevines, tasting some dried grapes as sweet as any in Italy. The time being early spring these must have been stored by the Indians. The text continued that the grapes "are esteemed by them, since wherever the vines are the growth about them is kept clear so that they may do well"—an interesting note suggesting incipient viticulture. They were within the range of *Vitis labrusca,* parent of American table and wine grapes, and used as raisins by the Indians. That vines were cared for suggests that such attention was given to vines of superior fruit, this species being notoriously variable in size, color, and quality.

The Indians of Arcadia grew crops as was learned by eating their food. "Their subsistence is largely of *legumi* which are abundant, differing in color and size from ours, very good and of delectable savor; for the rest they depend on game, fish, and birds, which they take by bow and net." Legume here is used in the sense of pulse or beans. They were given a mess of the New World kidney or navy bean (*Phaseolus vulgaris*), of the previous year's harvest, and found them excellent. There was no mention of maize or squash or of planted fields, perhaps because "we did not see their habitations, which were inland." Verrazzano here described natives working at making canoes, made of a single tree trunk, twenty feet long by four wide, and fashioned by charring to the desired concavity. The people may have been Nanticokes, "the tidewater people" as they were called by their Delaware kinsmen.

New York Bay swarmed with boat loads of welcoming Indians, some having donned feather headdresses for the occasion.

A score of boats came out to greet the *Dauphine* as it entered Narragansett Bay. After the preliminary salutations the natives clambered aboard, among them two "kings" of fine stature and carriage.

The elder had about his naked body a buckskin, worked with artifice resembling damask and with various adornments; the head was bare and the hair coiled at the back with various bindings; about the neck a large chain with stones of diverse colors . . . these are the most handsome people and most gentle in their manners of any we have met on this navigation. They exceed ourselves in size; are of bronze color, some inclining to white, others to tawny color; the profile sharp, the hair long and black and they give great attention to its care; the eyes are black and alert, and their bearing is sweet and gentle, much in the manner of olden days.

The women were described at some length as to attractiveness and conduct. Both sexes wore ornaments of plates of copper which they prized more than gold, the color of which they held to be inferior.

The things we gave them that they liked were small bells, blue crystal glass, and other objects of fantasy to put in their ears or hang about the neck. They did not appreciate cloth of silk or of gold or any other kind, and did not care to have such; the same was true of steel and iron, being shown our arms they did not admire or want any of them, looking only at their artifice. They did the same with mirrors, having looked at them they would be returned with a smile. They are very generous and give anything they have. We formed great friendship with them. One day when we were trying to come into port with the ship from a league at sea, the weather being contrary, they came to the ship with a great number of their boats, their faces painted and made up in different colors in token of friendliness, and bringing us of their food. They showed us where we should make port to save the ship and accompanied us to the place where we dropped anchor.

The Indian men made daily visits to the ship, the women staying in the boats. The native craft of a single tree trunk shaped "with marvelous artifice" held fifteen men. They were propelled by a short oar (paddle), broad at the end and worked wholly by strength of the arm. Thus they went out to sea without danger and at whatever speed they wished. The French made visits to the native houses, described as of circular form, fourteen to fifteen paces in circumference, semicircular in vertical section; the framework of poles was covered with skillfully made mats of straw. The houses were in random clusters and were relocated whenever desired by removing the mats to another frame of poles. Some houses were said to have twenty-five to thirty persons (multifamily).

The subsistence was as in other parts. In their cultivation they observed "in planting the influence of the moon, the rising of the Pleiades and many customs of the ancients." The party visited there at planting time. Verrazzano was impressed by the good order of cultivation but it is doubtful that he could determine an astrologic calendar. The natives enjoyed long life and good health and practiced compassion and charity. The account ended with telling of a long dirge for the dead that used "the Sicilian plaint."

The fortnight spent about Narragansett Bay provided Verrazzano with a first description of the life of an Indian people within the confines of the United States. The observations were made of the Narragansett nation living on the western side of the bay and the Wampanoag of the east side. Both nations were numerous and well practiced in agriculture, fishing, and hunting. The houses were the Algonquian wigwams in the form of a bell-shaped beehive, the frame of saplings set in the ground, bent together and lashed at the top, covered with mats or bark. The idyll of Narragansett Bay called to mind the virtuous life of olden times that men of the Renaissance learned from classical writings.

The last contact with natives was with *mala gente,* the bad people of the Maine coast, possibly Penobscots. "Whereas those seen before had been of gentle manners these were of rude and bad habits, so barbarous that we could converse with them only by signs. They dress in skins of bears, wolves, seals, and other animals. Their food, insofar as we learned by going through their habitations is game, fish, and a kind of wild root." Their bad name seems to be due to trading habits. They kept the French at a distance, letting down what they offered by cord from a rock, and accepting only knives, fishhooks, or edged metal. A French party that went inland to a settlement was shot at. Verrazzano was unaware that he had come to shores visited by Europeans. The Narragansett natives knew nothing of European goods, were not interested, and gave freely what they had without return. These people of the north wanted to trade, but only for sharp pieces of metal; also they were wary of ships and their crews. The implication is that codfishing ships engaged in trading peltry were accustomed to range as far as the shores of Maine.[13]

VERRAZZANO AFTER THE RETURN

When the *Dauphine* got back to France Francis I was a prisoner of the Emperor. Nothing is known of the original report of Verrazzano. Copies in Italian were circulated, one being

13. As for example the Basque traders who visited the Fagundes colony.

printed at midcentury by Ramusio. The declared objective of
the voyage to find a passage to Cathay was not carried out.
The supposed sight of the other ocean across the Hatteras
banks was not investigated. There was no entry or notice of
Chesapeake or Delaware Bay or the Hudson River. The reconnaissance of the Atlantic coast was made without misadventure and gave a favorable account of land and people.
The report might well have served as a prospectus for colonization, but no such plan resulted. After his release Francis
thought it the better part of wisdom not to risk another confrontation with Spain.

Verrazzano and his brother Girolamo turned to action in
Portuguese waters, or such as Portgual considered its own by
papal decree. In 1526 an association was formed at Rouen,
including Ango and the Verazzanos, to trade along and beyond
the coast of Africa. Three ships were manned by Normans,
the Verrazzanos were named captains.[14] Upon being caught
in a storm at the Cape of Good Hope, the ships turned about
to the coast of Brazil to load brazilwood. A later expedition in
1528, from Rouen to Brazil, resulted in the death of Giovanni
at the hand of natives. Mollat thus has disposed of the impossible tales that he was killed and eaten by cannibals in Jamaica, Darien, Coro, or elsewhere on the Caribbean coast. These
later Verrazzano voyages were part of French ventures to
Brazil for brazilwood and other tropical trade goods, prior to
Portuguese settlement there. When France renewed its interest in North America it was to latitudes higher than those
explored by the Verrazzano voyage.

VOYAGE OF ESTEBAN GÓMEZ

Whatever the Spaniards were doing about the Caribbean was
at individual initiative and expense; the Crown gave the
license to a petitioner for a share of the proceeds. The American Mediterranean seas were known to have no passage into
an ocean beyond. Magellan was sent by the Crown in 1519 to
look for one along the southwest trending coast of Brazil,
coming to winter quarters in a harbor of Patagonia. Here
discontent and mutiny were dealt with severely by him, re-

14. Michel Mollat, *Premières relations entre la France et le Brésil, des
Verrazane à Villegagnon,* Cahiers de l'Institut des Hautes Etudes de
l'Amérique Latine (Paris, 1964).

sulting in the desertion of officers in the largest ship. On their return to Sevilla they filed charges against Magellan in March 1521.[15] The pilot was Esteban Gómez, a Portuguese who had been sent to the East Indies in the service of Portugal.

It was by then apparent that if Magellan did discover a passage it would be in high southern latitudes and over a long and difficult route. This was confirmed when Sebastian el Cano returned in September 1522 with one remaining ship and the survivors from the first circumnavigation of the world. The strait discovered by Magellan was more than a thousand miles south of the latitude of Cape of Good Hope; its waters were cold and storm-vexed, and the land bleak. The route discovered by Magellan would not provide Spain with access to the East Indies.

Gómez offered to find a better alternative by going west to the eastern part of Cathay, continuing thence to the islands of the Moluccas, and staying within the domain assigned to Spain by treaty with Portugal. He was given the royal license March 17, 1523 with provision of a suitable caravel not to exceed fifty tons, a stock of trade goods, and victuals for one year.[16] The approach from the east to China meant a northwest passage. Gómara thus interpreted it, writing that Gómez had offered to find a strait in the land of Bacalaos (Newfoundland). Peter Martyr noted that in the summer of 1524 a *junta* of Spanish and Portuguese experts had been held at Badajoz and Elvas to resolve the delimitation of Spanish and Portuguese rights in the Far East, in particular as to the Spice Islands (Moluccas), Gómez being a participant for Spain. He would go by another route, he said, passing from Florida to Bacalaos to find the way to Cathay. A caravel was being made ready, Peter Martyr added, and Gómez carried no other instruction than to see whether in the twistings and turnings of the ocean sea he would discover a seaway to the land of the Grand Khan.[17]

The project was broached in 1522, authorized early in 1523, and undertaken early in 1525. The plan must have been known in France. Whether it influenced the Verrazzano voyage of 1524 is not known.

The Gómez voyage began and ended in 1525. Peter Martyr,

15. Navarrete, vol. IV, Doct. 21.
16. CDI, vol. 22, pp. 74–78.
17. Decade VI, chap. 10.

penning the final part of his *Decades* at the end of 1525, wrote
that Gómez, "without having been able to discover, as he had
promised, either the strait or Cathay, returned after ten
months. I have always thought that the notions of this good
man were vain and have said so." Gómez sailed from La
Coruña, the most northwestern Spanish port, and returned to
it.

Like Verrazzano, Gómez made his exploration from south
to north along the American coast, contrary to the usual
interpretations. His commission being to discover a strait to
China, if there was such, he began exploration somewhere in
the north of Florida. Peter Martyr and Gómara provide some
information as to where he sailed; more is gained from
cartographers of the time. Two of these, like Gómez, were
Portuguese in Spanish services, Diogo Ribeiro (in Spanish
form Diego Ribero) and Chaves, both employed by the Casa
de Contratación, the office of overseas affairs at Sevilla which
kept the *padrón general,* the official sailing chart, revised to
date. The third and last was the Spaniard Alonso de Santa
Cruz.

Ribeiro drew a series of charts, given dates from 1525 to
1532 (he died in 1533), five of which have been preserved in
European libraries (1525 at Mantua, 1527 at Weimar, 1529 at
the Vatican, another of 1529 also at Weimar, 1532 at Wolfen-
büttel). A part of the 1527 map is reproduced as Figure 6, of
the 1532 one as Figure 7. They are excellent in design and
record additions of knowledge.[18] It is inferred that Ribeiro
drew them from the current *padrón general.* Chaves, working
at Sevilla after Ribeiro, showed Oviedo a master chart corrected to 1536, from which Oviedo copied into his *Historia
General* place names and distances from Pánuco to Labrador.[19]
Santa Cruz completed his *Islario General* in 1541, consisting of
fifteen maps from Labrador to the Strait of Magellan, with
descriptive text. The coast from Chesapeake Bay to Florida is
omitted without explanation. The maps are indifferent and
less informative than the text.[20]

To the north of the peninsula of Florida the land of Ayllón
and the River Jordan were of earlier knowledge (see below).

18. In *Port. Mon. Cart.*
19. Vol. LXXI, chaps. 8, 9, and 10.
20. The *Islario* was first published by Franz von Wieser, *Die Karten
von Amerika in dem Islario General* (Innsbruck, 1908).

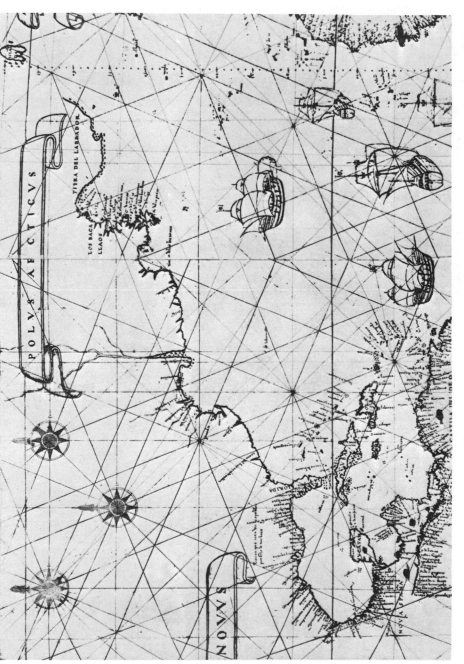

FIG. 6. Northern Atlantic portion of the Weimar map of 1527 (Anonimo-Diogo Ribeiro according to Armando Cortesão), *Portugaliae Monumenta Cartographica*, I, Lisbon, 1960.

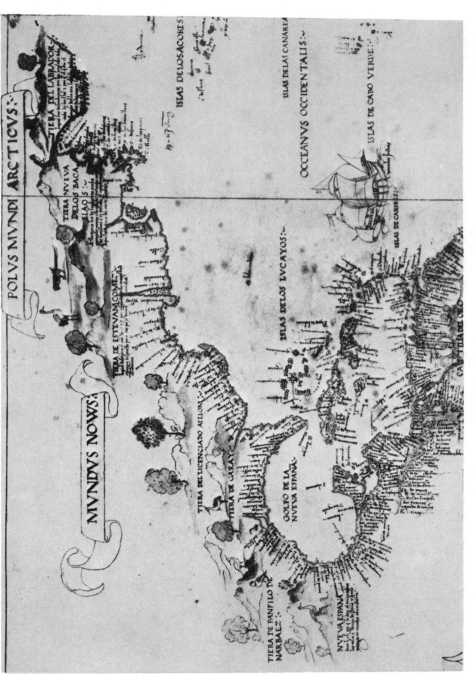

POLVS MVNDI ARCTICVS:~

MVNDVS NOVVS:~

TERA DEL LABRADOR

TERRA NVEVA
DELOS BACA
LLAOS:~

TERA DE ESTEVAM COME

TIERA DEL LICENCIADO AILLON:~

TIERA DE GARAY:~

TIERA DE PANFILO DE
NARBAEZ:~

NVEVA ESPANA:~

GOLFO DE LA
NVEVA ESPANA:~

ISLAS DELOS LVCAYOS:~

ISLAS DE CARBES:~

CA...TIA DEL ORO

ISLAS DELOS ACORES:~

ISLAS DELAS CANAREA

OCCEANVS OCCIDENTALIS:~

ISLAS DE CABO VERDE:~

Fig. 7. Northern Atlantic portion of the Ribeiro-Wolfenbüttel map of 1532. *Portugaliae Monumenta Cartographica.*

Thence to Maritime Canada (*Tierra Nueva*) the land on the Ribeiro maps was that of Estevam Gomez (sic). The trend of the coast is to northeast. As was true of Verrazzano's voyage, there was no notice of Chesapeake or Delaware bays. There is sufficient agreement as to place names to make a fair reconstruction of the Gómez voyage, with the aid of the distances and directions Oviedo took from Chaves. Beginning at the south, the order thus is:

Ribeiro	Chaves Oviedo	Santa Cruz	Present Name
C. de S. Juan	C. S. Joan 30 leagues NNE to	C. de S. Juan	Cape Charles
C. de Arenas	C. de las Arenas (38⅓°), 30 leagues N. to	C. de las arenas	Cape May
C. de Stiago	C. Santiago (39½°) 30 leagues WSW to	C. de santiago	Sandy Hook
B. de S. Xrval	B. de San Cristoval (39°) 30 leagues to	B. de s. Xroval	Lower New York Bay
B. de S. antonio	Rio de San Antonio (41°) 40 leagues ENE to	R. de sant antonio	Hudson River
Rio de buena madre	Rio de Buena Madre Thence east to	R. de buena madre	Connecticut River? Thames River?
B. S. Juan Baptista	B. San Joan Baptista (41½°) 50 leagues ENE to	B. de sant Juan baptista	Narragansett Bay
arecife	C. Arrecifes (43°)	C. de arrecifes	Cape Cod

The Ribeiro maps placed "Tierra de Estevam Gomez": southwest of and adjacent to the Newfoundland of the cod fishers: "there are in it many trees and fruits of Spain and many *rodouallos* (halibut) and salmon and *sollas* (sole)." They did not find gold: "in all this north coast the Indians are of greater stature than those of Santo Domingo and the other islands: they subsist on maize and fish, of which there is great abundance, and on hunting deer and other animals; they dress in the pelts of wolves and foxes."

Santa Cruz wrote of islands to which Indians came in summer to fish for salmon, *sávalos* (shad?), *bogas* (menhaden?) and many other kinds. (Salmon did not enter south of the coast of New England.) The land was of temperate climate, with many oaks, wild grapevines, and plants like those of Spain. The gold Gómez thought to have found turned out to be pyrite (*margarita*). The natives were tall; both sexes used bow and arrow. Santa Cruz introduced his account of a very wide and great river he called the river of deer (*Gamos*), which Gómez navigated "for a considerable distance, thinking it might be the strait he was seeking, but finally found it to be a notable river formed by great confluence of waters, from which the large size and expanse of the continent can be inferred." This River of Deer, which his map would appear to locate in Maine, may be the misplaced Hudson River.

As far as the river or bay of San Antonio, Gómez had been going in a northerly direction; there he turned briefly somewhat south of west, entering a bay (New York Bay). Gómez had about six months on our Atlantic coast against the scant three of Verrazzano. If Santa Cruz was correctly informed about the Gómez caravel sailing up a great river until they were assured it was not a strait, the Hudson River, which is a tidal fjord to Albany, is the best choice. Chaves placed the river San Antonio at 41°, which is close for the Hudson, and as being north of the *rinconada* (corner) formed by the cape of Santiago (Sandy Hook). Gómara, usually knowledgeable, headed his account of the Gómez voyage with the title "Rio de San Anton," indicating that this was the principal discovery. Oviedo added: "The land from forty one to forty two and a half degrees was discovered by Estevan Gómez in 1525, who brought the account of this coast of the North to Toledo the same year."

The Ribeiro maps indicated the limit of the Gómez coasting as *Rio de la buelta* (the river from which the return was made), the next notations beyond being of "land of the Bretons." The second map of Santa Cruz showed a large Isla de San Juan (Nova Scotia) with the bay of the Bretons to the northeast, the text adding "of this island there is nothing to relate except that the pilot Esteban Gómez says that passing along it he saw many smokes and signs of habitation." Nova Scotia was long thought to be an island. The bits of information seem to add up to a Gómez voyage around Cape Cod and along the east coast of New England, with a continuation by Santa Cruz to Nova Scotia. Knowing that he was getting to coasts familiar to the cod fishers (who probably had left for home before then), Gómez set sail for La Coruña, whence he made his report to Toledo before the end of the year.

Gómez had found neither strait nor gold, but he had brought back some Indians, to the disgust of Peter Martyr: "Not having attained anything he had thought to do, and not wishing to return with empty hands, he loaded the ship, contrary to the law, with innocent natives of both sexes." Oviedo's observation was: "The Indians the pilot Estevan Gómez brought to Toledo in 1525 were from the north coast, where he had been in forty two degrees; and I saw six or seven of them; all were larger than any Indians I have known and so tall as to exceed the usual stature of men we consider of medium height in Spain." These then were Algonquians from New England or Nova Scotia, probably enticed aboard the caravel. There is no mention of misadventure—storm, running aground, hostility, sickness, or lack of food.

The voyage was the only one to the Atlantic coast of North America that was planned in Spain and paid for by the Spanish Crown. Cortés meanwhile had thought of the alternative of sailing from the west coast of Mexico across the Pacific to the East Indies. Instead of one long sea voyage between Spain and the Far East there would be the greater convenience and security of a transfer by land carriage across a narrow part of New Spain. The exploration by Gómez was not followed up and its record largely was lost or forgotten.

THE LAND OF CHICORA (1521–1526)

Spaniards drifted from their earlier places in Española to Puerto Rico, Jamaica, and Cuba, and from there to new prospects on the mainland, which by 1520 meant Mexico. Those who remained in Española, or Santo Domingo as it was also called, had land but lacked labor, the natives having died out. Some stocked the empty land with cattle and horses. Sugarcane had been introduced and yielded well. The first sugar mills of the New World were built in Española and gave promise of large profit, if labor could be secured. Negro slaves were expensive. The islands, other than those of the Caribs, having been depopulated by 1513 by raids for Indian labor, slave hunters turned to various parts of the mainland.

Puerto Plata on the north coast of Española had engaged in capturing natives on the Bahama Islands. A local sugar plantation and mill procured Indians from the mainland beyond the Bahamas. Two caravels dispatched, in 1521 or 1522, finding no Indians in the Bahamas, went on to the mainland

in 32° to the district known as Chicora.[21] Many Indians came
to the coast to visit the caravels. Some were given Spanish
dress and sent to their chief who sent back fifty with a present
of food. Spaniards went to visit the "king" and were given
guides to see the country. After an exchange of presents the
natives were invited aboard the caravels for more entertain-
ment. When the ships were filled with guests they hoisted sail
and made for Puerto Plata. One caravel was lost, the other
delivered its cargo of captives. The trick had been used before on the coast of Venezuela.

Lucas Vázquez de Ayllón was one of the partners in the
venture, but did not take part in the voyage. He was part
owner of the sugar operation at Puerto Plata, also a judge
and member of the Audiencia of Santo Domingo, the overseas
governing body of the Spanish Indies.[22] In the division of the
captives Ayllón obtained a young Indian, perhaps a son of a
chief, who became known as Francisco Chicora. Ayllón became greatly attached to the Indian youth, who was quick to
learn Spanish and soon was baptized a Christian. Ayllón took
Francisco with him to Spain where he went on business of the
Audiencia. Oviedo saw both at court, Ayllón in the habit of
the Order of Santiago to which he had been appointed. Oviedo
thought that Ayllón left Santo Domingo in September 1523
and that he was at the court in Sevilla in January 1524, representing the Audiencia in the recall of Diego Columbus as
governor of Santo Domingo and also trying to secure for
himself the government of the newly discovered mainland to
the north.[23] Unless Ayllón was given such appointment before he returned to Spain, which is unlikely, Oviedo was off as
to timing, his colonizing contract having been issued in June
1523.[24]

At any event Ayllón and his Indian visited at their leisure
in Spain, telling of the discovery which, according to Ayllón,
who had not seen it, was a fertile land suitable for Spanish

21. Gómara, in Vedia, vol. 1, p. 179.
22. Gómara thought there were seven partners who underwrote the
Chicora expedition and that it took place in 1520. At that time Ayllón
was in Vera Cruz as representative of the Audienca in an unsuccessful
attempt to prevent a conflict between Narváez and Cortés.
23. Libro IV, chap. 8.
24. CDI, vol. 14, pp. 503 ff; again vol. 22, pp. 79 ff. In his petition Ayllón
said that he and two othe˙ members of the Audienca had found a land
to the north, unknown before, situated in latitudes 35 to 37 degrees
North. The latitudes given are too high unless these caravels also discovered Chesapeake Bay (Santa María), which is possible.

settlement, "for in it there are many trees and plants of the kinds of Spain and the people are of good understanding, in greater part ruled by a man of giant stature and there are pearls there and other things which they trade." [25]

Francisco Chicora played up very well to the attention he was getting and made up tall tales about the country and its different people. The aged Peter Martyr, who was usually not credulous, was completely taken in. He wrote the second and third books of his *Seventh Decade* about what he heard from the Indian. Beginning with his native land of Chicora, Francisco told of a score of tribes and territories, most of which have not been identified. (These were also named in the official grant to Ayllón. Some were identified later, more probably were inventions.) One country was inhabited by people who had come by sea. These had tails thick as an arm and a palm's span long. They were obliged to dig a hole whenever they sat. They had fingers as broad as they were long, a scaly skin, and they lived on raw flesh. Having put this one across young Chicora told of other tribes ruled by giant kings or queens, who were made to order by a special diet and by stretching their limbs. Some tribes kept domestic deer which were raised in the houses and returned to them at night. Also many kinds of domestic fowl were kept.

The Indian also told some things that were true—the earliest data on Carolina natives. They drank the juice of a plant called *guay,* which made them vomit bile and caused them to feel good. (This was the ceremonial black drink made of a native holly, *Ilex vomitoria.*) In place of the cassava bread of the islands they ate bread of maize, noted by Peter Martyr as like the panicum of Lombardy. They also cultivated another grain called *xatha* which Peter Martyr thought might be a millet, meaning a small-seeded plant grown as a cereal. (The second small-seeded grain grown may have been a *Chenopodium,* such being reported later from Roanoke in North Carolina.) A small tuber was eaten (*Helianthus tuberosus?,* the Jerusalem artichoke).

Oviedo thought that the young Indian was intelligent but was fooling his master by nonsensical stories: "I told him so but Ayllón believed him as though he had been one of the twelve apostles." [26]

The license to Ayllón emphasized that the occupation

25. CDI, *supra.*
26. Libro XXXVII, Proemio.

should be peaceful, protect the rights of the natives, and instruct them in the Christian faith. The brutalities and stupidities that had destroyed the island natives were not to be repeated. That the venture was undertaken in good faith was shown by the participation of Dominican friars, including Antonio de Montesinos, who had begun the demand for Indian rights with his famous sermon at Santo Domingo in 1511.

How Ayllón went to colonize the land of Chicora was told by Oviedo. Ayllón sailed in mid-July 1526 from Puerto Plata with six ships, carrying five hundred men and eighty to ninety very good horses. (Horses at the time were many and cheap in Española. That most of the participants were afoot suggests both the peaceful intent and their humble station.) The course was direct, northwest across the open sea to the land of Chicora, disembarking below the mouth of the river called Jordan. The latitude was given as 33 and ⅔ degrees, later amended by Oviedo to 33 degrees. (Jordan River was either the Santee or Waccamaw River in South Carolina. The latter appears preferable, a tidal stream entering Winyah Bay at the north end of the Sea Islands, Georgetown being the present town.) Seamen of Puerto Plata knew the way to Chicora, and the Indian had planted the idea in the mind of Ayllón that his colony should be located there (fig. 8).

Oviedo doubted that there was a land by that name or that any of the score of Indian territories named in the grant to Ayllón were other than inventions of Francisco. "Not one land was known by any such name, but Ayllón held them to be the treasure that had been granted him." John Swanton, however, best informed on the Indians of our southeastern states, thought that the name Chicora might be valid. A tribe known as Shakori, when displaced from their coastal home, became absorbed into the related Catawbas farther inland. In that case the earliest Spanish contact with Indians of Carolina was with a Siouan-speaking people.

The flagship ran aground as it entered the Rio Jordan and was lost and with it the greater part of the supply of food and equipment. A double mistake: the freight was loaded into the largest ship, and it was wrecked by negligence at the entry to the channel. Destitution faced the party at its beginning. Shortly Francisco and others of his tribe who had been brought back from Española ran away and were not seen

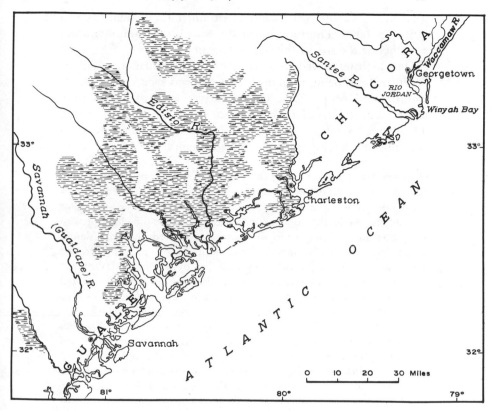

FIG. 8. The Sea Island coast of the Ayllón colony.

again. The Spaniards were left without guides or interpreters, and with little food. Instead of the land Chicora pictured, Ayllón found himself in a land of sand and swamp and without Indians to give welcome.

The party reembarked in the smaller ships, to follow southwest along the coast and its sounds for forty to forty-five leagues to a large river called Gualdape. Here there were scattered Indian huts and a dry place by the water on which to build their camp. The country all about was low and flat, with many swamps. The river, though great, had a shoal at its entry that could be crossed safely only at high tide. The Gualdape was the Savannah River. Swanton has shown it to mean the river of the Guale people, *guale* meaning southern in Muskogean speech, hence a southeast branch of the people, later known to the English as the Creek Nation. These occu-

pied much of the Sea Island coast until their removal two
centuries later. The location of the Spanish encampment was
at or below the site of the city of Savannah.[27]

Oviedo interviewed persons after their return, his Thirty-
Seventh Book being a synopsis of what was seen of the Guale
country and people. The Guale natives were of good build,
taller than the Indians of the southern islands (Arawaks).
They were excellent archers, using very strong bows made of
chestnut and having quivers of various pelts.

On some small islands along the coast there are certain temples or
mosques that contain bones of the deceased, those of children being apart from those of adults. These appear to be ossuaries or
charnel houses of the common people. The bones of chief persons
are placed in a chapel or temple apart, also located on small islands.
These latter houses or temples have walls of *cal y canto* [dressed
stone laid in mortar] which they make of oyster shells. [Were the
shells burned to make lime mortar, or did they use partly cemented
shells, a stone known as *coquino*?] The walls are half again as high
as a man, the part above being made of pine timbers, which trees
are common here. Along that coast are great houses, usually one to
a village. These are very large and are constructed of very tall and
excellent pine trees on which the upper branches and foliage remain, a double file of pine trees forming a wall, the space between
being fifty to thirty feet wide and three hundred feet long. The
branches meet overhead and thus there is no necessity of a roof or
covering. Nevertheless they do cover the entire structure with well
laid mats. [Oviedo continued with a somewhat repetitive account of
the great houses, their pine timbers and trees and walls.] In each
of the great houses there may very well be two hundred persons,
living there.

Oviedo heard at second hand of a society in which class
distinction extended to the storage of the deceased in particular ceremonial structures. The mortuary customs made an
impression as something strange to Spanish experience. The
great house, usually one to a village, was probably the assembly hall.

Oviedo named six informants, some of the data applying to
the Sea Islands, others to the mainland. Indian agriculture is
barely mentioned but there is a good deal on the flora of the
dry land and on the aquatic fauna, suggesting that the Spaniards ranged about rather widely. It was a land of pines and

27. Swanton, pp. 66 and 183.

of many oaks, some of the oaks forming galls, others being live oaks noted for their acorns. There were grapevines in the woods, small fruited chestnut trees, laurels, walnuts, mulberry trees, osiers, hollow canes, blackberries that were dried for winter use by the natives. There was much sumac and many palmettos, like the low-growing ones of Spain. There were thistles and sorrel. The vegetation seen was that of coastal Georgia and South Carolina. It was fairly well identified by Spanish names. In Spain there was only the Persian walnut; here there were native walnuts (*Juglans*) and the related hickories (*Carya*), all known to the Spanish as *nogal*. Sumac was first recorded here as *zumaque*, the Spanish-Arabic name for Mediterranean shrubs of the genus *Rhus*. *Sorvo* was reported to Oviedo from the Guale country. In Spain this is the mountain ash (*Sorbus*) which is not native to the southern coast plain. *Amelanchier*, of the same family and somewhat similar flower and fruit, is a native and has acquired there the name service-berry (by English derivation from *Sorbus* to service).

Some of the items suggest old fields abandoned from Indian cultivation. Staghorn sumac and the blackberry known as dewberry are active colonizers of worn-out fields and are unlikely to be conspicuous unless there has been serious disturbance of cover and soil.

Deer, rabbits, squirrels, and skunks were named. There were countless birds of many kinds—cranes, crows, thrushes, sparrows, partridges (bobwhite), turtledoves, geese, and ducks.

As to fish, there is much to be told. The Rio Gualdape is a matter of wonder as to the great abundance and excellence of fish, as the religious [Dominicans] and others affirm. They say that they saw more than six hundred mojarras taken in a single haul of the net, of which all the people ate and much was left over. They tell of one mojarra of which the Licenciado Ayllón and ten or twelve others ate and left some. It is a most excellent fish. There are many flatfish . . . , many acedias [flounder?], many lizas [mullet], very large and good, and many others . . . and of each great abundance. But with all this many persons died of hunger for lack of bread and because in their infirmity they were unable to fish.

Ayllón died October 18, 1526. Thereafter dissensions and strife broke out, resulting in killings. Some strayed off to Indian villages, got into trouble, and were killed. Of the five hundred who had set out from Española not more than a hundred and fifty got back, and these mostly sick and starving.

Ayllón had been the wrong man for the job, in Oviedo's judgment. Belonging to a good class of hidalgos, he had been well trained in law and civil service, but knew nothing of leading men on expeditions. He had come wholly under the spell of the Chicora Indian who, desiring to get back to his people, made Ayllón believe things that were incredible. The disaster began when the flagship with most of the supplies was lost on landing. Indian hostility broke out after the death of Ayllón when Spaniards began to wander off into the back country. Some of those who returned thought that the country would be attractive if the settlement were properly undertaken.

This ended for forty years Spanish interest in mainland settlement on the Atlantic coast.

5

Preview of Canada

(1534 to Midcentury)

CARTIER TO THE
GULF OF ST. LAWRENCE (1534)

Ten years after Verrazzano, France again took up the search for the western passage. Ships were prepared at and sailed from St. Malo in Brittany with Breton crews acquainted with Newfoundlands waters and a Breton captain, Jacques Cartier of St. Malo, who had been to Brazil loading brazilwood and trading with the natives.

The first two voyages were written from journals and log books, Cartier speaking as it were. The third is known only in the English version in Hakluyt's *Principal Navigations*.[1] The first voyage begins: "Under the command of Cartier we set forth from the harbor and port of St. Malo with two ships of about sixty tons each, the two manned by sixty men, on the twentieth day of April, 1534. Sailing in good weather we came to Newfoundland, sighting land at Cape Bonne Viste [Buenavista] in Lat. 48 ½ N." This was right on course for the desired landfall. The crossing had taken three weeks. They found a lot of ice about the cape and the next day (May 11) entered the harbor of Ste. Katherine (Catalina), where they spent ten days attending to the longboats and awaiting better weather. They then sailed north to the isle of birds

1. Biggar, *Voyages;* his map is here reproduced in reduced form as Figure 9.

(Funk Island), which was surrounded by cakes of ice and a
multitude of birds—in the air, on the sea, and on the island.
This was the famous rookery of the flightless great auks,
commonly visited by cod fishers. The two longboats were
filled in short order with bird carcasses, which were salted and
stowed in casks. They continued northwest across the open
sea to the harbor of Quirpon at the northern tip of Newfoundland (May 27), to be detained by ice until June 9. They
had started early in order to take full advantage of the season
of open water, awaiting which they spent a month on and
off the east coast of Newfoundland.

The entry of the Strait of Belle Isle was on June 10 along
the north shore past Blanc Sablon, still thus named, and now
marking the boundary between Quebec and Newfoundland.
At Brest harbor, now Bonne Espérance, they found a great
quantity of eggs of eider ducks (Labrador duck?) and of other
waterfowl. Here they met "a large ship from La Rochelle that
in the night had run past the harbor of Brest where she intended to go and fish." Thus far they had been on coasts
familiar to cod fishers. Cartier thought little of the land seen
thus far.

If the soil were as good as the harbors, it would be a good land; but
it should not be called New Land but one of stone and horrible
and rough rocks; for in all this north coast I did not see a cart load
of earth, though I landed at several places. Except at Blanc Sablon
there is nothing but moss and short, stunted shrubs. In sum I in-
cline to think that this is the land that God gave to Cain. There are
people in this land, well built but wild and savage. They wear their
hair on top of their heads, like a twist of straw, with a pin or something through the middle, and into it they fasten bird feathers.
They dress in skins of animals, both men and women, but the
women are wrapped more fully in furs and have a belt about their
waists. They paint themselves in colors. They have boats in which
they go to sea, made of the bark of birch trees; from these they
catch many seals. Since seeing them I have learned that this is not
their home but that they come from warmer lands to take seals and
other things for their sustenance.

The Indians are not further identified. The visitors from
"warmer lands" who had come in seaworthy birchbark canoes
perhaps were Iroquois from the St. Lawrence River.

On June 15 the ships left the harbor of Brest on a southern course to examine the west coast of Newfoundland for ten days. More than a hundred cod were taken at one place in less than an hour. Leaving that coast they turned west across the Gulf of St. Lawrence for about a hundred miles on direct course to three small islands, cliff-sided

. . . so that is impossible to climb to the top. Between them is a narrow passage. These islands were as completely covered with birds that nest there as a meadow is with grass. The large one was full of gannets which are white and larger than geese. On the others there are many such in one part; another was covered with murres, also great auks, as on the aforementioned island [Funk]. We landed on the lower part of the lesser one and killed more than a thousand murres and great auks and loaded as many as we wanted. One might have loaded thirty longboats in an hour. We named them the gannet islands. [These are the Bird Rocks northeast of the Magdalen Islands.]

Five leagues west of these islands is another, two leagues long and as wide. We went to stay overnight and to get water and firewood. It is surrounded by sand, has a good bottom and an anchorage all about at six to seven fathoms. This is the best island we had seen, an arpent of it being worth more than all Newfoundland. We found it full of fine trees, prairies, fields of wild wheat [lyme grass], and [beach] peas in bloom, as thick and fine as ever I saw in Brittany, appearing as though they had been sowed by husbandmen. There are many gooseberries, strawberries, and roses as in Provence, parsley and other aromatic herbs. About the island are numbers of large beasts, like great oxen, with two teeth in their jaw, like an elephant. They go about in the sea. We took our boats to catch one asleep ashore at the water's edge, but when we got near it threw itself into the sea. Also we saw bears and foxes.

The island was named Île de Bryon "in honor of the Admiral of France" (now Brion Island). The morainic northernmost of the Magdalen Islands was a pleasing contrast to what they had seen. Here they had their first acquaintance with walrus. The larger Magdalens were skirted as was Prince Edward Island, Cartier being under the impression that he was on a low mainland coast, of beautiful woods and prairies abounding in wild grain and berries, lacking nothing but harbors.

On July 3 they came to the mainland at Chaleur Bay, thus named because of the hot weather. Its size and westward ex-

tension gave hope that it might be the western passage they
were seeking. A lot of Indians came in canoes, bringing furs
and welcome.

We likewise made signs to them that we wished them no harm and
sent two men ashore to give them some knives and other iron goods
and a red cap to give their chief. Seeing this they sent to the shore
a party with some of their furs; and the two groups traded together.
The savages showed marvelous great pleasure in possessing and ob-
taining these iron wares and other commodities, dancing and going
through many ceremonies and throwing salt water over their heads
with their hands. They bartered everything they had to the extent
that all went back naked without a thing on them; and they made
signs that they would be back on the morrow with more furs. [Ten
days were spent in Chaleur Bay, exploring as far as its head]
whereat we were grieved and disappointed. At the head of the bay,
beyond its low shore were very high mountains. And seeing that
there was no passage we proceeded to turn back.

Another meeting for trade took place, more than three hundred Indians assembling to barter furs for knives, hatchets,
and the like. Their words for hatchet and knife recorded at
the time have been identified as Micmac, the principal
Algonquian people of New Brunswick.[2]

Having left Chaleur Bay they were held up by bad weather
to July 25 in a well-sheltered harbor (Gaspé Bay). During the
time two hundred Indians, men, women, and children, arrived by canoe to net mackerel.

They are not at all of the same race or language as those we met
before. They have the head shaved all around in a circle, except for
a tuft on top of the head, which they leave long like a horse's tail.
This they do up and tie in a knot with leather thongs. They have
no other shelter than their canoes, which they turn over to sleep
underneath on the ground. [The fishing nets were made of] hemp
(*chanvre*) that grows in the land where they live ordinarily, for they
do not come to the sea except at the fishing season, as I have been
given to understand. Also that they grow maize (*groz mil*) like peas,
the same as that in Brazil, which they eat instead of bread, and of
which they had a large quantity with them.

Cartier named other food items they had brought, dried
plums, beans, and nuts, giving their Indian names, which are

2. *Ibid.*, p. 57, note 8.

Iroquois-Huron.[3] Two sons of the chief accompanied the French from Gaspé harbor, served as guides, and told of their homeland where maize was cultivated, the same grain Cartier had known in Brazil.

From Gaspé they sailed north to the south shore of unnamed Anticosti Island, which they followed to its eastern end, and then west along its north coast into the narrowing channel now called Jacques Cartier Passage, a "marvelously high coast" looming to the north, the Laurentian highland Cartier had found so bleak in the Strait of Belle Isle. Looking "to see whether it was a bay or passage," they got to the west end of the island by hard rowing of the longboats against head winds and tides. They started back August 1 along the Laurentian coast. A dozen Indians came aboard from two canoes (off Natashquan Point) as they were returning to their western home and told that the fishing ships, loaded with cod, had already left the bay (the northeast arm of the Gulf of St. Lawrence). Blanc Sablon was entered August 9, left on August 15, and St. Malo was reached September 5.

The reconnaissance was well executed. The Atlantic was crossed in each direction in three weeks, remarkably good time for a voyage west. From Cape Buenavista, the usual landfall in Newfoundland, the ships took their way north through the Strait of Belle Isle, then known as Chasteaux, familiar to Breton fishers. Entering the unnamed Gulf of St. Lawrence by the northern strait, they made the clockwise circuit of the Gulf. The west coast of Newfoundland was followed south to the headland from which they crossed the open sea for a hundred miles to the Bird Rocks, then to low Brion Island, and from the Magdalen Islands the better part of a hundred miles to the lowland of Prince Edward Island. The assurance and directness of the course tells that they knew where they wished to go, that the Breton crew had been there before. The shoal waters of the southwest part of the Gulf were familiar fishing grounds and the shores provided places to prepare dry cod. Cape Breton Island, adjacent to Prince Edward and Magdalen Islands, was well known to Breton fishermen.

The welcome in Chaleur Bay by Indians who were ready to trade pelts tells that they were familiar with ships; fishing vessels also engaged in fur trading. Whether Cartier got beyond waters visited by European ships is not known.

3. *Ibid.*, p. 83.

The most important practical result of the reconnaissance was finding that Chaleur Bay offered no passage and that the strait between Anticosti Island and the Laurentian mainland might do so. Bearings, soundings, nature of bottom, and shore lines were recorded daily. Cartier returned to France with a sufficient knowledge of the Gulf to know where to direct the next exploration.

Also, in somewhat florid language, he brought good observations on the country, topographically properly placed, of cliffs and bare rocks, prairies and lowland, coniferous and mixed woods, islands that were bird rookeries and the home of walrus. There was note that the cod fishers stocked up on eggs and salted carcasses of waterfowl. Cartier took down Indian words by which the Indians were identified as Micmac on Chaleur Bay and the summer fishers at Gaspé as Iroquois. The fur trade, casually begun by codders, was to become the basis of New France in the next century; the Iroquois were to change into enemies.

CARTIER'S VOYAGE TO CANADA (1535)

Cartier sailed again from St. Malo May 19, 1535, in command of three ships, carrying provisions for fifteen months. A storm having separated the ships, Cartier landed at the bird island (Funk) July 7, "which island is so exceedingly full of birds that all the ships of France might easily load there without their disminution; and there we took two boat loads for our stores." Its latitude was given as 49°40', which is nearly correct. Cartier continued north to go again through the Strait of Belle Isle and await the other ships at the designated harbor of Blanc Sablon. Cartier arrived there July 15, the other two ships on the 25th, the voyage continuing on the 29th. Their entry to the gulf was almost as late as the start of their return the previous year. This time they were expecting to pass the winter in the New World, not knowing how hard that winter would be.

They coasted along the Laurentian shore to the far end reached the year before. Being at good anchorage behind the Mingan Islands, thought to have been at Pillage Bay, they celebrated August 10, the day of St. Lawrence, in honor of this favorite saint of Brittany. The day had added importance, for ahead of them lay unknown waters. The extension of the

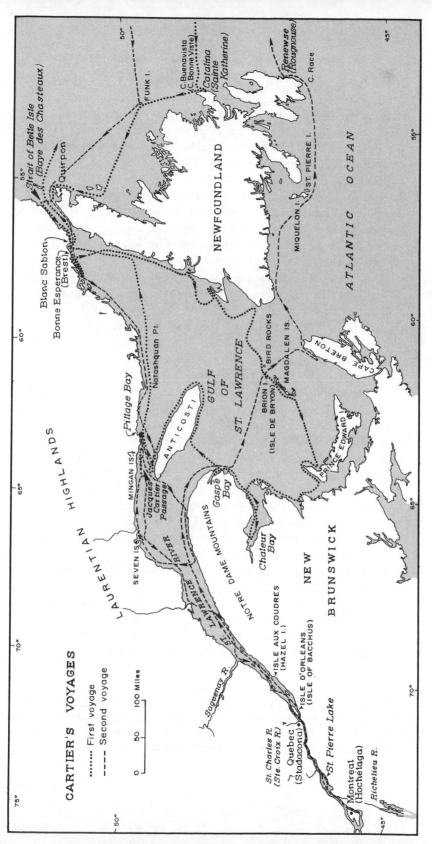

CARTIER'S VOYAGES

.... First voyage
– – – – Second voyage

0   50   100 Miles

FIG. 9. The Cartier voyages (after H. P. Biggar, *The Voyages of Jacques Cartier*, Ottawa, 1924).

LAURENTIAN HIGHLANDS

Strait of Belle Isle (Baye des Chasteaux)

Quirpon

Blanc Sablon
Bonne Esperance (Brest)

FUNK I.

C. Buenavista (C. Bonne Viste)
Catalina (Sainte Katherine)
Renewse (Rougnouse)
C. Race

NEWFOUNDLAND

ST. PIERRE I.

MIQUELON I.

ATLANTIC OCEAN

CAPE BRETON

Pillage Bay

Natashquan Pt.

MINGAN IS.

Jacques Cartier Passage

ANTICOSTI

GULF OF ST. LAWRENCE

BRION I.
(ISLE DE BRYON)
BIRD ROCKS
MAGDALEN IS.

PRINCE EDWARD

SEVEN IS.

Gaspé Bay

NOTRE DAME MOUNTAINS

Chaleur Bay

NEW BRUNSWICK

ST. LAWRENCE RIVER

ISLE AUX COUDRES (HAZEL I.)
ISLE D'ORLEANS (ISLE OF BACCHUS)

Saguenay R.

St. Charles R. (Ste. Croix R.)
Quebec (Stadacona)

St. Pierre Lake

Montreal (Hochelaga)

Richelieu R.

75°   70°   65°   60°   55°

50°   45°

name from a minor harbor to the great gulf, river, and mainland came later and was done by European writers and map
makers who chanced on the name in the Cartier records. López
de Gómara in his history in 1552 wrote "of the great river
St. Lawrence which some hold to be an arm of the sea." In
Italy Ramusio printed the voyage of Cartier in 1556 with the
caption "how the Captain had knowledge of the Bay of St.
Lawrence." Mercator's famous world map of 1569 showed it
as Sinus S. Laurentii, the gulf having been shown without
names on maps of earlier post-Cartier date and perhaps even
before his voyages. Cartier did not claim to have been the discoverer of the gulf nor did he give it its name.

Beyond the Mingan-Jacques Cartier Passage west of Anticosti
Island, Cartier relied on the two Iroquois youths whom he
had taken to France the year before. They were still a good
distance east of the land of the Iroquois but well within
waters visited by them. West of Anticosti they entered the
narrowing arm of the gulf, which in Canadian usage is called
the St. Lawrence River, though it is salt and deep for more
than three hundred miles. The exploration was made by zig-
zag course, Laurentian to Gaspé shore, back and forth (see
map, fig. 9). At the mouth of a river out of the north, great
enough to make the sea as fresh as spring water for a league
from land, they came again on walruses without knowing
what they were. "Up this river are a number of fish in the
form of horses which go on land at night and into the sea by
day, as we were told by our two savages, and of these fish we
saw a great number in the river." The Iroquois youths coming
back from their year in France provided the metaphor "horse
fish." The river was thus named R. de Chevaux by later map
makers, including Mercator, a "horse river" arising in the
Laurentian wilds.

Their guides had told of a Kingdom of Saguenay ahead
from which red metal was brought. Early in September they
came to a great fjord on the north shore which it was understood led to the land of Saguenay. It has since then borne
that name.

The river is between high mountains of bare rock having on them
but little soil, notwithstanding which many trees of several kinds
grow there on the rock as though they were in good soil, in such
manner that we saw a tree tall enough to make a mast for a ship of

thirty tons, as green as could be and growing on a rock without semblance of soil. At the mouth of this river we found four canoes that had come from Canada to take seals and other fish. While we were stopped in that river two of the canoes came hesitantly toward our ships, one turning back, the other coming close enough to hear one of our savages call out his name and identify himself, whereup they came aboard with confidence.

The glacier-scoured surface of the Laurentian Highland which they had first seen in the Strait of Belle Isle here bore scattered conifers of the size of small masts. The canoes were manned by Iroquois from the lower St. Lawrence Valley, of the same community that the year before had gone to Gaspé Harbor for summer fishing. The French made contact with these people hundreds of miles east of their agricultural settlements, as they ranged by canoe along the north of the gulf, hunting and fishing at sea.

Going on from the Saguenay "we discovered a kind of fish of which there is no record that it has been seen or heard of. These fish are as large as porpoises, without any fins, and in body and head are formed like a greyhound, as white as snow, without a spot, and they are in that river in very great numbers, living between salt and fresh water. The people of the country call them *adhethuys* and have told us that they are very good to eat and that in all this river and country they are found only in that vicinity." They had come upon a school of white porpoises or belugas, still a memorable sight of the saltwater St. Lawrence and of Saguenay fjord, found here far south of their general Arctic range.

On September 6 they anchored at Isle aux Coudres (Hazel Island), "the soil good and rich with fine large trees of several kinds, including hazels, that we found laden with nuts as large as ours and of better taste, the shells somewhat harder; for this reason we named it hazel island." There were white porpoises in abundance and "an inestimable number of great turtles in the vicinity of the island." [4] The island, still bearing the name given by Cartier, is formed of alluvial and lacustrine

4. I am told that this cannot be true. Cartier had not seen walrus before and their description is strange but recognizable. His voyages in the tropics surely had made him acquainted with sea turtles. What was familiar needed no descriptions, only recognition. Cartier was a pretty fair naturalist and I should leave his turtles at the head of salt water on the St. Lawrence, the month being September, as unexplained.

deposits of the lowermost part of the St. Lawrence Valley and is of that vegetation. Its growth of hazel suggested the name, the vegetation being unlike the country to the east.

The following day they came to fourteen islands, "the beginning of the country and province of Canada. One of these is large, about ten leagues long and five wide, where the people engage in fishing of all kinds in season." Here the two youths were reunited with their families and a celebration followed in which the Frenchmen were given eels, other kinds of fish, and several loads of maize (*groz mil*), "which is the bread by which they live in that country," also many large "melons" (pumpkins). There were numerous huts, occupied during fishing time. The island had a fine stand of trees, "oaks, elms, pines, cedars, and other kinds like our own; and also we found there a great number of grapevines, which we had not seen before anywhere, and for this reason we named it the Isle of Bacchus." It is Île d'Orléans, in mid-river below Quebec, later occupied by gardens and dairy farms.

On September 8 Donnacona, "Lord of Canada," came down the river with twelve canoes for ceremonial welcome. The surroundings were attractive, the natives friendly, and it was time to look for winter quarters. Cartier sent the longboats up the river to find a suitable place where the ships would be laid up over winter.

We came to a fork of the waters, very beautiful and pleasing, where there is a small river and a harbor with a bar at a depth of two or three fathoms. We found this a proper place to put the ships safely and named it Ste. Croix. The people of whom Donnacona is lord live around here and he has his residence of Stadacone near by. This is as good land as can be found and is highly productive, with many fine trees of the nature and kinds of France, such as oaks, elms, ash, nut trees, plum trees, yews, cedars, vines, hawthorns with fruits as large as damson plums, and other trees, beneath which there grows as good hemp as that of France, and it grows without sowing or labor.

This is the original description of the site of Quebec, at the junction of the St. Charles River (Ste. Croix of Cartier) with the St. Lawrence adjacent to the Indian village of Stadacona.

The Iroquois land of Canada was the lowermost St. Lawrence Valley, including the islands below Quebec. Cartier gave a fair description of this most northerly extension of the northeastern mixed hardwoods and hemlocks, omitting from this first list maple, birch, and beech. Wild grapes reached their highest latitude in these deciduous hardwoods. His yews were eastern hemlocks (*Tsuga canadensis*), conifer companions of the hardwoods. The nut trees included the butternut (*Juglans cinerea*), of fertile valley floors. Arborvitae (*Thuja occidentalis*) of wet lowlands is still commonly known as white cedar. Wild plums and hawthorns grew at the borders of woodland and fields. The wild hemp has been identified as the wood nettle (*Laportea canadensis*), a local fiber of Indian use.[5]

Taking the smallest ship and two longboats, Cartier started up river on September 19 to explore the valley. He was charmed by the landscape in early autumn, its promise of productivity, and the hospitality of its natives. "Along the banks we saw the most beautiful and fertile lands, as level as a body of water, full of the finest trees of the world, and along the river so many vines loaded with grapes as though planted by the hand of man, although not being cultivated or pruned, the grapes are not as sweet or large as ours. Also we found many houses along the banks of the river, the people at the time busily engaged in fishing. They came over to our boats in as friendly and familiar a manner as though we had been their countrymen." The kinds of trees were again named, adding birches, willows, and conifers, also naming a score of birds as being like those of France, including *outardes*.[6]

The river was extremely low, two fathoms below the high water mark shown along its banks. Having come to the head of a lake (St. Pierre), they were obliged to leave the ship and continue up river in the longboats. At the riverside settlements they were greeted with dancing and were brought food, fish and other kinds, and thus were introduced to the taste of broiled muskrat.

The island on which the town of Hochelaga was located was reached October 2. More than a thousand natives came to receive them "with as good a welcome as ever a father gave to

5. Jacques Rousseau, "La botanique canadienne à l'époque de Jacques Cartier," in *Contributions du Laboratoire de Botanique de l'Université de Montréal*, no. 26 (1937).

6. Outarde is the French name for bustard, a large terrestrial game bird not found in the New World. It is one of the names for the Canada goose in French Canada, perhaps thus given because it is disinclined to or incapable of flight during the molting or nesting season. A river *aux outardes* flows into the St. Lawrence two hundred miles northeast of Quebec City.

his son." After a ceremony of dancing they were brought quantities of fish and of the bread made of maize (*groz mil*) and then followed a well-worn road, noting

oaks as fine as in the forests of France, the ground beneath covered with acorns . . . the land cultivated and beautiful, large champaigns full of the corn of their country . . . and in the midst of these fields stands the town of Hochelaga, near and adjacent to a mountain, cultivated round about and fertile, and from the top of which one can see far. We named this mountain Mont Royal. [They viewed the surrounding country] for more than thirty leagues about. To the north is a range of mountains running east and west [the escarpment of the Laurentian Highland] and to the south another [the Adirondack and Green Mountains]. Between these mountains one sees the most beautiful land, arable, smooth, and plain. And through the middle of these lands we saw the river, above the place where we had left our longboats, with very turbulent rapids beyond which we could not pass [Lachine Rapids].

They were looking out over the broad lowlands that had been the floor of a Pleistocene lake. The description of the town of Hochelaga follows:

The town is circular and enclosed by timbers in three *rangs* [rows or tiers?] in the manner of a pyramid, interlaced above, having the middle row forming a vertical line, then timbers laid lengthwise, well joined and lashed together according to their manner; and it is of the height of about two lances. And there is but one gate and entry to this town, closed by bars, above which and at several places along the enclosure there are galleries with ladders to mount to them, where stones are kept for protection and defense. There are some fifty houses in the town, each fifty or more paces long and twelve to fifteen wide, made of timbers and covered, roof and sides, by large pieces of bark and rind of trees, some as wide as a table and artfully tied according to their manner. And inside are a number of rooms and chambers and in the center of the house is a large room or space upon the ground, where they make their fire and live together, the men thereafter retiring with wives and children to their private rooms. Also houses have lofts on high in which they store their corn.

The houses were grouped about an open central area, about a stone's throw across. Here the visitors were seated on mats to listen to an address of welcome by a chief, to be followed by a meal.

Cartier saw a good deal during the single visit within the palisade town. It is the first notice of the Iroquois longhouse and its interior arrangements for the families that shared it. The brief look he had at the manner of enclosure of the town was inadequate to give a clear description. It is all that Ramusio had available when he had an artist draw the plan of Hochelaga that has been reproduced many times as though it were an authentic representation.

The two days on the Island of Montreal provided a lot of information. "They have large containers like tuns [7] in their houses into which they put their fish, such as eels and others, which they dry in summer by smoking and on which they subsist in winter; and of such they have great store, as we have seen by experience. All their food is eaten without salt."

The main crop was maize. Hochelaga was entered by way of "champaigns full of the corn of their country, like the *mil* of Brazil, of the size of peas or larger, on which they subsist as we do on wheat." Cartier had been to Brazil and knew maize from there. It was known to the Portuguese as *milho*, with or without qualifying adjective, which was translated into French as *mil* or *gros mil*. At Hochelaga he observed corn fields in autumn ripeness and learned that corn was stored in house lofts (the ears hung under the roof). Of it, he continued, "They make the bread they call *carraconny* and they do so by this manner. They have wooden mortars like those used for braying hemp and pound the grain into meal with wooden pestles; they then mix this into a paste and make *torteaux* (cakes) thereof, which they place on a hot stone and cover with heated pebbles, and thus bake their bread instead of in an oven. They also make diverse pottages of their corn, some with beans and peas of which they have plenty, and also large cucumbers and other fruits." (The cultivated crops will be noted below.)

In résumé of the life of the Hochelagans:

They sleep on the bark of trees spread on the ground and covered with poor pelts. They make their clothes of the pelts of otter, beaver, marten, fox, lynx, deer, stag [wapiti], and others; but for the most part they go quite naked. Their most prized possession is

7. Arthur W. Parker, "Iroquois Uses of Maize," *64th Ann. Rept. N.Y. St. Mus.*, vol. 2 (1911). Plate 5 shows a Seneca storage barrel of elm bark; Plates 11, 12, and 20 are wooden post mortars used in grinding grain. Parker was a Seneca ethnographer.

esnoguy [wampum], white as snow, which they procure in that river. [A fanciful account follows of the qualities and getting of wampum.] All these people engage in cultivation and fishing solely to sustain themselves; they do not value worldly goods, being unacquainted with such and they do not go out of their own country, not roving about as those of Canada and Saguenay, although the Canadians and eight or nine other tribes along the river are subject to them.

The return down river was made in a week, the ships rejoined at Stadacona on October 11. Winter quarters were prepared by building a fort at the anchorage. "Made of large timbers planted upright," it was the prototype of later French log building as far west as the Mississippi River. "From mid-November to the fifteenth day of April we were continually frozen in by ice, thicker than two arms' length, with snow on land to the depth of four and more feet, higher than the sides of our ships. This lasted to the above date, all our beverages frozen in their casks, and the ice four fingers thick within the ships, below as well as above deck. The fresh water of the river was frozen as far as Hochelaga and beyond."

In December a great sickness broke out among the Indians of Stadacona, more than fifty dying. Fearing contagion, Cartier stopped the Indians from visiting the fort and forbade their coming close to any Frenchman. "Not withstanding that we had chased them away, the sickness broke out among ourselves." The sickness of the French was described in detail and was scurvy, strange to their experience. (Having broken contact with the Indians, the Frenchmen were no longer provided with fresh fish and game but depended on the ships' stores of flour, biscuit, salt pork, and the like. The deficient diet resulted in making the scurvy more severe.) By mid-February not ten of a company of a hundred and ten French remained in health. Twenty-five had died and forty were thought to be dying. Then one of the Indians who had been taken to France taught them the remedy, *anedda,* probably the shoots of the hemlock tree (*Tsuga*).[8] A decoction brought rapid recovery and continued use kept them in health. Hemlock was easily at hand, was used in massive draughts and had an antiscorbutic effect. Cartier made marginal note that the Indians were again making visits and bringing freshly killed game and fish (which may have been the principal cause of the recovery).

8. Rousseau, pp. 41–43.

The first drastic experience of scurvy was quite misunderstood. The Indians did not suffer from it, having a proper diet without which they could not have lived there. The French were not stricken by contagion from the Indians, but the Indians were infected by the French, as was commonly the case when natives first came into close contact with Europeans. In this case the sickness broke out among the Indians in early winter, after they were confined by cold weather to close quarters and new pathogens brought by Europeans found optimal reception and propagation.

The voyage home began May 8, 1536, with Chief Donnacona and four of his Indians aboard. They took the ice-free southern way out of the gulf to the islands of St. Pierre (St. Pierre and Miquélon), where they stayed from June 11 to June 16, meeting ships "from France as well as from Brittany." Cod fishing off the south shore of Newfoundland was well under way at that season. Passing Cape Race they made a last stop for water and wood at the harbor of Rougneuse (now Renews). They reached St. Malo July 16, 1536, having made the longest and most informative exploration of the north of America.

SCOPE OF CARTIER'S REPORT

Cartier dealt with "the River." "This river begins above the island of Assumption [Anticosti] between the high mountains of Hongueda [the Notre Dame Mountains of Gaspé Peninsula] and the Seven Islands, the distance across being thirty-five to forty leagues, with a depth of more than two hundred fathoms in the middle." The "river" is still as Cartier defined it: the lower half the long deep arm of the Gulf of St. Lawrence, the upper the St. Lawrence Lowland built mainly of glacial lake sediments, drained by one of the world's great rivers.

Hochelaga he reported as having authority over all of the St. Lawrence Lowland, the lower part of which was the province of Canada under a chief Donnacona who lived at Stadacona (now the City of Quebec). The marine St. Lawrence River below the province of Canada was ranged over by Iroquois fishing and hunting parties from Canada.

Cartier's Kingdom of Saguenay signified the Laurentian Highland both north and west of the St. Lawrence. About the Seven Islands large rivers flowed "from the mountains of Saguenay." Farther west "the Saguenay River issues out of high mountains and enters the [salt St. Lawrence] river on the north side, before one comes to the province of Canada, and is very deep, narrow, and difficult to navigate." While in Saguenay fjord they were told that it led to a land from which copper came. The Saguenay River was said to be a way of getting to far lands. By means of light canoes they were told that one could thus travel northwest for more than a month (by portages to James Bay?). Another route of which they were informed was up river from Hochelaga, thus ascending for a month a river that flowed down from Saguenay. This was the first notice of the great canoe route up the Ottawa River to Lake Nipissing and the Great Lakes. Cartier was told: "Beyond western Saguenay the river entered two or three large lakes and then one came to a fresh water sea [Great Lakes] the end of which no one is known to have seen." Somewhere in the far interior "they gave us to understand that the people dressed in cloth as we do and that there are many towns and people of good disposition and that they have a great amount of gold and red copper." Rumors of Mexico or of New Mexico that had spread across the continent?

There was also information concerning lands to the south. Where they left their bark on Lake St. Pierre on the way to Hochelaga a river entered from the south (Richelieu River). By it they were told that one could travel for a month and come to "a land where there is no ice or snow; but that in that country there are continual wars between tribes; and there are oranges, almonds, nuts, plums and other kinds of fruits in great abundance. Being asked whether those people had gold or copper, they said no. I think, from what they told, that this land lies toward Florida." The canoe route up the Richelieu led directly to the Hudson River and to numerous Algonquian tribes farther south.

The hearsay geography of distant lands, partly understood by Cartier, told him that the ship passage he had been sent to find did not exist but that one could travel far and easily on inland waterways by light canoes carried from one waterway to another. Cartier was given an outline of the hydrography of the northern continent that later would be used in establishing New France.

Both for marine and riverine St. Lawrence Cartier assembled legible data on the native economy, its agriculture, and fishing and hunting on the waters. Little is said of taking land game, which was a lesser source of flesh and pelts.

This river abounds with more kinds of fish than man has ever known; for from beginning to end you will find in their season most kinds, both of salt and fresh water. As far up as Canada you will find many whales, porpoises, and [here repeating description of walrus and beluga]. . . . Also in July, June, and August there is great quantity of mackerel, mullet, sea bass, sartre, large eels, and other fish, and when their season is past there are smelt as good as in the Seine River. In spring there are many lampreys and salmon. Above Canada [Quebec] there are many pike, carp[!], bream, and other freshwater fish. All such fish, each according to season, are taken in quantity by the natives for their sustenance and food.

The crop complex maize-beans-squash, of Mexican origin, was seen here at its polar limit. Warm summers, long days, and mellow and fertile soil enabled an agriculture that succeeded at Quebec and was impressive about Montreal. Planting was done by wooden dibble "sticks half the size of a sword." The beans and peas, of different colors and sizes, were varieties of the common navy and kidney beans, *Phaseolus vulgaris.* The cucurbits were of such diverse forms as to be called not only *courges,* the French equivalent of the English pompion/ pumpkin, but also melons and cucumbers. All probably were forms of *Cucurbita pepo,* grown in greatest variety by the Indians of the Eastern Woodlands.

Cartier's description of tobacco is the earliest account out-side of the tropics:

They also have an herb, of which they collect a lot in summer for use in the winter. They esteem it greatly and it is used only by the men, in this manner. They dry it in the sun and carry some about their neck in a small skin pouch, in lieu of a sack, and with it a tube of stone or wood. They crumble the leaf at all hours and put it into one end of the tube, then place a live coal on it and suck on the other end, so as to fill their body with the smoke until it comes out of mouth and nose as though from a chimney. And they say that it keeps them warm and in good health, and they are never without these things. We have tried this smoke. Having it in one's mouth is like having it full of pepper.

Nicotiana rustica, high in nicotine, is a cultigen taken from northwestern South America as far as the St. Lawrence Valley and later grown by French Canadian farmers. According to Cartier its use was not restricted to the ceremonial passing of the pipe. He mentioned having seen it in Brazil.

Cartier recorded a native vocabulary by which the language

is known as Iroquois, closely related to Seneca and to Huron. Otherwise, we should not know that the Iroquois had occupied the valley. When Champlain came early in the next century they had been replaced by Algonquians, traditional enemies of the Iroquois.

ATTEMPT AT A FRENCH COLONY (1541–1543)

Cartier brought back a negative report on a sea passage to Cathay, supported by log and soundings of gulf and river. It was a prospectus of a country greater than France with waterways north, south, and especially west that were traversed by light, fast, and portable birchbark canoes. Cartier's great "river" was the prospective gateway to the wealth of a continent and perhaps beyond. Its people were friendly, intelligent, and attractive, in evidence of which the chief Donnacona and some of his subjects joined their return to France. Donnacona became somewhat of a celebrity at the French court and an advertisement for the colonial venture.[9]

The plans to establish a French colony had advanced by 1538 to drawing up the list of personnel and of equipment and supplies. Francis I, not noted for piety, now proclaimed his mission to bring the Christian faith to the Indians, as the Spanish monarchs had done in their avowed responsibilities as Catholic kings. At the moment Francis was not at war with the King Emperor, giving him occasion to push a diplomatic advance. He told the Spanish ambassador in Paris that he would respect all territory in actual Spanish possession but that he did not acknowledge discovery as giving title. The ambassador reported that Francis had said "the sun warmed him as well as it did others and that he desired greatly to see the testament of Adam to learn how Adam had partitioned the world." In another letter the ambassador reported that Francis acknowledged "that the popes have spiritual jurisdiction but not the right to divide lands among kings, and that neither the French nor other Christian kings had been called in when such partition took place," also that thirty years before ships of Spain or Portugal had sailed to the western

9. The late French literature is large, comprehensive, and excellent. Ch. A. Julien, *Les Français en Amérique* (Paris, 1946); also *Les Voyages de découverte* (Paris, 1948); Gustave Lanctot, *Histoire du Canada des origines au régime royal* (Montreal, 1960); Marcel Trudel, *Les Vaines Tentatives* (Montreal, 1963).

Indies, ships of the French crown had gone there. This was the claim that Bretons had gone to fish in American shores before the discovery of Columbus, a claim that has not been substantiated. Spanish and Portuguese agents at northern French ports sent intelligence how France was preparing a formidable fleet, causing concern that an attack might be impending against either the West Indies or Brazil.[10] Thus Francis kept Spain and Portugal worried about his next move while the expedition to colonize Canada was being prepared.

Cartier was named Captain General in the fall of 1540; the Sieur de Roberval, a nobleman of Picardy, several months later was given overall authority. Roberval had been active as a corsair; Cartier also is thought to have been thus engaged. Roberval was given authority to grant seignories, the Spanish ambassador writing that in effect he was made King of Canada. A Spanish agent, watching the loading of the ships at St. Malo, took count of the military supplies, tools, foodstuffs, and livestock, noting twenty cows, four bulls, a hundred sheep, a hundred goats, and twenty horses and mares. The major difficulty was to find colonists; jails were drawn upon in different parts of France, and a few noblemen in disfavor were added to the deportees. Cartier sailed from St. Malo with five ships in May 1541. Roberval delayed his departure to the spring of 1542, leaving from La Rochelle. Both men had experienced overseas crews.

Cartier sailed directly to Stadacona where he was festively welcomed. He thought it prudent to locate at some distance from the Indian town and chose a townsite nine miles above Quebec at Cap Rouge, where he built Charlesbourg-Royal. Again he took the longboats up river to find out more of the nebulous kingdom of Saguenay.

What Cartier had to say of the prospects of the colony is known only from an English version made years later by Richard Hakluyt while in Paris, a tract written in promotion of the colony:

Oaks the most excellent that ever I saw in my life, which were so laden with Mast that they cracked again . . . fairer Arables [maples], Cedars, Beeches, and other trees than grow in France. . . .

10. Documents in H. P. Biggar, *Pub. Public Archives of Canada,* no. 12 (Ottawa, 1930). The international play is well presented by Trudel, *Les Vaines Tentatives,* pp. 129–138.

Vines which we found laden with grapes as black as Mulberries, but they be not so kind as those of France because the Vines be not tilled.

There was a great extent of tillable land, and they had come in time to reap a fall sowing of cabbages, turnips, and lettuce. Best of all, the future was assured by the discovery of great mineral wealth:

We found there good store of stones, which we esteemed to be Diamonds. On the other side of the said mountains and at the foot thereof, which is towards the great River, is all along a goodly Mine of the best iron in the world, and it reacheth even hard unto our Fort, and the sand which we tread on is perfect refined Mine, ready to be put into the furnace, and on the water's side we found certain leaves of fine gold as thick as a man's nail. . . . There is a rising ground, which is of a kind of slate stone clean and thick, wherein all that stone there are veins of mineral matter, which shew like gold and silver; and throughout all that stone there are great grains of the said Mine. And in some places we have found stones like Diamonds, the most fair, polished and excellently cut that it is possible for a man to see. When the sun shineth upon them, they glitter as it were sparkles of fire.

Cartier was a good observer of plants, animals, and natives. His ignorance of minerals was almost total. André Thevet, the author of one of the first natural histories of Brazil, *Singularités de la France Antarctique,* appended chapters on Cartier's discovery. They were at second hand, partly from Cartier and Donnacona, both of whom he had known. The stones, Thevet said, that resembled gold in color and weight turned to ashes under heat. Iron and copper mines, he thought, might be found. As to the stones thought to be diamonds, "those who first found them thought themselves suddenly rich, thinking they were true diamonds, whence the current saying known to everyone: 'This is a Canadian diamond.' " He knew them to be rock crystal. The supposed gold was an iron pyrite that turned to ashes. Crystals, colors, and weight of minerals in the metamorphic and vein-laced rocks of the margins of the Laurentians were mistaken for gems and ores.

During the long winter of confinement within the fort scurvy again ravaged the French. Also mistrust developed between Frenchmen and Indians. Nothing had been heard of Roberval. When the river became free of ice Cartier abandoned the fort to start back to France. The ships put into the harbor of St. John's in southeast Newfoundland, a rendezvous of cod fishers, and found Roberval at anchor there. Roberval ordered him to turn back to Canada, but Cartier slipped out of the harbor at night and took his ships to St. Malo. He had no further contact with Canada.

Roberval stayed at St. John's to the end of June, partly to settle a quarrel between French and Portuguese fishers. He then took the northern course to Canada by way of the Strait of Belle Isle, the more roundabout and foggy route, but familiar to his La Rochelle crew. He repaired the fort Cartier had abandoned and settled his party in it. There was casual reconnaissance of the vicinity. The natives were friendly and brought food, mainly freshly caught fish. When winter closed in there was again the suffering of scurvy and, increasingly, hunger. (There is no report of either party as to what became of the livestock.) At the beginning of June 1543, he started up river with six boats rigged with sails. There is no record of how far they got or when the fort was evacuated. Roberval's party was back at La Rochelle prior to September 12, 1543. The year he had spent in the New World resulted in no new exploration, no planting of crops, no opening of trade, no initiative of any kind.

THE GEOGRAPHY OF JEAN ALPHONSE

Roberval's pilot, known as Jean Alphonse, was rated a great navigator. Thevet held him to be such, as did Hakluyt. Champlain gave him first place among the French navigators of the time. Alphonse finished writing his *Cosmographie* the year after he got back from Canada, stating that he had been voyaging for forty-eight years. The volume gives sailing directions overseas and may represent the extent of French knowledge in 1544.[11]

11. It was published by George Musset (Paris, 1904) with biography and bibliography. He was also known as Alphonse de Saintonge, Saintonge being a district near La Rochelle. The Canadian section was reproduced by Biggar as appendix to his *Voyages of Jacques Cartier*. Hakluyt made use of parts of the *Cosmographie*. Musset thought that Alphonse was killed in 1545 in an engagement with Spaniards, which would mean that he served as corsair at an advanced age.

The *Cosmographie* is a collection of information of his own experiences, of hearsay, and of other rutters or sailing accounts, the sources mostly unacknowledged. He copied freely from Fernández de Enciso's *Suma de Geographia,* printed at Sevilla in 1519, thereby giving an obsolete account of the town of Darien. Indications are that Alphonse did not get to that part of the Caribbean. Other items on other parts of the Spanish Main suggest that the information came from French corsairs operating in those parts. La Rochelle was a major base for such raids, in which Alphonse may have taken part or of which he was appraised. The maps of the *Cosmographie* are of little value, being very poorly drawn and badly oriented.

Champlain credited Alphonse with having gone in search of a western passage by which he got beyond Labrador until stopped by ice. Alphonse made no such claim in his volume but did give seventy leagues as the distance from Belle Isle to the beginning of the frozen sea whence came the ice masses that drifted south to Newfoundland; also, the northern sea was in large part fresh and extended to the North Pole. French knowledge of Labrador and the cold Labrador current is indicated. Belle Isle was the name for the island, not as yet for the strait. (The name had nothing to do with its appearance; the island was named for an island off the coast of Brittany.)

The *Cosmographie* took Cape Race as the beginning of the description of the North American coast; Alphonse outlined it as he piloted Roberval's ships with the benefit of what his La Rochelle crew knew of those fishing waters. The north shore of the Gulf of St. Lawrence was entered competently and in detail. "And on this coast are found falcons and birds of prey, and fowl that keep to the woods and resemble pheasants" (uncertain reference to ruffed grouse?). Anticosti Island (called Ascension): "a flat island, all covered with trees down to the sea, composed of white and alabaster rocks; and there are all kinds of trees like those of France. And there are on land many wild animals such as bears, porcupines, stags, hinds, does, and birds of all kinds, and many wild fowl that keep to the woods." About this island, and south to Chaleur Bay, there was great fishing of cod, of better quality than in Newfoundland. Two to three leagues above its narrow entry the Saguenay "seems to be an arm of the sea, for which reason I

think that this sea goes into the Pacific or to that of Cathay."
Shore and channel of the St. Lawrence were noted in detail.
Past Île aux Coudres, where Cartier had come to the beginning of fertile land at the beautiful isle of Orleans, "begins the
fresh water of France Prime and ends the salt water."

The land of Canada was praised as Cartier had done, with
the comment that "they are cold lands, much subject to snows
and to sickness of the limbs [scurvy] because the ground underneath is all frozen to a depth of two to three feet." The remark that the inhabitants "have no fixed abode, for they do
nothing except run from one land to another" is gratuitous
and wrong. The country about Hochelaga he considered much
better than that of Canada and its people more rational.
Recapitulating observations of the St. Lawrence, lowland
and maritime, "In that country much maize (*milg*) is harvested, on which they subsist together with the fish that they
take in the river and in the sea; for they are great fishers of all
kinds of fish, such as eels, seals, salmon, shad, porpoises large
as whales, and others of lesser size." Elsewhere he added stur-
geon and a confused description of walrus and beluga. Of
mineral resources he said "in these lands there is nothing but
crystal and tin, as I have seen."

"All these lands of Canada properly should be called New
France because they lie in the same latitudes. And if it were
as well peopled as France, it is my opinion that it would be
as temperate." [12] The trees were like those of France, but the
country was covered with forest, the removal of which and the
tillage of the soil would ameliorate the climate so that it
would be as mild as about La Rochelle.

The lands toward Hochelaga are much better and warmer than
those of Canada; and this land of Hochelaga trends toward Figuyer
and Peru, in which gold and silver abound. I saw also that its
natives say that in the town called Cebola, which is in thirty-five
degrees of the height of the north pole, the houses are all covered
with gold and silver, and they use vessels of gold and silver. These
lands lie towards Tartary and I think this to be the extremity of
Asia by the roundness of the world. And therefore it would be good
to have a small ship of seventy tons for discovery of the coast of
Florida; for I have been to a bay as far as forty two degrees, between

12. He also used the name France Prime, derived from Verrazzano.
Canada was applied by him to a larger reach than the area about
Stadacona (Quebec).

Norumbega and Florida, but did not see its end and do not know
whether it leads beyond.

This is a greatly confused geography that scrambles some
knowledge of Spanish reports with observations, imaginings,
and hearsay. Figuyer was Higueras, an early Spanish name of
Honduras, like Peru an important source of precious metals.
The legend of Cibola was ascribed to New Mexico by Fray
Marcos in 1539 and shown by Coronado in 1541 and 1542 to
be in reality the modest towns of the Pueblo Indians without
any wealth of metals. That Alphonse knew the tale made up
by the friar is shown by the name Cibola, which he attributed
to Indians of Hochelaga. How he came up with the correct
latitude for Cibola/Zuñi I do not know. The St. Lawrence
Valley he thought trended toward the Pueblo country as well
as to Central America, but he also thought it an extremity of
Asia, south of which a passage west should be sought. Previously he had proposed the Saguenay to the north of the
St. Lawrence as a prospective waterway to China.

Norumbega, which he placed between Canada and Florida,
was, more or less, New England. It was thus named on the
Girolamo Verrazzano map of 1529 and was so called until its
English settlement. The bay, which he claimed to have visited,
and thought worth exploring to see how far it led west, may
have been Long Island Sound. Alphonse was informed on
latitude. The bay he gave as at 42° N., the cape of Norumbega
at 41° and as being a hundred forty leagues southwest of Cape
Breton. "The said coast is all sandy, the land low, without any
mountain, and along the coast are several sandy islands.
[Nantucket Island is near 41°.] Beyond the cape of Norumbega
the river Norumbega enters, about twenty five leagues from
the cape," the town of Norumbega fifteen leagues inland. The
people here were of good disposition and "had a lot of furs
of many kinds. [Either the Thames or the Connecticut River
may be indicated.] In general, the people of this [Norumbega]
coast and of Cape Breton are bad people, strong, great bowmen, and people who live on fish and meat and have some
maize, and speak almost the same language as those of Canada,
and are a numerous people." The summation applied to the
Algonquian tribes of New England and the Maritime Provinces.

The legendary islands thought to lie in the North Atlantic

Ocean disappeared as that sea became familiar to fishing fleets of different nationalities. Alphonse however retained a place for them, including the famous Brendan and Seven Cities islands:

To the southeast of cape Ratz [Race] there are two lost islands, which are named the isles of saint Jehan d'Estevan and are lost because they were of sand. And it is forty leagues from them to cape Ratz; and are in forty five degrees north latitude; and are very dangerous. Sixty five leagues at sea south of cape Ratz, there is another island named Sainte Croix; and is at forty one degrees north latitude. To the southwest of Cape Ratz, eighty leagues at sea there is also an island named Bardan, and is all sand; and is at forty two degrees north latitude. To the southeast of cape Breton, thirty leagues out at sea is another isle, which also is of sand and lies northwest-southeast with the isle of Bardan, and it is thirty leagues from one to the other. And is at forty four degrees of north latitude. And to the south of cape Ratz a hundred and five leagues at sea, is another isle, called Heron, and is at thirty eight and a half degrees north latitude. And to south-southeast of cape Breton, at about three hundred leagues there is a large island, called the Seven Cities, which is a large island. And there are numbers of persons who have seen it, as also I have done, and thus certify; but I do not know what there is within it, for I did not go on land.

The one oceanic island of the north is Sable Island, which he identified as a number of islands reported by different names. His Ste. Croix was Sable Island, the Santa Cruz of Fagundes. It had acquired the alternative name of Juan Esteves from another Portuguese (under the section on Fagundes, above) and became the two lost islands of St. Jehan d'Estevan for Alphonse, named after a nonexistent saint. His Bardan isle, all of sand, is given a position not far off the location of Sable Island—probably mythical St. Brendan's Isle. The unnamed isle, also of sand, is in the latitude of Sable Island and not far off proper direction from Cape Breton. Heron Island was placed at about the distance of Sable Island from Cape Race, but in the wrong direction and latitude. One real island of sand was construed into a half dozen, spaced about the ocean south of Cape Race and east of Cape Breton.

The island of Seven Cities of medieval legend he placed in the approximate position of the Bermuda Islands. It was an island that had been seen by numerous persons including him-

self, he certified. Being a navigator of repute, his claim of
having seen it is acceptable, and probably means that he saw
it during a raid to the Spanish Indies. The Bermudas were
named after an early Spanish pilot at the beginning of the
century. They were known as lying in the Sargasso Sea of
quiet water and floating vegetation and usually were bypassed
after Spanish ships discovered the Gulf Stream.

SABLE ISLAND AT MIDCENTURY

The bleak wind-piled sand ridge of Sable Island was involved
incidentally in the attempt in 1598 by the Marquis de la
Roche to colonize New France, thereby revealing an earlier
history. The story was told by Marc Lescarbot, who lived from
1606 to 1607 in Acadia (Nova Scotia): [13]

In the year 1598 the Marquis de la Roche, a nobleman of Brittany,
seeking to colonize New France and to plant there French settlement . . . led thither a certain number of folk, whom (having as
yet no knowledge of the country) he disembarked on Sable Island.
. . . Meanwhile he went off to reconnoitre both the inhabitants and
the country. . . . On his return he was overtaken by a contrary wind,
which carried him so far seaward that, seeing himself nearer to
France than to his company, he continued his journey thither [to
France]. . . . His men remained on the island for the space of five
years, living on fish and on the milk of some cows carried thither
some eighty years ago, in the time of King Francis I, by the Baron
de Leri and de St. Just, Viscont of Guet . . . who was constrained
to disembark there his live stock, cows and pigs, for want of fresh
water and pasture. And on the flesh of these animals, now greatly
increased in number, the colony of said Marquis lived the whole
time they were in this island. At length the King, when at Rouen,
ordered a pilot to go to their rescue when he went to the Newfoundland fishery. This he did and out of forty or fifty brought
back a dozen, who presented themselves before his Majesty clothed
in walrus-skins.

Lescarbot knew about the cattle left on Sable Island, but not
the time and manner. The reputed Baron de Leri seems to be

13. *Histoire de la Nouvelle France* [1608, third edition 1618, republished
by the Champlain Society (Toronto, 1907–1914) and cited here in
English translation], vol. 1, pp. 44–45.

apocryphal. A colony sent out by Francis under a nobleman of high lineage would hardly have passed without notice.[14]

The proper explanation of wild cattle on Sable Island is that they had been brought by Portuguese. Champlain, writing of his voyage of 1613, told that Portuguese had taken cattle to Sable Island about sixty years before. Hakluyt had the account of Sir Humphrey Gilbert's voyage in 1583 in search of a location for an English colony, which told that Gilbert, inquiring of fishermen in the harbor of St. John's, Newfoundland, heard of Sablon (Sable Island). "We determined to go upon intelligence we had of a Portugal (during our abode in St. John's) who was himself present, when the Portugals (above thirty years past) did put into the same island both neat [cattle] and swine to breed, which were since exceedingly multiplied." By independent testimony of Champlain and Gilbert, Portuguese had stocked Sable Island at midcentury. Prince Henry had thus prepared the Azores for settlement. Portuguese continued the practice on uninhabited islands where there were no human or other predators. Sable Island was unsuited for settlement but might serve cod fishers with fresh meat. The cattle survived and reproduced, the swine as well were said to have done so, though this seems unlikely.

14. L. Scisco (*Transactions R. Soc. Canada*, 1911, Sec. II, pp. 247–251) and Robert le Blanc (*Rev. d'hist. de l'Amérique française*, vol. XI, 1958, pp. 563–569) found no one of that family unaccounted for at the time or at sea.

Part II

Spanish Entries to the Interior
and the Far West

6

Spanish News
of the Northern Interior
(1524–1539)

Cortés presented the King Emperor with New Spain, largely the domain of Moctezuma—known to the Spaniards as the great lord of Mexico—the Aztec state, a feudal empire of numerous peoples under central control. Its component parts mainly were of a high and similar culture, known to ethnology as Mesoamerica. On the Gulf of Mexico the Aztec domination extended to Pánuco. Cortés promptly secured control there and thwarted Garay's attempts to move against him from the north coast of the Gulf of Mexico.

The confrontation of Garay and Cortés in Pánuco resulted in the first report, recorded by Peter Martyr in 1524, that north of its mountains there was a great plain and a people who lived in cities and pueblos.

Three years later (1527) Nuño de Guzmán took advantage of Cortés' absence from Honduras to capture slaves about Pánuco and ship them to Española. Nuño had been a *vecino* in that island, knew the good price slaves and forced labor brought there, and used the opportunity to go into the illicit business. A class of Indian merchants (*pochteca*) ranged far beyond the Aztec domain to bring in goods of high value.

Turquoise was prized throughout Mesoamerica, and most of it was procured from one small district near Sante Fé in New Mexico (of which more later). An Indian merchant in the Huasteca (Pánuco region) told Nuño of this other Mexico to the north, meaning another land of civilized people to which he knew the long road. Nuño did not then undertake the thousand-mile march to the Pueblo country but remembered the direction he had been given.

While Cortés was away in unknown parts to the south and was unheard from, Nuño de Guzmán moved to the Spanish capital Cortés had founded at the former seat of Moctezuma. A Guzmán of ancient and high nobility, he was made head of the First Audiencia, which ruled with unbridled rascality. When it became known that Cortés had survived and was on his way back to Mexico, Nuño with his soldiers and his partisans departed for the unoccupied west, where they left a dreadful trail of devastation as far as the end of the land of high culture in the Culiacán valley. Here Villa San Miguel de Culiacán was built (1530–1531), to be for years the northwestern Spanish outpost, as Pánuco was on the east coast. Both were gateways to the Pueblo country, the route from Culiacán north being the major one used by Indian commerce. Nuño knew this and tried to follow it north from Culiacán. However, beyond the civilized people of the Culiacán valley he and his ruffians ran into a tougher breed, formidable bowmen, kinsmen of the Mayos and Yaquis, who blocked his way. Nuño de Guzmán set up his own government from Guadalajara to Culiacán, which he called Nueva Galicia.

With the return of Cortés order was restored in Mexico. The Second Audiencia called Nuño de Guzmán to account and sent him to Spain for trial. Nueva Galicia remained largely in the hands of his former followers, those of Culiacán continuing to engage in slave raids to the north. In 1535 Antonio de Mendoza was sent to Mexico as the first Viceroy of New Spain.

THE RETURN OF THE
CABEZA DE VACA PARTY IN 1536

In the spring of 1536 Melchor Díaz, alcalde of Culiacán, while on a slave hunt to the north saw a large party of Indians approaching, neither hostile nor afraid. They were Pimas Bajos from the middle Yaqui Valley, and with them were three Spaniards and a Negro, all in Indian dress. Such was the return after eight years of the only survivors of the Narváez expedition: Alvar Nuñez Cabeza de Vaca, Alonso Castillo Maldonado, Andrés Dorantes, and the latter's Negro slave Esteban (Stephen). They reached Mexico City in July to tell Viceroy Mendoza the story of their long and desperate wandering from the Gulf of Mexico to that of California.

Cabeza de Vaca wrote his famous narrative after his return to Spain, and it was first printed in 1542 at a time when the expeditions of Coronado and De Soto were of great public interest. His odyssey of shipwreck and hardships among strange peoples and in unknown lands, and of finding a round-about return to a Spanish outpost has been often reprinted and retold.[1] The narrative tells of the Narváez expedition, its shipwreck, the long stay in Texas, and the long journey over-land to the Spanish frontier at Culiacán.

Because Narváez' expedition had been under the authority of the Audiencia of Santo Domingo, the three Spanish survivors gave a written report to it in 1537, Dorantes being the principal deponent. He and Castillo were separated from Cabeza de Vaca in 1529 and did not rejoin him for more than five years. The Joint Report gave more information on the nature of country and natives in Texas, was more specific on the crossing of New Mexico, and was more objective. The report was excerpted and condensed by Oviedo in Libro XXXV of his *Historia General,* omitting only the superfluous and repetitious passages. Oviedo noted "in some respects I hold the relation of the three as better and more than the other" (that of Cabeza de Vaca, of which Oviedo appended to the Joint Report a competent résumé).

The long wandering from Galveston Bay to Culiacán was reconstructed by Fanny and Adolph Bandelier as having gone from Texas across Chihuahua and the western Sierra Madre.[2] The Bandeliers paid little attention to the Joint Report and their route has been accepted by most writers. More than forty years ago I began field studies in northwestern Mexico and adjacent parts of the American Southwest. I thus had the opportunity to observe all parts of the state of Sonora as to

1. A late annotated translation of merit is by Cyclone Covey, *Cabeza de Vaca's Adventures* (Collier Paperback, New York, 1961).
2. *Journey of Alvar Nuñez Cabeza de Vaca* (New York, 1905).

physical geography, vegetation, and settlements and became interested in what it had been like in the past. It became apparent that the Spaniards who came from the south followed the same route north by which the Cabeza de Vaca party had come out of the north, and that this was the ancient Indian trade route between Mexico and the Pueblo country. Knowing the country and the historical records, I plotted the recurrent use of the same road, which I described in *The Road to Cibola*.[3]

I backtracked the route taken by Cabeza de Vaca north from Culiacán through Sonora into the high grassy plains of southeastern Arizona and thence across southwestern New Mexico to the crossing of the Rio Grande about Rincon, where I left off. The Cabeza de Vaca route kept well to the north of the Sierra Madre, and did not cross it as projected by the Bandeliers. Independently Cleve Hallenbeck tracked the longer and more obsecure stretch of their wandering west from Galveston Bay and arrived at the same crossing of the Rio Grande as I had.[4] Hallenbeck lived at Roswell, New Mexico, and was well acquainted with the seasons, terrain, vegetation, and game of West Texas and eastern New Mexico. He inquired of old settlers what former conditions were and read the accounts of pioneer botanists in Texas, in particular George Engelmann.

SIX YEARS ON THE
TEXAS COAST PLAIN

Cabeza de Vaca's boat piled up on the beach of Galveston Island or on an adjacent bar, the one with Dorantes and Castillo some miles away (November 5–6, 1528). In all, there were about ninety survivors of the shipwreck. The weather was uncommonly cold, as the following winter seems to have been. Indians came to the survivors to give help, bring food, and take them to shelter. A small Spanish party started south to find a way by land to Pánuco and failed. Most of the men spent the winter about Galveston Bay, moving with the Indians, small bands of Karankawas, as they shifted camp.

3. *Iberoamericana*, No. 3 (Berkeley, 1932). It is reprinted in the volume of my essays *Land and Life* (Berkeley, 1963; paperback edition, 1967). In the latter the map has been reduced so that the route symbol for Cabeza de Vaca is difficult to distinguish from that of Fray Marcos.
4. Hallenbeck, *Cabeza de Vaca*.

The numerous Spaniards soon overtaxed both the native hospitality and resources.

The castaways spent a bad winter learning to forage for food. The accounts told of misery, hunger, famine, even of cannibalism among the Spaniards, to the horror of the natives. They were wasted also by "a sickness of the stomach" that affected the Indians much more severely, half of whom were said to have died. By the spring of 1529 there were only a dozen refugees able to move on. Cabeza de Vaca, who was gravely ill, was left behind with one companion on the island that he named Malhado, the wretched island (Galveston Island).

After his recovery Cabeza de Vaca found acceptance and freedom of movement by turning to trade. He took shells and other things found on the coast to people of the interior, going inland as far as fifty leagues and bringing back red ochre for face paint, wood shafts, flint for projectile points, and skins. Galveston Bay was divided between Karankawas at the west and Attakapas at the east, both of whom were primitive collectors and fishers with hunting as a secondary occupation. Partly agricultural Caddoan tribes inhabited the interior to the north. Hallenbeck suggested that the red ochre may have been brought from Nacogdoches in Caddo country. Cabeza de Vaca was engaged for about two years in moving between coast and interior of East Texas.

A party of twelve, led by Dorantes and Castillo, started south along the coast in April 1529. They lived with various Karankawa bands, were treated as subjects by them, and at times were driven out or departed on their own to find another band. They remembered the time as one of degradation to the life of slaves. Dorantes, referring probably to Matagorda Bay, said that "there they were treated as slaves, used more cruelly than by a Moor, naked and barefoot on a coast that burns like fire in summer . . . , and since they were hidalgos and men of standing and new to such life it was necessary to have patience as great as their labors." The accounts agree that their initial reception by a new band was always friendly. Oviedo noted: "Those Indians, in whose company these few Christians were, tired of giving them to eat, as happens always when the guest stays longer than the host wishes and in particular if they have not been invited nor contribute anything."The castaways had been saved by the Indians, sheltered, and fed. They brought no useful skills and were a burden on the scant resources of their hosts. Their place was therefore at the bottom of the economy, to fetch wood and water, dig roots, do servile labor, and occasionally to suffer taunts and abuse. The Spaniards considered themselves treated as slaves, but they were not captives; they moved from band to band, camp followers in groups or singly, looking for a share of the native provisions.

Hunger was the outstanding memory of the years on the Texas coast. The Indians moved frequently, taking down the poles and mat covers of their huts to set them up at a new camp in the seasonal circuit of food gathering. Some of the encampments lacked drinking water, which had to be carried in. The Joint Report gave a calendar of the food supply through the year. At its beginning (January) they depended mainly on oysters for three to four months. Thereafter, for four months they ate herbs and *zarzamoras* (dewberries and the like). Then for two months they sucked roots and ate large spiders, other vermin, snakes, rats, and took some deer. In the last two months of the year they lived on fish that were taken by canoes, and they dug roots resembling truffles that grew under water (*Sagittaria,* duck potatoes?). The report continued, "They have no fixed abode because of the great hunger in all that land while they search for roots. They have no maize, nor can they procure any, nor do they sow anything. The country is very healthy and temperate, except when there is a norther in winter, at which time even the fish are frozen in the water."

The digging of roots provided starch food, repeated mention being made of one such growing in shallow fresh water and harvested in winter—probably arrowhead (*Sagittaria*). The Joint Report told of Cabeza de Vaca as "digging from morning to night to procure roots by a *coa* or pole which the Indians use under water for that purpose and also for digging in the soil." [5] In his own account he told how he dug these roots into February, at which time they began to leaf out, also that they grew among canes that cut his hands.

Of the coast to the south (Matagorda or San Antonio Bay) the Joint Report told of fires set in the plains to hunt *venados*

5. Coa is the Mexican name of the blade-pointed planting stick.

(deer or antelope). Here there was good seasonal fishing in the river (Colorado River of Texas), especially while it was in flood in April or again in May. "Then they kill a great quantity of fish and very good ones and they dress many but the greater part is lost because they have no salt." The manner of fishing was not described except for the use of dugout canoes and the mention of weirs by Cabeza de Vaca. The accounts may have had nothing to say of the manner of fishing because the Spaniards, as unskilled labor, took no part in it.[6]

The coast from Galveston to San Antonio Bay was Karankawa territory. The low and sandy coast plain was a savanna of drought-resistant bunch grasses and hardwood scrub. Its series of lagoons are largely shut off from the gulf by great sand bars. The lagoons, their branching estuaries, margining marshes, and lower river courses provided the natives sustenance.

While Cabeza de Vaca remained in the north, about Galveston Bay and up country, the others were with bands farther south, identified by the name Espiritu Santo as the country about Matagorda and San Antonio bays. The inlet connecting the two bays still has the name Espiritu Santo, given by Pineda in 1519 on the voyage he made for Garay. As Pineda sailed along that coast he named and charted features from a distance. The refugees recognized an inlet thus named from a chart, perhaps a copy of the padrón on which Pineda's entries were recorded.[7]

The Colorado River of Texas discharges into the northern part of Matagorda Bay. Though marshy in its lower part, it has a large and fertile flood plain that extends upriver to Austin and was formerly covered by mesophytic hardwoods, including many pecan trees.[8] According to Hallenbeck, the Colorado River bottoms, now cleared for crops, held the greatest stand of pecan trees between Wharton and Austin, the

6. William W. Newcomb, *The Indians of Texas* (Austin, 1961), cited later accounts from their eastern neighbors, the Attakapas of similar culture, of torchlight fishing with spears and of mass killing by plant stupefacients ceremonially prepared and applied.

7. Oviedo, copying names of the Texas coast on the Chaves map of 1536, had these items: From Cabo Bravo (at the mouth of the Rio Grande) 30 leagues to Rio Pescadores (inlet to Corpus Christi Bay?), thence 65 leagues to Rio Espiritu Santo (inlet, not river).

8. *Carya illinoensis*, because first described from Illinois at its northeastern limit.

Brazos valley being second. The well-drained alluvial valleys of the Texas coast plain still had pecan trees in a great number when American farmers began settlement.

At the beginning of cold weather, when the husks split and drop the nuts, Indians came to gather pecans, enjoying a time of plenty. The Joint Report told that during the nutting season Indians came from as far away as twenty to thirty leagues to live on the nuts. These nuts were not borne in abundance every year, but in good years the Indians lived for a month on nothing else except for some hunting of game. Cabeza de Vaca described the nuts as the size of those of Galicia (Persian walnuts) and the trees as of great size and number. In early winter when the nuts dropped, bands of collectors came both from coast and interior to share in the bounty, implying that territorial rights were not in effect. It is also inferred that Castillo, Dorantes, and the Negro, who shifted about among Karankawa bands of the Matagorda Bay region, went repeatedly to gather pecans in the Colorado River bottoms.

In the winter of 1533–1534 Cabeza de Vaca, according to his own account, rejoined the others for the first time after a separation of five years. This happened during the harvesting of pecans in the middle Colorado valley. Hallenbeck made a reasonable construction of the obscure data, suggesting that the refugees moved jointly up the valley to overwinter in the vicinity of Austin. While together, they agreed to meet again the next summer and get out of that country. In his narrative Cabeza de Vaca took credit to himself for the plan to be on their way to Christian lands and for the agreement to wait until summer when the *tunas* (cactus fruits) were ripe in another region, to which people would come from afar bringing bows and other articles to trade. Meanwhile they split up to return with their several hosts to their localities on the Gulf coast.

Large as was the winter gathering of people for pecans, there was an even greater assemblage in summer when the cactus fruits were ripe. This harvest attracted people from even farther parts, was an occasion for trade, and presented the refugees with an opportunity to leave the coast to start in search of Spanish settlements. The Spaniards who had made the attempt the first winter to follow the Gulf coast south had come to grief. They would try another direction.

THE TUNA COUNTRY

Prickly pears (*tunas*) are mid- and late summer fruit of different species of *Opuntia* of robust growth, often forming great thickets in semiarid lands from south Texas south through the Mexican Meseta. Thus about Mezquital in southern Durango a great *tunal* has been the immemorial scene of annual gathering to reap its fruits. Cactus fruits are still a summer staple in Mexico, the name *tuna* usually referring to pad or pancake stemmed *Opuntia* species, *pitahaya* to columnar and climbing cacti.

In early summer Indians from the coast began to move to the country of the tunas. According to the Joint Report they would come from more than forty leagues to feast on tunas for a month and a half or two months, having "the best food of the year." August was the time of greatest plenty. Cabeza de Vaca gave the tuna season as three months, during which they were eaten out of hand, the juice was drunk, and some were dried to be stored.

The South Texas Plains, thus named as ecologic association, have their northeastern limit about San Antonio.[9] To the south the country is progressively more xerophytic, a thorn scrub savanna. During the past century commercial agriculture and stock raising have cleared and otherwise altered much of the vegetation south of San Antonio. Hallenbeck, plotting the course of the castaways into and out of the tuna country, concluded that this began about or a short distance south of San Antonio. Dr. George Engelmann made botanical studies there early in its period of American settlement and identified the various species of *Opuntia* and their occurrence. These studies and records of early settlers and naturalists confirmed Hallenbeck's interpretation that the great tunal to which the Indians assembled lay south of San Antonio. The reconstruction is reasonable and acceptable.

While gathering tunas the Indians also hunted. Dorantes stated in the Joint Report that he had seen sixty Indians kill several hundred deer in eight days and that they might get as many as five hundred in one drive. Hallenbeck thought the large number thus taken indicated pronghorn antelope rather than white-tailed deer, the former congregating in large herds

9. H. O. Kunkel, *Texas Plants* (College Station, 1969).

to graze, whereas the deer browse in small groups. This was indeed once a major antelope range. Early Spanish notices did not commonly distinguish between deer and pronghorns, the latter unknown in Spain.

The extraordinary massing of cactus useful to man suggests that man had been concerned in its increase. The annually populous campgrounds served to distribute seeds and segments. Recurrent fires eliminated woody growth but did little or no damage to cactus. Campfires occasionally spread. Fires were set to drive game. The long recurrent occupation by numerous Indian bands, it is inferred, had reduced the vegetation to a cactus savanna. The long and numerous camps required convenient access to fresh water, freely available in the San Antonio area; thus this area would have been most visited and most subject to the alteration of vegetation to cactus thickets.

The South Texas Plains are the northern extension of what the Spaniards called the Grand Chichimeca, a large semiarid land inhabited by many small bands of collectors and hunters, moving about according to the seasonal availability of food. Little is known of their culture. A Coahuiltecan language was spoken by many; this was true also of South Texas and perhaps of the inner coast plain farther to the north.[10]

The great tunal, like the stands of pecan trees farther east, was freely available to visiting bands from distant parts— Karankawas who came from the coast and other tribes out of the north. When the tunas were in season Indians of various tribes shared the bounty in peace, each group in its own encampment.

DEPARTURE FROM THE TEXAS COAST

In the summer of 1534, according to the Joint Report, Castillo, his Negro, and Dorantes met in the tunales, the fruits being in great abundance that year. They came with several Indian groups from the coast and shortly met Cabeza de Vaca. Each appears to have remained with his Indian "master," meanwhile conferring as to how they would break away and join some band as it returned to its inland home. The interpretation, largely due to Cabeza de Vaca, that they were captives is

10. Newcomb has thus interpreted this as the Coahuiltecan area of Texas.

improper, their movements and contacts being as they willed.

At the end of the tuna season each Spaniard joined a home-ward bound party that was heading north. Cabeza de Vaca dated the "escape" as September 22, most of the tunas then being gone. The leaving was not escape, nor do they seem to have been under restraint during the tuna collecting. They rejoined shortly. On October 1, the Joint Report related, "they came at sunset upon the Indians they were seeking, who were very gentle and had some notice of Christians, though very little." This would explain why they took the direction to the north, farther to the interior. The Indians were called Ava-vares and have been thought to be a Caddoan tribe that lived in the rough hill country north of San Antonio, the fretted southern edge of the Edwards Plateau known as the Balcones Escarpment.

They overwintered in the hill country and stayed on into the summer of 1535. The Indians continued friendly. There was much hunger. Lacking fishing streams, the people de-pended mainly on digging roots. The children had potbellies like toads. Game was taken and provided the Spaniards with buckskins which they made into clothes against the cold weather.

THE LONG WESTERN JOURNEY

The long trek west to the country of Christians began in August 1535. The Joint Report, made when memories were fresh, is less obscure than the relation of Cabeza de Vaca.[11] Carrying packs of buckskin, the travelers covered seven leagues the first day, being well received by Indians who were friends of those they had left. The next day they went on to meet other Indians, all joining to gather small seeds ripening at the time, there being great groves (*montes de arboledas*) bearing fruits (pods of mesquite?). They continued on to a people who lived in a direction "more convenient to their route and intent." Hallenbeck inferred reasonably that they had been skirting the upper Colorado River and continued to do so

11. Cabeza de Vaca at this point digressed into recollections of Indian customs without regard to location. Thus he told of a hot ceremonial drink, apparently the black drink of Muskogean tribes of the Southeast, made from yaupon, an *Ilex* that grows also in the Texas Coast Plain, but is not known to have been used there, nor is it likely to have been a practice of its primitive tribes.

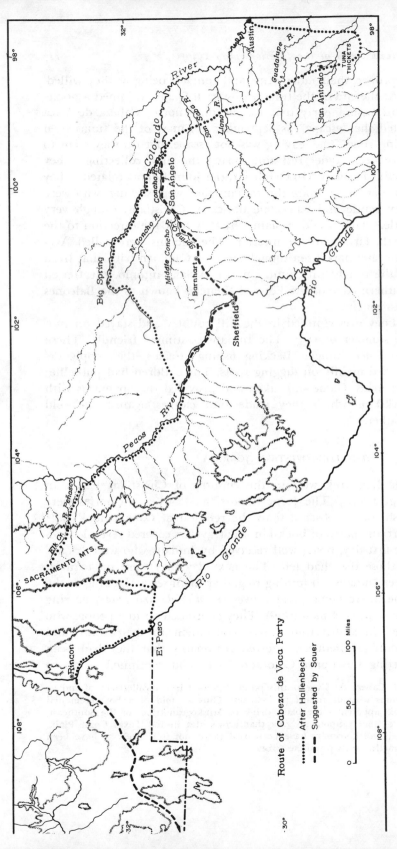

Route of Cabeza de Vaca Party

····· After Hallenbeck
▬ ▬ Suggested by Sauer

FIG. 10. Route of the Cabeza de Vaca party (after Hallenbeck and Sauer)

above San Saba, where its course changes to a west-east direction. They stayed eight days with Indians who were living on the cooked pads of prickly pears, awaiting the ripening of the "seeds." They were moving into higher elevation and later season. In the extremity of their hunger the Christians traded buckskins for two dogs which they cooked and ate and thus regained strength. Distances and dates are not given.

After changing direction, inferred as to the west, still along the valley of the Colorado of Texas, there is no further mention of hardship. They arrived at a settlement of forty to fifty houses: "It was here that first began the show of awe and reverence in which those few Christians were held, though these had been more accustomed to labor than to perform 'miracles' " (Joint Report). Henceforth they cured sick of all kinds by laying on of hands and making the sign of the cross. Cabeza de Vaca related at length his own healing powers. From this village, where they stayed fifteen days, their journey was a procession of Indians bringing their sick to be healed and leading them to the next village. At a distance of two leagues they came to another village where they were received with great celebration and given very good tunas and game that the Indians brought for the Christians. Indian women came from farther on bringing gifts and accompanied them so that they should not lose the road. And thus they came to "a water (*agua*) and a small river" which Hallenbeck thought was Big Spring, one of the sources of the Colorado River at the edge of the High Plains and a major crossing of Indian trails.

After their change of direction west they traveled at their ease through a country that lacked neither sustenance nor people. According to Hallenbeck, they went westward up the valley of the Colorado, in the southern part of the Rolling Plains. Perhaps they did not continue to Big Spring as Hallenbeck thought. The desired direction was west. Going to Big Spring meant turning northwest above the entry of the Concho River into the Colorado. By taking a course up the Concho, on the other hand, they would continue west to the site of San Angelo and thence west up the Middle Concho to one of its spring-fed headwaters, on the most direct route to the Pecos River. The Joint Report gave the distance from the spring to the river as eight to nine long leagues, far short of that from Big Spring to the Pecos River but proper from a Concho headwater such as Spring Creek.

On this leg of the journey, tentatively inferred as west by way of San Angelo, they were greeted noisily by a multitude from a village consisting of about a hundred ranchos. The people came up to touch them with reverence, as one might the body of a saint. In the ceremonial reception gourd rattles were used, mentioned here for the first time. A league and a half on they stayed two days at another village of seventy or more ranchos where among other things they were given twenty-eight loaves made of mesquite meal. This being the first mention of that name, perhaps the small seeds noted earlier were something else. The word rancho suggests that these were seasonal encampments. The distribution of Indian tribes in the interior of Texas is largely unknown. The account gives no help in their identification. They were numerous, friendly, in good circumstances, and they treated the visitors as great shamans.

From the spring, accompanied by a troop of men and women, they went eight or nine long leagues to a river that seemed to be of the width of the Guadalquivir at Sevilla, Hallenbeck making the case for the Pecos. Well before they got to the river they could see a line of mountains extending north-south, on the western horizon. They came to the river "at the foot of the end of the sierra" (Joint Report), where there were forty to fifty ranchos. After a reception, with dances, a council was held as to which road they should take. The native advice was to go downstream. The Spaniards "wished only to go up stream farther inland," not to go to the sea to which the river would take them, apparently with the correct conclusion that this would be the gulf from which they had started. By the San Angelo option via a southwestern headwater of the Concho (such as Spring Creek) the Pecos River would have been reached where it changes from a northwest-southeast to a more southerly direction and enters a deep canyon (below Sheffield). (Because Indian trails take the most direct course, one such is inferred from permanent water in the Concho drainage to some point above the beginning of the Pecos canyon.)

As they took the road up river they were accompanied by many people "including women who carried water for the road because of the lack of it, and there was very great heat." This is the only mention of carrying water on the journey, and this was while they traveled along a river. Hallenbeck explained that above the canyon, north to the border of New

Mexico, the Pecos River is saline and lacks tributaries of fresh water. There is no mention of the kind of containers. "They went along the flank of the mountains for eighty leagues," passing numerous ranchos along the road, suggesting that they were on an Indian trail. At the end of this long stretch up valley they came to four ranchos at the foot of a sierra, "of another nation and language, who said that they were from farther on (*mas allá*) and were on their way home," confirming that they were on a traveled road. These new people gave the Christians some cotton *mantas* (woven cloth) and a small brass bell. In his account Cabeza de Vaca mentioned women who were carrying cornmeal and medicine men who gave a present of two gourd rattles. Whether this applies to the same place and people is uncertain; Cabeza de Vaca added the remark that they were traveling through so many places of different tongues that his memory was confused.

Hallenbeck, here on home territory that he knew intimately, placed the meeting with the homeward bound Indians on the Rio Peñasco near Carlsbad. "They turned into the sierra to the west, toward sunset, and [having crossed its crest] were taken to some ranchos on a beautiful river, where they were given much margarita and alcohol [marcasite and galena or other light and dark colored metallic sulfides] and were told that those who had previously given them the cascabel had much therof [of such minerals] but had not given any. From which it is inferred that whence this is brought, whether it be gold or not, there should be mining and smelting (though by reason this should be on the South Sea)." Thus the Joint Report in its only reference to minerals and metal, mentioned neither as being locally produced but as coming from farther west. The cascabel perhaps was one of the jingle bells that are found archaeologically in the Southwest and were of Mexican origin.

The "beautiful river" was identified by Hallenbeck as the Tularosa, in rapid descent of the western side of the Sacramento Mountains into the Tularosa Basin. The travelers turned south at the base of the mountains to have the most enjoyable part of the journey. They were taken to "five clusters or congregations of ranchos, accompanied all along the way by more than two thousand souls; and along the road many deer and hares were killed for them, the Christians blessing the game and taking for themselves what they wished.

. . . They were provided with a great quantity of piñon nuts, as good as those of Castile, or better, because they have a [thin] shell that is eaten with the nut; the cones are very small and the trees in these mountains bear heavily." As far as the southern end of the Sacramento Mountains they fared well.

Farther on the going got bad. "For more than fifty leagues they were led, [in part] by some desperate sierras, in great hunger by reason of the poverty of the country, which had neither tunas nor anything." How they skirted the Tularosa Basin and got to its southern end is not said. Indian guides conducted them all along. Since there was no mention of thirst, the guides appear to have known adequate watering places. Distances and intervals were not noted. Their fame as medicine men still preceded them. At one camp in the plains people gathered into a hundred ranchos awaited them, having come from afar, bringing piñon nuts. Indians accompanying them then fell sick, many dying and more than three hundred taken ill. Women who had been sent ahead to find a certain people returned with the word that they had gone to hunt buffalo, which would have been on a winter hunt east of the Pecos, a hundred miles or more distant. At the end of this stretch of three days' hard travel they were "taken to a river, where they found people and houses and stopped and had beans and squashes to eat, though only a little."

AT THE RIO GRANDE

The river to which they were led was the Rio Grande and the vicinity was that of El Paso, as Hallenbeck traced the route. Here they saw the first planted crops. "They were taken up that river to four clusters of houses. There was little to eat, mainly beans and squash and a very little maize, and they had nothing in which to cook but made stew in containers of calabashes." A description of cooking by stone boiling follows, the earliest account of cooking by dropping heated stones into a container. Their hosts, a riverside tribe that did some farming, were later known as Mansos because of their gentle ways. The guests were given many robes of buffalo, which they understood to be numerous and nearby. (This was a misunderstanding; the buffalo herds were east of the Pecos River.) Asking about what route they should take, they were told that ahead (to the west) they would find neither cornmeal nor beans for thirty to forty days' travel but that they should go up river for eight to nine days without finding food, and then cross the river and go west until they got to where there was maize, and a great deal of it.

They followed these instructions and went up the river for nine days, "each day traveling until night, in great hunger, and always at night they slept in houses with people who gave them many buffalo robes." The natives ground a tree fruit between stone, a poor nourishment. (Since the Spaniards were familiar with mesquite, Hallenbeck surmised that juniper berries might have been ground for food.) At that time most of the Indians had gone to hunt buffalo. The Spanish party was supplied with pieces of deer fat.

The crossing of the Rio Grande was made at Rincon, according to Hallenbeck. In *The Road to Cibola* I had traced the Indian trade road from Culiacán north. Independently Hallenbeck and I, working from opposite ends of the route, came to the same crossing of the Rio Grande. My study having been published before his, he accepted my reconstruction for the route west of the Rio Grande.[12]

FROM RIO GRANDE TO SONORA

Beyond the Rio Grande they went for more than twenty days before they came to the people who grew maize, "passing folk who were less hungry, eating dried herbs and killing many hares [jackrabbits]," the Christians always being supplied with more than they needed. This traverse was made without hardship. The Joint Report passed briefly over this stretch, the relation of Cabeza de Vaca adding that the hares were clubbed and deer (three kinds) were taken by bow and arrow. Those of the size of *novillos* (young bulls) of Castille would have been mule deer, the others antelope and white-tailed deer.

South of the International Boundary they came to the country of the Opatas, the people who, they had heard, had much maize. The southward trending valleys of Sonora were

12. His outline of the route west to the Rio Grande replaces what I wrote in *The Road to Cibola* concerning the segment of the journey from the Pecos River to the Rio Grande. I knew that the Bandelier crossing of the Rio Grande, Chihuahua, and Sierra Madre was wrong but not that their crossing of western Texas also was in error.

intensively cultivated and the harvest was large. They still had hundreds of miles to go before they reached a Spanish settlement, but the hard trek was over.

SUMMARY

The Joint Report, the preservation of which is owed to Oviedo, is the main source. Oviedo added a proper abstract of the relation of Cabeza de Vaca, calling attention to discrepancies. For example, the margarita they were given became Cabeza de Vaca's bag of silver: "Cabeza de Vaca says that in all the mountain country they saw great indications of gold and alcohol, iron, copper, and other metals. I wish this were made more clear and that there were better explanations." The Joint Report had said nothing of the sort. Oviedo was politely questioning the story told by Cabeza de Vaca, which was published six years after their return, at the time that Coronado was in the north looking for treasure.

Cabeza de Vaca, the ranking member of the party, wrote the book by which their journey became known. For six of the eight years he lived mostly apart from the others. When they reassembled the three hidalgos shared in the plans and conduct of their journeying, which was neither escape nor undirected wandering. They had some word of a Spanish frontier settlement when they started from Texas, and they followed a trail under Indian guidance that took them to the Spanish outpost of Culiacán. Always they were led and accompanied by Indians, being passed on from one group to the next and received with honors as strangers and great medicine men.

Their recollection of the route was most vivid as to the food they had or lacked, the times of plenty and times of hunger. They told of the game with which they were supplied—one means of identifying the areas they crossed. There is no mention of having seen buffalo, perhaps because they kept south of the high plains as they went from the Colorado-Concho River across the Edwards Plateau to the Pecos River. Cabeza de Vaca wrote of having eaten buffalo meat, but this was before he was one of the traveling party. West of the Pecos they were often given buffalo robes that had been procured by hunting parties accustomed to go east of the Pecos on seasonal hunts. Buffalo robes were a major article of trade south to the agricultural peoples of Sonora.

While far from any place where agriculture was known they were given cotton mantas and gourd rattles, by inference traded from the Pueblo lands. When they reached the Rio Grande and saw their first planted fields, they heard of another country far up that river to the north where maize was grown. These are the only indications of a northern country of agricultural Indians, the Pueblos. No mention of houses, towns, wealth, or different culture. They were interested not in finding out what might lie to the north but in getting to the maize people to the south and so to the Spanish frontier. Having come directly from Spain, they probably knew nothing of the rumors current in Mexico of a land of precious metals to the north.

They were given a copper jingle bell which they surmised rightly to have come from the Pacific side, and they noted heavy minerals, one light and one dark colored, given them at one place. There is nothing in the Joint Report of a higher native culture or of precious metals. When Viceroy Mendoza tried to engage one of them in a return exploration he found none interested.

Their return to Mexico City in the summer of 1536 was a sensation—three hidalgos and a slave had survived from the long-lost host of Narváez. While living with and in the manner of unknown and primitive Indians tribes, they had walked from the Texas coast to Culiacán. They also gave the new viceroy thoughts about what lay north and northwest of the undefined limits of New Spain.

THE OPPORTUNE MOMENT
FOR VICEROY MENDOZA

The return of the castaways came at an important time in the affairs of the Indies. The first viceroy had made a good beginning in New Spain by revising the grants of encomiendas so as to ease Spanish demands and give some protection to the Indians. The hazard of autonomous authority had been reduced by the removal of Nuño de Guzmán from the northwestern frontier. Guzmán's followers still remained in control of Nueva Galicia, but they would accept the rule and protection of the viceroy. Cortés had been embroiled with Nuño de Guzmán for the possession of that frontier and if Cortés should take over they would be thrown out. Cortés was again asserting his interests in that direction, having crossed the Gulf of California in 1536 to the pearl beds at the lower end of the "Island of California."

Cortés had taken New Spain without being given authority or support by the Crown. The King partially acknowledged his great services by making him Marqués of Oaxaca, but it was never forgotten or forgiven that he had seized power by insubordination. The first and the greatest of caudillos, his loyalty was suspect to some, his lack of patent objected to by others. Cortés had a devoted following of veteran soldiers who had marched with him across Mexico. He had great wealth and the ambition and energy to discover and possess more lands in the northwest. He had just done so in Lower California. If Mendoza was to be the viceroy in fact he had to stop Cortés from going on his willful way.

Pedro de Alvarado had been Cortés' first lieutenant in the conquest of Mexico, had then gone south to seize Guatemala and had done there as he willed. Having no more need of Cortés, he changed over to the side of Mendoza, as will be noted later.

To the viceroy's concern about Cortés on the Gulf of California was added the revived prospect of trouble from the side of the Gulf of Mexico. Cortés had turned back Garay and Narváez in their attempts to establish themselves in Pánuco. Narváez and his host, authorized to found a government of Florida extending west to New Spain, had been lost. The four survivors brought word to Mexico in 1536 of how they had crossed the continent from Florida to the farthest outpost of New Spain on the Pacific. They had been part of the expedition licensed by the crown to set up a government of Florida independent of that of New Spain, and with undefined limits. What four castaways had done could be done with ease by a properly led force based on the north coast of the Gulf of Mexico. The danger was real and imminent that New Spain would be hemmed in at the north by a rival Spanish government. Hernando de Soto, meanwhile, had returned to Spain, rich with the loot of Peru and ambitious to have a land of his own to govern. He offered to undertake the conquest of Florida at his own expense and was thus licensed in April 1537, being named Governor of Cuba and Adelantado of Florida, to have and hold whatever part of the northern mainland he might take. De Soto might cause real trouble for Mendoza.

After Mendoza failed to engage one of the three returned Spaniards to take an expedition into the north, he bought the Negro from Dorantes to be used as guide when a leader of the exploration should be found. Mendoza had the account given by the three, which outlined a route north through a populous and well-provisioned country, through the length of Sonora to the International Border. The account by the Joint Report said nothing of the Pueblo country, and almost nothing of metals. The castaways, having come directly from Spain, probably were uninformed of both. Mendoza knew the tales of the north and Nuño de Guzmán's intentions. A convenient approach to the northern lands was now manifest. Time was of the essence, De Soto being prepared, perhaps already under way, to take possession of Florida, and he might push its limits into any unoccupied part of the northern mainland.

In 1538 the viceroy appointed Francisco Vázquez de Coronado, one of the higher nobility who came with the viceroy, to be governor of Nueva Galicia and to prepare for the exploration of the north. Fray Marcos de Niza, a companion of Pedro de Alvarado, was brought into the plans and was given the Negro Esteban as guide. He left Culiacán on March 7, 1539, the Negro going ahead. On May 9 the friar came to the northern *despoblado,* which I placed in the high grassland of the Sonora–Arizona border, about four hundred miles from Culiacán. By the end of June he was back in Compostela, then capital of Nueva Galicia, a good three hundred miles south of Culiacán. He gave his formal report to the viceroy in Mexico City on September 2. Having done field work throughout that stretch of country, I plotted the friar's account in detail and concluded that, by his own calendar, he got no farther than the southern border of Arizona. If he got that far he made a formidable return journey of seven hundred miles in seven weeks at the season of extreme heat. His reconnaissance was by the Indian road along which the Cabeza de Vaca party had come south from the maize country of the Opatas of the Sonora Valley.

The friar's relation is a strange tissue of hearsay, fantasy, fact, and fraud. He said that he had seen the city of Cibola (Zuñi) from a distance and that it was greater than the City of Mexico. Also, he had met a native of Cibola in the valley of Sonora who told of cities greater than Cibola, one having houses of ten stories. Fray Marcos added nothing to the exploration of the Southwest. His fictions were believed in

Mexico and assured the supply of recruits and funds to the
expedition. Their effect is told in two letters of October 1539.[13]
The viceroy reported the return of the friar with very great
news of a large country with many towns, to which a strong
expedition was being sent. The second letter by Rodrigo de
Albornoz, treasurer of New Spain, gave particulars of the
stir in the capital:

News of the new land discovered in New Spain in the part that
Nuño de Guzmán had held on the South Sea, which is adjacent to
the island [California] which the Marqués del Valle [Cortés] has
newly found and to which he has sent three or four fleets. The Lord
Viceroy having such news and notice of such land sent a friar and
a negro, the latter having come from Florida with the others who
had come thence as survivors of the party taken there by Pánfilo
Narváez. These [two] set out with the knowledge the negro had
in order to go to a very rich country, as the latter declared, and told
the friar (who has already returned) that there are seven very populous cities with great buildings. Of one of these the friar brought
news by sight, of those farther off by hearsay. The name of the
one where he has been is Cíbola, the others are in the Kingdom of
Marata. There is very great news of other very populous country,
both of their riches and good order and the manner of their living,
also of their edifices and other matters. They have houses built of
stone and lime, being of three stories, and with great quantity of
turquoises set in doors and windows. Of animals there are camels
and elephants and cattle of our kind as well as wild ones, hunted
by the natives, and a great number of sheep like those of Peru,
also other animals with a single horn reaching to their feet, for
which reason they must feed sidewise. They say that these are not
unicorns but of another kind. The people are said to go clothed to
the neck in long vestments of camlet, girdled in the manner of
Moors. In sum, they are known to be people of good understanding,
unlike those here.

The tale heard by Albornoz from Fray Marcos made this
the land of Seven Cities of medieval legend, current in Spain
and Portugal. One of these cities was called Cibola, others belonged to the Kingdom of Marata. Both names were accepted
by European map makers, such as Ortelius, who still depended on Fray Marcos a generation later. The Pueblo people did dress in long woolen garments spun and woven from

13. Oviedo used them to begin his fortieth volume. They were not
cited in *The Road to Cíbola.*

the hair of dogs, mountain sheep, and bison, the latter hunted in the high plains to the east. Buffalo skins and turquoise were customary objects of trade to the Opata settlements of Sonora. Information about the Pueblo manner of living was heard by Fray Marcos in the Opata villages and elaborated by him into the tale of the Seven Cities. The role of the Negro is obscure. He knew only what the Cabeza de Vaca party knew. He went ahead of Fray Marcos and did not return. The friar told that the Negro sent word back of great discoveries and it was found later that he got to Zuñi. The tale told by the friar had the desired effect. Mendoza gave a large sum to equip the expedition. Coronado invested a fortune, largely that of his wife. Spanish gentry joined up with their horses and gear to seek their fortunes.

7
The
Journey of Coronado
(1540–1542)

RECONNAISSANCE BY MELCHOR DÍAZ

The friar's story had told wonders about Cibola but not how
to get there. Mendoza promptly sent instructions to Melchor
Díaz, alcalde of Culiacán, to find the way that Coronado
should take. Díaz had met the party of Cabeza de Vaca in 1536
as it came out of the *monte* and was the most experienced
veteran on that frontier. He set out from Culiacán with fifteen
horsemen and a number of Indians on November 17, 1539.
The report of his journey reached the viceroy four months
later and was sent to the emperor April 17, 1540,[1] Coronado
in the meantime having reached Culiacán with his host of
horsemen, foot soldiers, Indians, and baggage.

Díaz took the main Indian road north into the Sonora Valley,
across the *despoblado* of southeastern Arizona, and up the
Mogollon Rim of the Colorado Plateau until stopped by the
cold, snow, and ice of winter, a number of his Indians dying
of exposure. Since he was to guide Coronado it was not
necessary for him to describe the route in detail. Having left
the Opata villages of Sonora he gave brief notice of southeastern Arizona:

1. CDI, vol. 2, pp. 356–361.

The people found along the road have no permanent seat, except in one valley that is a hundred and fifty leagues from Culiacán, well populated and having flat roofed houses, with many people along the road, but these are of interest only to be made Christians.

He was following the road along a well-populated valley. The only such valley was that of the San Pedro, which drained north into the Gila, possibly including the adjacent Aravaipa Basin. The former and perhaps the latter were occupied at that time by Sobaipuri Pimas, sedentary people who farmed as much as the limited land and water permitted. Those who had no permanent seat perhaps were Apaches, who later drove the Pimas out of the eastern valleys.

Most of the Díaz report dealt with the Pueblo country, which he did not enter but about which he gathered information from the Indians in his service. Largely these Indians were brought from Culiacán and were well informed about the north. His account was greatly different from that of Fray Marcos; it was the first factual presentation of Pueblo life and it was given by natives of the south who had been accustomed to trade with the north:

Beyond the great despoblado [the Mogollon Rim] there are seven settlements, each a short day's journey from the other, all called Cibola [the Zuñi pueblos, Cibola perhaps the name used by the Opatas]. They have houses of stone and mud (*barro*) rudely fashioned and made in this manner: A long wall, partitioned in rooms to both ends, the rooms about twenty feet square and roofed with unhewn beams. Most of the houses are entered by ladders, reaching from the street to the flat roofs. The houses are of three or four stories; they say that only a few are of one or two stories. Each story is of one and a half *estados* [the height of a man] except the first which is low, scarcely more than one estado. Ten to twelve houses are reached by one ladder. They keep stores on the ground floor and live in the upper ones. Beneath the houses they have some chambers (*saeteras*) made at one side (*al soslayo*) as in Spanish fortresses [i.e., kivas]. The informants say that when attacked all the people gather in the houses, from which they fight, and that when they go to make war they take shields and jackets made of dyed buffalo skins, and that they fight with stone arrows and mallets (*macetas*) and with other arms of wood the nature of which I have been unable to understand. They eat human flesh and those they take in war they keep as slaves. [The report of cannibalism was in error.]

There are many tame turkeys (*gallinas de la tierra*). They have a great deal of maize, beans, and squash (*melones*). They keep some shaggy animals like large hounds (*podencos*) of Castile in their houses. These they shear and make of the clip colored wigs they wear, like the one I sent Your Lordship and also they make clothes of the same. The men are of short stature, the women of light color and good appearance and wear dresses that reach to their feet, their hair parted on the sides and in ringlets that leave the ears exposed. They hang many turquoises in the ears and also about the neck and wrists. The dress of the men is a *manta,* over which they wear a buffalo robe like the one Cabeza de Vaca and Dorantes brought Your Lordship. On the head they wear a toque (*toca*). In summer they wear shoes of skin, painted or dyed, and in winter long boots (*barcequies*). I have been unable to get any account of metal or of its possession. They have a good deal of turquoise, but not as much as the friar says. They have small stones of crystal, like those I sent Your Lordship, of which you have seen many in New Spain. [So much for the tale of fabulous wealth.]

They work the soil as is done in New Spain and carry loads on the head as in Mexico. Men weave the cloth and spin the cotton. Salt is procured from a lake two days' journey from Cibola. [A description follows of dances, accompanied by chanting and flutes.] The land they say is productive of maize and beans. They have no fruit trees nor do they know of such. There are excellent woods (*montes*); the province has little water; cotton is not grown locally but is brought from Totonteac [the Hopi country]; they eat from plates of pottery (*cajetes*); they harvest a great amount of maize and beans and another seed resembling *chia* [the Mexican name for a cultivated *Salvia,* which may have been grown here]; they do not know what sea fish are nor have they heard of such; of the buffalo (*vacas*) they know only that their range lies beyond Cibola. There is great abundance of wild goats of the color of roan horses. There are a lot of such where I am, but when I ask the Indians whether these are like those, they say no. [Díaz was writing on his return. The animals he knew were pronghorn antelopes in the grasslands of Arizona or Sonora. The different ones he was told about to the north would have been bighorn sheep.]

Three of the seven places are very large, the other four not. They indicated to me that each was of the reach of three crossbow shots. Taking into account the houses, their size, and how they are connected, and the people living in each house, there must be a great multitude.

It is known that Totonteac is distant seven days' short journeys from the province of Cibola and is of the same nature of houses and people, also that it has cotton; I doubt this for they tell me that it is a cold country. They say that there are twelve pueblos, each greater than the largest in Cibola. Also they tell me that there is a pueblo at one day's journey from Cibola, warring with the others, houses, people, and trade being the same, but affirming it to be larger than the rest. I take it that there is a great multitude of people who are widely known because they have such houses and food and turquoises in abundance. I have been unable to learn more than I have said, although I have taken Indians with me who have been there from fifteen to twenty years.

The Indians with Díaz were well informed about the Zuñi (Cibola), Hopi (Totonteac), and another pueblo (Acoma) at a day's journey from Zuñi. He was told that the Zuñis did not grow cotton but imported it from the Hopis. This he doubted because he was also told that the Hopis lived in a cold country. The information, however, was correct on all counts. The Hopi country has severe, long winters and a short growing season. Until recently the Hopis grew a special kind of cotton, of quicker maturity than any other elsewhere in America. The Pueblo natives were "widely known" because of their dwellings, cultivation, and turquoises, as Díaz said when he wrote down what he learned from his guides. What Díaz reported was all relevant and true except for eating human flesh.

THE JOURNEY OF CORONADO TO CIBOLA

The grand expedition assembled at Compostela, then the capital of Nueva Galicia, now a quiet small town off the main road, notable for its old church bearing the Hapsburg double-headed eagle. The start was made on February 23, 1540, without awaiting word from Melchor Díaz. The viceroy rode along briefly to bid them farewell.[2]

2. George Parker Winship, *The Coronado Expedition* (1540–42). This is the first and still the basic monograph and was done by a scholar in his early twenties. Winship secured and published the Spanish text of the *Relación* of Pedro de Castañeda, a *vecino* of Culiacán, who joined the expedition and wrote as a simple soldier trying to give a true account. See also George Hammond and Agapito Rey, *Narratives of the Coronado Expedition*, a collection of translations made for the Coronado Cuarto [sic] Centennial Commission of New Mexico; A. Grove Day, *Coronado's Quest* (Berkeley, 1940), which has good notes, chronology, and references; and Herbert Eugene Bolton, *Colonado on the Turquoise Trail, Knight of Pueblos and Plains* (Albuquerque, 1949), a competent narrative history with outline of the route, partly by personal inspection.

The known sources include letters by Coronado, the relation of Castañeda, and that of Juan Jaramillo (CDI, vol. 14, pp. 304–327). The

Melchor Díaz met the party at Chiametla in southern Sinaloa. At Culiacán Coronado went ahead of the main contingent with seventy-five horsemen, some foot soldiers, and a number of Indians, Díaz being their guide. They departed on April 22, 1540, following the Indian road up the Sonora Valley to the Pima settlements of the San Pedro or Nexpa, as the stream was known. The time was June, nearing the end of the long dry season. The natives gave them only cactus fruits (*pitahayas*) and roasted maguey, according to Jaramillo. Probably they could give no more, being at the end of the previous year's harvest. Beyond the Pima settlements they came to Chichilticalli, the red house or temple as this first archaeologic ruin of the Southwest seen by Europeans was called. Its name was Nahua, the language of Mexico, perhaps given by traders from the south. This was an important landmark on the road to Cibola, toward the far end of the thorn scrub grassland of southeastern Arizona. Shortly beyond it the nature of the country changed and the road climbed into the high country. No walls such as the Spaniards saw remain today, but there are remains of numerous pueblos with heavy walls in that area, abandoned long before the time of Coronado. By Jaramillo's account Chichilticalli would seem to have been in the Aravaipa Basin; by that of Castañeda, it was somewhat farther on where the road crossed the Gila River and "the spiky vegetation" ended.[3]

Ahead lay the dissected margin of the Colorado Plateau, the Gila River flowing along its base at about twenty-four hundred feet above sea level, the Mogollon Rim above rising to seven thousand feet. The road continued in the same direction, east of north, as it had led from the head of the Sonora Valley across the eastern Pimeria, deviating locally to get across mountain passes. The route was outlined by Jaramillo: From the reedy river (Gila) they took three days to the San Juan River (San Carlos, northern affluent of the Gila). (North of the Gila are the greatly dissected Gila Mountains, almost impassable. The barrier is avoided by going up that river and

latter, a veteran soldier of the conquest of Mexico, wrote a terse and objective account on his return from the expedition. Castañeda wrote years later, with excellent recall and at greater detail. Both are in general agreement and provide the greater part of our information on country and people.

3. In *The Road to Cibola* such a ruin was noted above Geronimo on the Gila River and an alternate one on the Aravaipa.

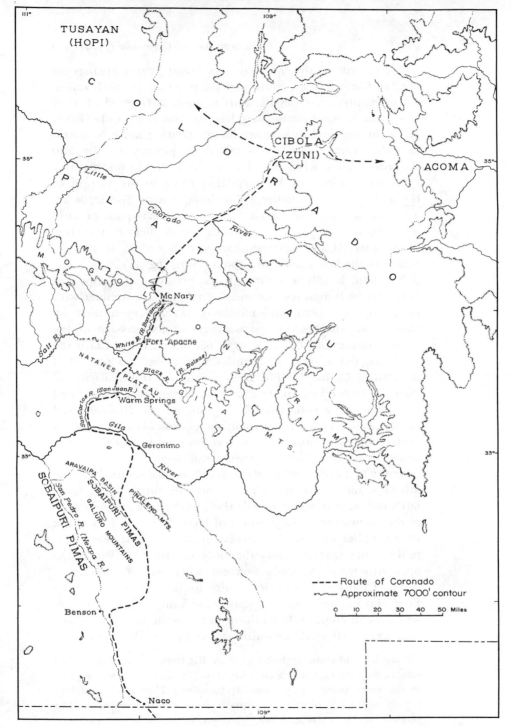

FIG. 11. Route of Coronado to Cibola, constructed from the narratives of participants.

turning north to the open country about Warm Springs on the San Carlos.) They continued for two days through rather rough country (Natanes Plateau) to another river which they called the Balsas because they had to cross it by rafts (Black River, at the time in summer flood). Bearing more to northeast they came after two short day's journey to the Rio Barranca (White River near Fort Apache). Going up this river for a day (vicinity of McNary) they came to the margin of the high plateau. In extremity of hunger some Spaniards ate a poisonous plant, of which three died (green pods of locoweed lupine?). A journey of two days took them to the river of red water (Little Colorado), whence they went on straight course to the first pueblo of Cibola (Zuñi) (fig. 11).

The road largely was through the present San Carlos and Fort Apache Indian reservations, a land green in summer with pines, alders, aspens, and meadows, perhaps even then inhabited by Apaches, unseen watchers of the passage of the strange procession. U.S. Highway 66, officially the Coronado Highway, lies a good many miles to the east, no part of it traveled by Coronado. The Indian road was traveled without difficulty by the large party of mounted men, pack horses, and Indians afoot. Spaniards suffered hunger, the Indians lived off the land. There is no mention of loss of horses, which found ample food and water in a region that is now fine cattle country, used by white and Apache stockmen.

At the first Zuñi pueblo of Hawikuh, named Granada in the accounts, the inhabitants tried to prevent entry of the Spaniards but were quickly routed, the invaders taking possession of the houses and of large stores of food. As it was July 7, the food supplies were of the harvest of the previous year. Jaramillo wrote that this was the only occasion on which the Spaniards were not made welcome wherever they went.

The Cibola of reality was quite unlike the fabulation of Fray Marcos, who foolishly had come along and shortly was sent back in disgrace. In addition to the main pueblo in which they were quartered, Jaramillo noted five smaller ones:

All are built of stone and clay and are flat roofed, their houses and *estufas* showing that it is a cold country. [Estufa (stove) was applied to the *kivas*, subterranean council chambers.] They have abundant supply of maize, beans, and squash for their consumption. The pueblos are at a distance one from another of a league or more, [the Zuñi basin] being about six leagues in extent. The ground is somewhat sandy and not covered by much vegetation and the wood-lands (*montes*) about are for the most part of junipers (*sabinas*). The Indian clothing is of deerskins, very well worked. They also have dressed buffalo (*vaca*) hides which they wear as mantles and which give good protection. They have sheets of cotton, some larger than others, about a yard and a half long. These the Indian women wear thrown over their shoulders, like gypsies, and they also wrap girdles of the same cotton about their waists. [The buffalo skins and cotton were secured by trade.]

Jaramillo also notes that from Cibola the waters drained to the South Sea (Pacific), from the other side to the Sea of the North (Gulf of Mexico of the Atlantic).

Coronado sent out parties to reconnoiter the Colorado Plateau. One went seven days west to Tusayan (the Hopi country) and found seven pueblos, the houses with flat roofs as in Cibola, having more and better food, a larger population, and mantles of cotton and of deer and buffalo skins. Another party, going farther west, discovered the Grand Canyon as barring crossing and descent: "The barranca of a river, to which it was impossible to find a descent anywhere by beast or man, the barranca so buttressed by cliffs that it was hardly possible to see the river, which from above appeared like a mere arroyo." [4] The hope was to find a river that could be used to communicate with a port on the west coast.

SUPPORT BY SEA OF THE
CORONADO EXPEDITION

While the Coronado party was being assembled and equipped, the viceroy also directed preparation of a supporting fleet. Ulloa, sailing under orders from Cortés, had newly discovered (1539) that California was a peninsula. He had followed the coast north from the known part of Nueva Galicia to the head of the gulf (of California) and the mouth of a large river (later named Colorado), the sediment of which colored the sea red, for which reason Ulloa named it Mar Bermejo (red sea, the earliest name of the Gulf of California). He then turned back along the west coast of the gulf to the end of the peninsula of California and sailed partway north along the Pacific coast of the peninsula. The discovery was important

4. Anon., *Relación del Suceso*, CDI, vol. 14, pp. 321–329. Canyon is a later Southwestern vernacular.

and might give Cortés a greater claim to the territory than the bit of California he had discovered and named in 1536. Cortés meanwhile having left for Spain, Mendoza took the occasion to send ships to the river at the head of the gulf, hoping to supply Coronado in the interior.

The river that colored the sea red gave evidence of a large drainage basin. The Cibola road crossed a river of red water (Little Colorado) southwest of Zuñi, Jaramillo observing that its drainage was to the Pacific. Coronado sent a party west from Zuñi to find that the river was in a mile-deep canyon. Melchor Díaz had been given true information about the geography of the Colorado Plateau; shortly Indians would take him across the Sonoran desert to the junction of the Gila and Colorado rivers. Mendoza and his men had a fair idea that the unnamed red river system led from the plateau pueblos to the head of the gulf discovered by Ulloa.

Hernán de Alarcón sailed from the port of Navidad in Jalisco with three ships, putting into Guayabal, the port of Culiacán, to load equipment left there by Coronado and to pick up Indians who were to serve as interpreters. On their arrival at the head of the gulf they transferred to boats for a trip up river, begun August 26 and continued for two weeks; the return was made within three days. A second boat trip followed. The visit of the lower Colorado River, named Buena Guia, took four weeks in all.[5] Alarcón wrote that they went more than thirty leagues up river, as far as "certain high mountains through which the river took a narrow course," that is, to the vicinity of Yuma, Arizona.

The villages along the river were many and populous (probably all of Yuman tribes). On the second day of boat travel they were given ears of maize and bread made of mesquite. (The Cocopas occupied the terminal stretches of the river.) Farther on (among Yumas proper) they found large supplies of maize, small squashes, and a kind of millet. (The Yumas grew a small grain, a domesticated *Panicum*.) The tortillas were noted as being poorly made, perhaps referring to meal ground of dry grain in contrast to the *nixtamal* (wet-ground hominy) of central Mexico. Cotton was mentioned but was not made into cloth. Other people (Mohaves?) came to the valley in summer to grow crops but lived in the mountains. Alarcón made

5. Alarcón's report to the viceroy is known in Italian translation (1556) by Ramusio.

the earliest observations of Indian farming on the Lower Colorado.

The purpose of the voyage was to find another way to Cibola, as far as possible by water, to be followed, it was hoped, by a short journey overland. On September 2 Alarcón met a man who said that he had been to Cibola, knew of its houses, manner of dress, and blue stones, also that the Negro had arrived there with a dog and later had been killed. On September 5 they interviewed a chief who had been to Cibola, knew nothing of any gold or silver there, but remembered the Negro. Two days later the natives had news of the arrival of the Christians at Cibola and of the battle that had occurred. (This was two months after Coronado got to Hawikuh.) On September 15 they were informed that the local villagers traded with Cibola, which was two moons' travel distant. Alarcón relayed the bits of information without comment. It was apparent that Cibola lay far inland from any approach by water.

THE LAST JOURNEY OF MELCHOR DÍAZ

Coronado sent Díaz back to Sonora, bearing word for the viceroy that Cibola had been reached, ordering the main party to move up to Cibola, and telling Díaz to go in search of Alarcón's ships. Díaz took the familiar road back to the Spanish base midway in the Valley of Sonora and thence with a small party of horsemen and Indians went west across the desert to the Colorado River about Yuma, in part along the course of the Gila River. The journey was direct, without mishap and without detail. A message from Alarcón was found at the river, left there two months earlier.

Díaz then crossed to the California side, roaming about and roughing up the natives, as known by later account. An anonymous report spoke of the natives along the river as vigorous and well supplied with maize, "the houses in which they live are huts or hovels, mostly underground, and covered with straw." The Colorado River was reached at thirty leagues from the coast; the journey continued on west, where there was neither water nor herbage, but many sand dunes, perhaps to the desert base of the mountains of San Diego County.[6]

While thus riding about Díaz fell by accident on his own

6. CDI, vol. 14, pp. 321 ff.

spear and died of the wound. Thus ended Spanish interest in the Lower Colorado Valley, not to be resumed until the following century.

THE EASTERN PUEBLOS AND
THE RIO GRANDE VALLEY

Late in August Coronado sent a party, with Hernando de Alvarado as captain, on the road east from the Zuñi basin. They noted impressive ruins along their way, visited the pueblo of Acoma on its cliff-rimmed mesa, a natural fortress, and continued to the Rio Tiguex (Rio Grande), "flowing through a very broad plain, planted to maize, with occasional groves of cottonwoods. The people appear to be gentle, more like farmers than warriors. There are twelve pueblos of earthen houses of two levels and flat roofs (*terrados*); they have much food of maize, beans, and squash (*melones*), and turkeys; they dress in skins of buffalo and wear turkey feathers. They wear their hair short." Seven more destroyed pueblos were seen in the valley, which they attributed to painted Indians from the east out of the buffalo country (Apaches?).[7] Delegations came from other pueblos to visit; they estimated that they came from about eighty places. "One of these, situated in a very cold country that lacked cotton and turkeys, was a memorable sight, with its houses of three stories of *tapia* [tamped earth], above which were three more stories of wooden planks set back. It seemed that there were about fifteen thousand persons in this pueblo." [8] Apparently the visitors got up river to Taos and were greatly impressed.

After scouting the pueblos of the Rio Grande valley they turned east, much as the Santa Fe Railroad does, and came to the fine pueblo of Cicuye (Pecos) where they were well received. They went on four days farther to enter the buffalo plains beyond the Pecos River. Cicuye was the easternmost pueblo, well beyond which was the grassy sea of the buffalo plains. They had come to the beginning of the Indian trade road over which buffalo hides were carried to Tiguex, Cibola, and Sonora. Without notice they had passed close by the turquoise mines of Los Cerrillos (southeast of Santa Fe) that supplied this prized stone to the civilizations of the south.

7. The abandonment had been centuries before.
8. Alvarado and Padilla, in CDI, vol. 3, pp. 511–513. The *Relación del Suceso* is similar, claiming eighteen quarters (*barrios*) in the town.

Having good report of the pueblos to the east, Coronado prepared to move from Cibola to the Tiguex pueblos for winter quarters. Tristan de Luna y Arellano had come up meanwhile from Sonora with the main contingent, in a snowstorm that marked the beginning of winter on the high plateau. Pedro de Castañeda was one of the new arrivals, henceforth to be the most observant reporter. Coronado left Zuñi for the Rio Grande late in November, Arellano in December.

Several hundred Spaniards, a large number of Indian servants from the south, a greater number of horses and mules, and herds of sheep and swine were quartered on the Tiguex pueblos. The reception was hospitable but soon the visitors became a burden to the hosts. The sharing of food with men and animals became forced levies and violent seizure. The winter was unusually severe and long—the Rio Grande was frozen solid. The Spaniards had not come prepared for a hard winter, nor were the Mexican Indians accustomed to the cold. The natives had warm houses and warm clothes, and were forced out. One pueblo was seized to serve as Spanish quarters and all its people were evicted.

A dozen pueblos of the valley revolted. Horses and mules were killed as they ranged about the fields. One pueblo, reputedly the strongest, was besieged for two months and surrendered for lack of water. Castañeda, perhaps reporting the same pueblo, told of its surrender when offered peace. Instead, claiming that the offer had not been authorized, the defenders were cut down or tied to stakes and burned. Those who escaped, he wrote, "spread throughout the country the word that the strangers did not respect the peace they had made, which later proved a great misfortune." Coronado did not order or direct the outrage but did nothing to stop the violence of his subordinates. Ravages continued throughout the winter. There was no treasure of gold or silver, no prospect of wealth to be gained in any part of the Pueblo land.

CROSSING THE STAKED PLAINS

The party that had gone the previous fall to Cicuye and the buffalo plains brought back a strange Indian acquired from his owners at Cicuye. A native of the plains, perhaps a Pawnee from Kansas or Nebraska, he was called the Turk because of his headdress. His new masters found him a willing informant who entertained them with tales of distant countries to which he would guide them.[9] The Turk told of a land rich in gold, called Quivira, lying in or beyond the plains to the northeast. Having come a long way to disappointment, and, perhaps thinking that Indians told the truth, they put their trust in the Turk and had him guide them to Quivira.

Coronado left the Rio Grande Valley late in April 1541 with his host of horsemen and Indians, taking the road by way of Cicuye (Pecos), the prosperous unravaged gateway to the Great Plains. Thence they followed the Pecos River downstream until they were clear of the mountain spurs and then turned east to take an unmarked course, almost due east across the high plains, later called Llano Estacado.

The experience of the vast plain, like a sea of grass, pastured upon by great herds of buffalo (*vacas*), was vividly recalled. Jaramillo noted that at first they saw bulls in number (aged and immature males apart from the herds), but soon found themselves "among a vast mass of cows, calves, and bulls, all intermingled." The Anonymous *Relación* said: "There are so many that I do not know with what to compare them except to fish in the sea, because as well on this journey [the preliminary exploration by Alvarado] as on the one thereafter, made by the whole force on its way to Quivira, there were so many that often we passed through their midst and though we wished to take another way we could not do so, the plains being covered with them. Their meat is as good to eat as beef of Castile, and some think it better. The bulls are large and brave but do not attack readily." A second anonymous account told that four days' journey beyond Cibola they "came to land as level as the sea, in which plains there are innumerable cattle like those of Castile, some larger. [A detailed and proper description follows.] The land is so flat that men get lost if they draw apart by half a league. Thus one horseman was lost, as were two saddle horses. There remains no trace of where one has gone and for this reason they had recourse to marking the road traveled with buffalo dung, there being no stones or anything else." [10] Castañeda also said that markers

9. There appears to have been no difficulty of communication anywhere. Melchor Díaz and Alarcón were well informed about Cibola and other distant parts. Coronado and his men obtained specific data repeatedly from people of different languages. Whether by sign language or linkage of interpreters, the news service worked and did so over large distances.

10. *Relación Postrera de Sívola,* the manuscript sent Winship from Mexico by Garcia Icazbalceta.

of buffalo bones and dry dung were made by the advance scouts to guide the main party.

Crossing the buffalo plains the Spaniards had their first contact with Plains Indians whom they called Querechos (probably Apaches). These Indians met the Coronado party without fear, hostility, or show of surprise and communicated freely by signs.

Traveling many days over those plains they came to a rancheria of about two hundred houses, with their people: The houses were of buffalo hides, for these neither sow nor harvest maize: Of the hides they make their houses, of hides they dress and shoe themselves, of hides they make ropes as also of the wool: of tendons they make thread with which they sew their clothes and houses as well: of the bones they make awls: the dung serves them for firewood, for there is none other in that country: the stomachs served as jars and cups for drinking: they live on the meat which they eat half broiled over buffalo chips. . . . These people have dogs like ours, although somewhat larger, which they load as beasts of burden with small pack saddles, cinched with cords: when they are traveling the dogs drag the poles [on which the skin tents were packed], a load of perhaps two arrobas [fifty pounds]. (*Relación Postrera.*)

Jaramillo noted of the Querechos that "these lived without houses, having bundles of poles they carry with them to make huts that serve them as houses." The *Relación Postrera* wrote of the tents as being like *pabellones* (army tents), loaded on dogs, of which there were many; also that there were two kinds of people who traveled about the sea of grass, Querechos and Teyas, very well built and painted, enemies to each other.

MEETING WITH A TEXAS TRIBE

As the Coronado party neared the eastern end of the high grassy plain it was joined by another kind of Indians who were called Teyas—the first appearance of the name Texas. These Indians had been on a buffalo hunt and were returning home; they took the Spaniards to their valley homes farther east in barrancas, Castañeda wrote, as great as those of Colima. The topographic comparison gives the approximate location of the Texas settlements; one of the main roads from central Mexico to the Pacific coast still follows a spectacular gorge in Colima, of easy gradient between highland and lowland. The high smooth plain that the Coronado party crossed, now called

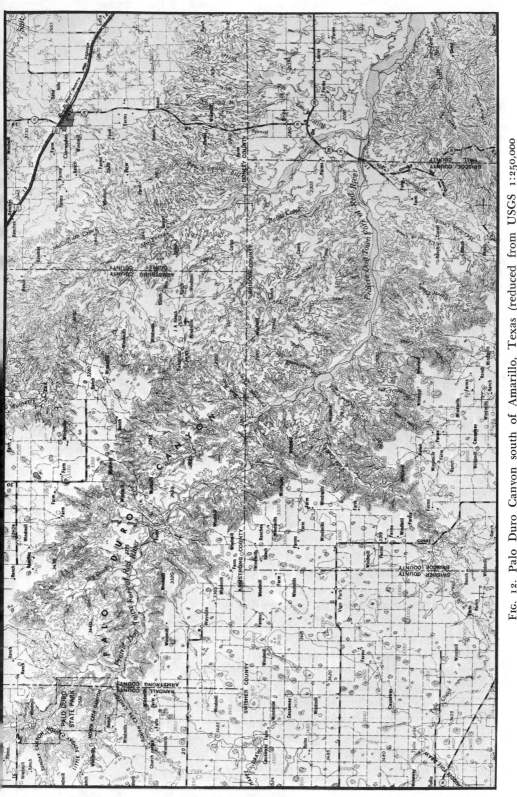

FIG. 12. Palo Duro Canyon south of Amarillo, Texas (reduced from USGS 1:250,000 Plainview sheet).

Llano Estacado, has at its eastern margin the Cap Rock Escarpment. Amarillo, on the high plain, is 3,650 feet above sea level; the plains below and east of the escarpment are at less than 2,000 feet. South of Amarillo the cap rock is deeply dissected by headwaters of the Red River. The longest of these, Prairie Dog Town Fork of the Red River, has cut Palo Duro Canyon to a depth of 1,500 feet, a spectacular barranca part of which is now a state park. It is adjoined to the south by the lesser Tule Canyon, indicated by Professor Bolton as the Coronado entry to the lower plains (fig. 12).

The valley floors within the Cap Rock Escarpment held more or less permanent settlements of Texas Indians. Castañeda remembered it as

a well populated land where there were beans (*frisoles*) in quantity and plums like those of Castile and grape vines. These settlements of rancherías extended for more than three days' journeys . . . the last barranca being more than a league in width, with a small river on its floor, and having much pulse (*aba*), mulberry trees and rose bushes like those of France, their sour fruits being ripe at the time and eaten. There were fowls like those of New Spain (turkeys) and plums like those of Castile, and in abundance.

Nut trees also were noted. The party took its ease for a number of days in the northern barranca (Palo Duro), enjoying the hospitality of its rancherías. In contrast to the semiarid and arid country in which they had been, these verdant valleys reminded them of Europe.

The rancherías were well located. To the west were the prime buffalo hunting grounds of the high plains. The barrancas gave snug shelter from winter storms, permanent water, abundant firewood, and various uses of the mesophytic woodlands. The usual interpretation that the people were mobile hunters without agriculture is unsatisfactory. *Frisol* has been construed as meaning mesquite, but *frisol* or *frijol* was the Spanish name for the cultivated *Phaseolus* beans. Castañeda had lived for years in the mesquite country about Culiacán and knew the tree by that name as did other members of the expedition. When they spoke of frijoles in the Pueblo lands or elsewhere they meant the garden beans of Indian cultivation, not the leguminous tree familiar to them as mesquite. The visit being in early summer, the abundant supply of beans indicates a surplus from the harvest of the previous year. The friable valley soils were well suited to Indian cultivation, the rancherias were large and numerous, its people were well acquainted with their kinsmen to the north who farmed as well as hunted and lived in permanent villages. (The Texas are thought to have been a Caddoan tribe, as were the Wichita to the north, next to be visited.) [11]

Castañeda remembered the people of the barrancas as of good understanding, the men as great archers, the women well treated and dressed in well-worked skins from shoulders to feet, and the reception of the visitors friendly.

THE RIDE TO QUIVIRA

Coronado was informed in the barrancas that Quivira lay to the northeast and was offered guides who would take him by direct route across the plains. He therefore sent most of his party back west across the buffalo plains to the Pecos River, which they reached well below the place where they had crossed before. Castañeda, with the returning party, told how they ate buffalo meat until they were sick of it.

Coronado rode north with thirty horsemen, one of whom was Jaramillo. The month was June, a pleasant time to cross the rolling plains of the Panhandle of Texas and Oklahoma. Their guides took them across the Canadian and Cimarron rivers to the Arkansas River at the ford below Dodge City, where in later years Texas cattle drives came to the town of Ford. Buffalo herds, "some days more and some fewer, according to water," pastured on the young growth of the prairies.

They followed the Arkansas River downstream on its northeasterly course to Great Bend. Here they met a band of Quivira Indians who had been on a buffalo hunt. Coronado gave them a letter to present to the presumed governor of Quivira and Harahay, "understanding that he was a Christian of the lost armada of Florida," that is, of the fleet of Narváez. They were in the land of Quivira, the territory of the Wichita Indians of Caddoan speech. Harahay was the Pawnee country, also Caddoan, of northeastern Kansas and beyond.[12]

11. The reference to the abundance of plums "like those of Castile" is to an American species of *Prunus*. Castañeda, low keyed, thought them superior fruits, suggesting that they had been improved by selection.

12. The State of Kansas got its name from a Siouan people living about the Kansas River, eastern neighbors of the Wichitas. The westward-

Leaving the Arkansas River and continuing northeast, they came to a half-dozen villages of good size situated on *arroyos* that carried little water but had good alluvial land, and so to a larger river with a larger settlement. This was the end of Quivira, beyond which lay the land of Harahay. They were in the Smoky Hills and probably got to the Saline River and the vicinity of Salina.

The Wichita and Pawnee Indians lived in villages, cultivated fields of maize, beans, and squash in the valleys, and hunted buffalo, antelope, and deer in prairie and woodland. Jaramillo described the country as

a land of very fine appearance, such as I have seen none better in all of our Spain or Italy or in part of France or elsewhere that I have been in the service of His Majesty. It is not very hilly, but a land of gentle slopes and of plains, with rivers of good aspects and waters. It pleases me greatly and I think that it will be very fruitful of all kinds of products. [There were wild cattle in vast numbers.] We found plums of Castile, one kind not red all over, but red, black, and green: Tree and fruit assuredly are from Castile and are of excellent flavor.

Another reference to superior plums, of such quality that Jaramillo thought them to be the European *Prunus*. There were grapes in the valleys, of fair quality considering that they were not taken care of. The houses, many of which were round, were covered with straw to the ground so that roof and wall were one (more or less hemispherical cross section on circular base). An extended entrance gave place for the people to sit. Coronado agreed with Jaramillo on the agricultural potential of the fertile dark soil.[13]

Coronado had come to the humid mesothermal heart of the continent and found that its attractions were not those of his expectations. Quivira had no rich cities, no wealth of metals, none of the things the Turk had promised. Coronado took formal possession for Spain, planted a cross, and left, getting

moving American frontier of the nineteenth century met the Kansas Indians west of the Missouri River and adopted the name.

13. The anonymous *Relación del Suceso* reported that they took thirty days after leaving the Texas barrancas to get to the Rio de Quivira (the Arkansas at Ford) and that it was thirty leagues from there to the settlements, where the houses were of straw in the manner of the Tarascans of central Mexico, also that the natives did not "make baked bread except under hot ashes."

back to the Rio Grande pueblos at the beginning of October 1541.[14] The horse party was well provided in Quivira with shelled maize, freely given. The return was by direct route to Cicuye, approximately the Santa Fé Trail of later time.

The long ride from the Rio Grande of Mexico to central Kansas and back was made without misadventure, hardship, or lack of food. The natives had been friendly, gave them food, were well informed of distant parts, and provided guides. From the Pecos to the Saline the route was through buffalo country and its great bounty was shared by various tribes. Pueblo Indians crossed east of the Pecos to hunt. Querechos lived on the plains, subsisted on buffalo, and followed the moving herds by dog-drawn travois. From the east, Caddoan tribes—Texas, Wichitas, and Pawnees—lived in farming villages and sent hunting parties to the buffalo plains.

END OF THE VENTURE

Tristan de Luna y Arellano meantime had restored order in the pueblos of Tiguex and extended Spanish control up and down the Rio Grande Valley. Winter was again at hand and there was ample store of food and shelter in the pueblos. A second winter would be spent there. In December "the general fell off his horse while exercising it and was injured in the head, whereafter he gave evidence of a ruined disposition" (Jaramillo). The return march began in April 1542. The detachment that had been left at the Sonora Valley base had mistreated the friendly Opatas who had risen in anger and wiped it out. Arrived at Compostela, the returnees found the country suffering the effects of the Mixtón War, a formidable Indian revolt that was made possible in part by the absence of the Spaniards who had gone with Coronado. The army that had set out gaily two years before to gain wealth and renown dragged back to Mexico in the fall of 1542, destitute and dispirited. The viceroy, Coronado and his wife, and a lot of gentry had lost fortunes to find that the fables of northern riches were only fables.

14. The Franciscan Juan de Padilla returned with lay brothers to Quivira to undertake missionary work. On being well received by the Wichitas, he extended his labors to the neighboring Siouan Kansas tribe, offended them somehow, and was killed by them. Years later his three companions walked into a Spanish outpost at Pánuco, having made as long a journey from north to south as the party of Cabeza de Vaca had done from east to west.

HOW REMEMBERED

The Cibola expedition was the viceroy's idea; the extension to Quivira was added by Coronado. The entire business was thought up and carried out in New Spain without support or control by any authority in Spain. No participant hurried to publish a narrative. There was little publicity.

López de Gómara a decade after the event gave it several well-informed pages, especially about the plains and their vast herds of wild cattle. A fairly representative woodcut of a bison was added, drawn from verbal account (fig. 13). He told how

FIG. 13. Woodcut of an American bison in Francisco López de Gómara's *La historia general de las Indias,* Anvera, 1554.

Spaniards who traveled on the trackless plains "made mounds of buffalo dung in the absence of stones and trees, so as not to get lost on their return." Gómara also reported the return of friar Padilla's companions from Quivira to Pánuco.

Documents were collected by Ramusio and appeared in the third volume (1556) of his *Navigationi e Viaggi,* some in translation, some as abstract. The voyage of Alarcón is known only by his report to the viceroy that Ramusio found and printed. Ramusio also used letters of Mendoza and Coronado, the relation of Fray Marcos, and other items from Spanish archives. This earliest and monumental publication of overseas discoveries later provided Richard Hakluyt with much material.

López de Velasco completed the official *Geografía y Descripción de las Indias* in 1574. It gave six short paragraphs to the northern interior, gleaned from the archives: Cíbola had good store of maize, beans, and squash. Turkeys were kept, mainly for their feathers. Its people were dressed in mantles of fiber and of skins. They were idolators who worshipped water (rain ceremonies?). The pueblos of Tusayan (Hopi) were of larger size than those of Cíbola, its people of similar customs, and also grew some cotton. The pueblo of Acoma was built on the world's strongest rock, had mantles of cotton and skins, had turquoise, and kept turkeys. There were sixty to seventy pueblos along the Río Tiguex. The natives on the plains of the wild cattle were very well built, painted, and moved about with skin tents and many dogs. For Quivira the absence of cotton and domestic fowl was noted, also that their bread was baked in ashes.

Antonio de Herrera y Tordesillas began publishing his official *Historia* in 1601. The Coronado expedition in the main is the relation of Jaramillo, the Alarcón voyage is based on a report to the viceroy.

The American Southwest became of national interest during and after the Civil War. There was newly discovered mineral wealth to be exploited in a country of strange land forms and vegetation, of Indians living in ancient ways, of many ruins such as had attracted attention at the time of Coronado. A new generation of explorers came—geologists, naturalists, archaeologists, and ethnographers.

First of these American scholarly pioneers was Major John Wesley Powell. His descent of the Colorado River through the Grand Canyon (1868) resulted in his founding of the U.S. Geological Survey. The Indians of the Southwest, living and past, became his greater interest, which led to his forming the Bureau of Ethnology in 1879. New Mexico and Arizona were for decades the major field of discovery and training of American ethnology and archaeology. Thus the young librarian Winship, who had seen no old ruin or living Indian pueblo, was given the opportunity to collect and interpret the records of the Coronado expedition that first observed the nature and culture of the Southwest beyond the trail taken by the Cabeza de Vaca party.

The Santa Fe Railroad, late comer to the transcontinental rail lines, promoted the scenic attractions along its route, including the Indians. It built a branch line to the south rim of the Grand Canyon to view the great barranca about where the Spanish discoverers had seen its awesome depth. The side trip to the Grand Canyon became a principal attraction of transcontinental travel. Hotels of modified Pueblo design were spaced at convenient intervals on the main line, and passenger trains stopped at them for meals. These hotels displayed and sold Indian craft products, turquoise jewelry, blankets, pottery, and baskets and often had authentic Indians amiably present. A leisurely way of enjoying travel at a time when leisure was one of the enjoyments of travel.

8
Discovery
North Along the
Pacific Coast
(1539–1543)

Cortés, after taking the Aztec capital, hastened to send parties
to the Pacific Coast. By 1526 he had established control from
Tepic south to Guatemala, the latter occupied by his chief
lieutenant Pedro de Alvarado. In 1529 Cortés was given authority by the king to discover and settle on the South Sea
(Pacific Ocean) and on the mainland coast of New Spain beyond its previously established dominion. He was the first to
see that Pacific ports of New Spain would give the access to
the East Indies that Magellan's voyage had shown not to be
in reach by an all-sea route. He was also the first to plan the
northward exploration and possession of the Pacific Coast.
[Given both rights, he ran into trouble to the north when
Nuño de Guzmán invaded the northwest to proclaim himself
governor of New Galicia. Guzmán was recalled, and Mendoza
shortly was appointed first viceroy of New Spain (1535).]

The contest between viceroy and captain general was inevitable and immediate. Cortés exercised his briefed rights in
going to the discovery of California in 1536, and followed it
with the despatch of Ulloa in 1539 to run out the Gulf of

California. Ulloa found that California was not an island but a long peninsula, and traced its ocean shore to Cedros Island. The new geographic knowledge was used by Mendoza to send Alarcón to the head of the gulf, named the Red Sea by Ulloa. Cortés protested the trespass on his rights and took his claims to court.

Meanwhile Pedro de Alvarado had got into the act, at first alone, then by making common cause with Mendoza. Lieutenant to Cortés in the conquest of Mexico, Alvarado went his independent way in Guatemala. Also his wealth became second only to that of Cortés. Cortés had proposed discovery across the Pacific and had been given license to undertake it. Alvarado built a fleet in Guatemala to go to the Spice Islands on his own. Hearing of the riches Pizarro was finding in Peru, he interrupted his plans and instead sailed south in 1534, to cut in for his share there. He was blocked at Quito, but sold his fleet at a good price. Fray Marcos had accompanied him on the march to Quito, made at dreadful cost of Indian lives. Returned to Guatemala, Alvarado built another fleet, for which he got authorization to explore the South Sea. Mendoza being engaged in the Cibola venture, Alvarado saw the opportunity to form a partnership with the viceroy to share the profits of the land and sea expeditions and to keep Cortés out of the action. The final contract of association and division of profits was signed at Tiripitio in Michoacán on November 29, 1540, at which time Alarcón was back from the Colorado River and Coronado had left Cibola for the Rio Grande.[1]

Alvarado moved his fleet of a dozen ships and a thousand men north by easy stages, with a Portuguese pilot, Juan Rodríguez Cabrillo (Spanish spelling), in charge. The main fleet entered Puerto de Navidad in Jalisco on Christmas Day, 1540, whence the name it bears to the present. From it the easiest road leads to the interior of Jalisco. Here the great Indian rebellion, known as the Mixtón War, was then spreading fast, encouraged by the absence of many Spaniards who had gone with Coronado. Alvarado gave sorely needed help, putting detachments at endangered places and taking his main force north of Guadalajara into the Mixtón mountain stronghold. He died there in June 1541 of injuries from a fall. Mendoza was occupied into the winter of 1541–1542 in breaking the revolt.

1. CDI, vol. 16, pp. 342–355.

The fleet had a long wait at Navidad while Mendoza and Alvarado were subduing the Jalisco Indians. After the death of Alvarado, Mendoza as surviving partner had fleet and crews at his disposal. The greater part of the fleet, he decided, should carry out the planned voyage across the Pacific. Cabrillo was given a detached assignment to explore the Pacific coast north of Cedros Island, beyond where Ulloa had ended his discovery for Cortés. The northern exploration was urgent, a letter from the king to the viceroy having reported that Portuguese were said to have discovered a strait connecting the two oceans in the far north. (This imagined passage later was known at the Strait of Anian.) Cabrillo therefore was sent on maritime exploration north, sailing from Navidad June 27, 1542. Ruiz López de Villalobos left with the larger fleet November 1 to cross the Pacific.[2]

THE VOYAGE OF CABRILLO

Cabrillo's voyage is well reported in a *relación* based on a log.[3] Cedros Island, discovered and named by Ulloa, was left August 10, 1542. Beyond they skirted the desert coast of Lower California to enter San Quintín Bay August 23, naming it Puerto Posesión in token of its new discovery and possession by Spain. On the Island (San Martín) north of that bay large driftwood, resembling cypress, was piled onshore. (These were logs of conifers carried south by coastal current from northern forests.) They were moving into a coast of lesser aridity, coming to a good port September 7, which they named San Mateo (Bahía de Todos Santos, or Ensenada). More large and heavy timbers were seen stranded on its beach. Inland were savannas, the vegetation like that of Spain. There were herds of grazing animals, recognizable by their description as pronghorn antelope. Three uninhabited islands were passed next (Los Coronados, south of the International Border).

The port of San Miguel (San Diego) was reached September 27, and Indians informed them by signs that men with beards and swords had been in the interior and killed many people (the visit of Melchor Díaz to the Yuma region). Farther on they saw many smokes inland (signal fires or brush fires set during the dry season). On October 7 they landed at an island

2. Henry Raup Wagner, *Spanish Voyages; Cartography; Cabrillo.*
3. CDI, vol. 4, pp. 165–191. Wagner made competent identifications of route and place names.

(Santa Catalina) where many Indians came to greet them, singing and dancing. The next day they entered "the bay of smokes" of plains, groves, and valleys (area of Los Angeles).

From October 9 into early November the Chumash natives were visited, from Point Mugu to Point Concepción, the length of the California riviera along Santa Barbara Channel. On the mainland they noted fine plains of groves and savannas, with mountains in the distance. Acorns were at harvest time, as was an unnamed large white seed. Maguey was a food, the turgid stems of *Agave* baked in pits. The channel was busy with canoes out fishing. The first village at the side of Point Mugu they called Pueblo de Canoas, a large one toward the far end of the channel, Pueblo de Sardinas. The canoes were large and well-made dugouts that held a dozen people. Villages were strung along both mainland and islands in extraordinary number. Their names were written down, twenty-five in the first list, seventeen more farther on, and additional ones on the Channel Islands, all well populated; the island villages were poor in comparison with those on the mainland. "Always there came many canoes, for all the coast is greatly populated." Mugu is the only village name that has survived.

The houses were large and round, the roofs extending to the ground; in one place they were said to be built in the manner of those in New Spain. Ordinary houses were clustered about large houses, some of which were circular. In front of these many thick timbers had been planted in the ground and covered with many paintings. (The suggestion is of a kind of totem pole.)

This was a land and sea of plenty, the most populous part of California; its "gentle" natives were hospitable and provided the visitors with an abundance of fish. The Chumash were the best fishers at sea and builders of boats in California, with other traits that appear to link them with Indians of the Northwest Coast of America.

The fall storms and rains began at the end of October. On setting out to explore farther, they were caught in a storm on November 11 and were driven about for a week by wind and waves along a bold and shelterless coast at the base of high mountains. By their reckoning, usually about two degrees too high, they reached forty degrees north latitude, where they saw a point of land covered with pines. (Point Reyes has been inferred.) Their means of determining where they were, while riding out a storm in undecked ships, were poor. They passed

by the Santa Lucia Mountains, named by them Sierra San
Martín: "All this shore is very dangerous and has great swells
of the sea and very high land; there are mountains that reach
to the sky, the sea beating against them. Sailing close to shore
it would seem that the mountains might fall on the ships."
To the north they saw snow on the mountains. Returning
south they entered a large bay on November 16 where pines
grew down to the water's edge (thought to have been Monterey
Bay). The trip was rough, vexed by unusually early winter
storms.

Winter quarters were taken November 23 in a very well-
sheltered harbor on the northernmost Channel Island, which
they named Isla de Posesión (Cuyler Harbor on San Miguel
Island). It was inhabited by poor fishermen, said to be naked
and filthy in contrast to the natives of the mainland. From the
Bahía de Posesión (San Quintín Bay in Lower California) to
Isla de Posesión at the far end of Santa Barbara Channel,
Cabrillo thus declared that he claimed California for Spain.

Cabrillo died at the winter harbor January 3, 1543, of an
injury incurred before the voyage north. The command passed
to one Ferrelo or Ferrer, probably a Christian Levantine.[4]
On January 19 another attempt was made at northern exploration, but again a storm drove them back after eight days
to the island harbor. On February 14 they made their last
try, sighted the cape of pines (Point Reyes?) on the 22nd, and
recorded their farthest north as 43° (by usual correction Cape
Mendocino). There was no landing or act of possession. They
were back at the winter harbor March 5, then renamed Juan
Rodríguez for the captain who was buried there. The return
was made without incident and in good time: March 9 at
Canoas (Mugu), March 11 to 15 at San Miguel (San Diego),
March 21 at Posesión (San Quintín), March 23 at Cedros Island
where the exploration had begun, and April 14 at the starting
port of Navidad.

The discovery of a thousand miles of California coast was
not followed up and was little remembered. Herrera made a
brief excerpt of the Cabrillo *relación*. When Sebastian Viz-
caino rediscovered the coast in 1602 he gave new Spanish
place names that are still applied.

4. A Corsican and another Portuguese were other officers of foreign
nationality.

9
The
De Soto Expedition
(1538–1543)

The prior grants of Florida lapsed with the deaths of Pánfilo de Narváez and Vázquez de Ayllón, the former having been given possession to the north of the Gulf of Mexico, Ayllón along the Atlantic Coast. Hernando de Soto petitioned for the vacant title and was given it in 1537.

De Soto was unacquainted with the lands he sought to possess. He had gone to Darien with Pedrarias in 1514 as a youth in his teens, owning only his sword and shield, according to the Fidalgo de Elvas.[1] Pedrarias gave free rein to plunder and violence in Darien, Panama, and Nicaragua in the search for gold, found in native possession in the houses of chiefs, in temples, and largely in tombs. De Soto prospered so well in this ravage that when Pizarro and his companions left Panama to start on the conquest of Peru he joined them in the Gulf of Guayaquil, bringing two ships and a hundred men (1532). He went ahead of Pizarro's troops across the Andes, met the Inca Atahualpa at his seat in Cajamarca, and shared in the huge ransom Atahualpa had collected, although he was not implicated in the imprisonment or killing. After the sack of Cuzco he stayed on as lieutenant governor. He returned to

1. A participant in the expedition, as noted later.

Spain a very rich man and married a daughter of Pedrarias. He was accepted by the higher nobility, and was ambitious for more wealth and fame.

The royal orders given in April and May 1537 gave him authority to conquer, pacify, and settle whatever he wished within the ample limits of Florida.[2] He was to choose two hundred leagues of coast for his government, to be called the Province of Florida, and also was named Governor of Cuba. He was to raise within the year five hundred men with arms, horses, and equipment and would have four years to explore and select the two hundred leagues of coast frontage. He was authorized to build three fortified towns and allot *solares* (town lots) to the citizens. He might bring fifty Negro slaves. All these expenses were to be borne by him or his men.

The crown share of revenues was specified, in particular, the gold, silver, precious stones, and pearls found. If these were gained in the usual manner in battle, on entering towns, or by trade with the Indians the Crown was to have a fifth. If they were taken from graves, sepulchres, temples, places of religious ceremonies, or buried in a private or public place the Crown was to get half. The lack of any mention of mining is to be noted.

Grave robbing and the plundering of temples and "palaces" had been the chief sources of gain in Peru as they had been in Panama. Buildings were stripped in a hurry, but graves furnished with the precious possessions of the dead continued to be found and to yield wealth (as they still do in those parts). De Soto expected his new domain to hold treasures of like kind, the accumulations of generations of artisans in precious metals.

Cabeza de Vaca returned to Spain after De Soto had secured his license, met De Soto, and was solicited to participate in the the expedition. It has been said that the negotiations failed because Cabeza de Vaca asked to be second in command. The inference is uncertain and I think unlikely. The Narváez survivors brought no word of opulent civilizations or of mineral deposits. Cabeza de Vaca, like his companions, had declined Viceroy Mendoza's request to go on northern exploration. De Soto knew that Mendoza was preparing such an expedition, and he wanted to forestall the viceroy. All previous Spanish attempts from the Gulf or Atlantic Coast had

2. CDI, vol. 22, pp. 534–546; CDU, vol. 4, pp. 431–437.

ended in disaster. Cabeza de Vaca as a survivor would be a valuable guide, but he knew the brutality of the proposed conquest that was written into the grant—a projection of the past career of De Soto and the opposite of his own life—for which reason I doubt that he would have joined such a company.

The project is remarkable in the annals of colonialism for the shameless manner in which it announced its objective as unlimited plunder. De Soto made a remark to the Gentleman of Elvas that where there was much land, referring to the large area he hoped to range over, some of it would prove to be rich. By that he meant riches to be taken from the inhabitants, as had been done in Peru, not resources of soil or mine.

THE RECORD OF THE EXPEDITION

The Congress of the United States in 1937 passed a Joint Resolution, beginning "Whereas we are approaching the four hundredth anniversary of the expedition of Hernando de Soto, the first and most imposing expedition ever made by Europeans into the wilds of North America . . ." to be followed by establishing the United States De Soto Commission. The body, headed by John R. Swanton of the Smithsonian Institution, made an admirable study of the historical record and of the terrain over which the expedition passed. Its final report was submitted in 1938 and was published in 1939.[3] The little-known document of four-hundred pages and ten maps is about as definitive as to route and calendar as is possible. The route as plotted is shown later in fig. 14. The interest of the Congress was in the landing of De Soto at Tampa, which was to have been the seat of the next Pan American Exposition (not carried out because of the Second World War). The resolution, saying that the expedition was the most imposing penetration into the wilds of North America, was in the popular American tradition that the white man found this country a wilderness sparsely inhabited by savages.

There are four primary sources.[4] Hernández de Biedma, factor of the expedition, gave a terse, factual account to the Council of the Indies in 1544. His report remained in manuscript for three hundred years, though it was not entirely un-

3. Cited as U.S. De Soto Comm.
4. Commented on in the first chapter of the U.S. De Soto Comm. report.

known. The mid-nineteenth-century publication was by abridged and inadequate translations.

Rodrigo Rangel (or Ranjel), De Soto's secretary, kept an accurate and detailed account. This fullest relation of the expedition, with candid observations on the conduct of De Soto and others, was transcribed almost verbatim by Oviedo in his *Historia General,* as he had done also for the Joint Report of the survivors of Narváez. Oviedo's great history was first published in 1851 and had been used somewhat by Spanish historians, but with little attention to northern explorations.[5] Rangel became known to historians in the United States, in English translation and excerpt, only in the present century.

In 1557 a printer at Evora (Ebora), Portugal, published an anonymous account of the De Soto expedition, *Relaçam verdadeira . . . por hum fidalgo Delvas.* The Gentleman of Elvas has not been identified. There were at least eight Portuguese from Elvas (on the border of Spanish Extremadura) who joined the expedition, largely made up of Extremeños from De Soto's homeland. For half a century this was the only published version of the De Soto venture. The sprightly and "true relation" was reprinted and translated in numerous editions from the seventeenth to the present century.[6]

The last, least reliable, and best known account is *La Florida del Inca,* by Garcilaso de la Vega, written at the end of the century and first printed in 1605 at Lisbon. Son of a conqueror of Peru and of an Inca princess, Garcilaso came to Spain twenty years after the return of De Soto's men. He heard one of the veterans, a known but undistinguished hidalgo, tell the adventures of the great march. These gave Garcilaso the idea of writing the book, to which end he collected a manuscript of "peregrinations" written by a common soldier and another by a tailor who had been on the expedition. *La Florida del Inca* is a romantic narrative of the daring and virtues of the Spanish conquerors, with sympathy for the conquered Indians. The high-born mestizo, accepted into Spanish society and a good Catholic, needed to believe that Christianity would come out of the conquest. His information of the country and people of Florida was at second hand and poorly understood by him. Nor was he interested in description other than to

5. The Rangel account is in Oviedo, Libro XVII, chaps. 21–28.
6. Facsimile and translation by the Florida Historical Society in 1933. Facsimile edition by the Ministry of Colonies of Portugal in 1940.

embellish his narrative. Garcilaso acknowledged his difficulties
in arranging the events in their proper sequence and place.
He wrote a dramatic story as he believed it to have happened.
It has enjoyed long popularity.

THE START

The expedition sailed from San Lúcar de Barrameda at the
mouth of the Río Guadalquivir on April 7, 1538. The place
of origin of 653 participants has been determined; 45 more
are unlocated.[7] More than 600 landed in Florida, 330 being
foot soldiers, the majority of the rest having mounts. Four
priests, four friars, and four women are named. There were
diverse artisans, including two Genoese and a Sardinian, who
were skilled at building bridges and boats. Unlike the feckless
Narváez expedition, care was taken in the selection of personnel and equipment.

Cuba, which had been granted to De Soto, was to provide
food. De Soto arrived with the fleet at the capital, Santiago de
Cuba, early in June and sent the fleet on to Havana at the far
end of the island, the horsemen following by land. The main
body of horsemen took its ease on the way, getting to Havana
late in March 1539, the Gentleman of Elvas reporting that the
governor, whom he accompanied, had arrived there about
three months earlier. While supplies were being collected, De
Soto sent ships from Havana to Florida to select a suitable
harbor. Five ships of five- to eight-hundred tons remained at
Havana for the transport of the men, horses, equipment, and
provisions.

Cuba furnished a goodly store of food, three thousand loads
of the durable ships' bread called cassava prepared from bitter
manioc, five thousand bushels of maize, sides of bacon, and
most important of all, live hogs. These range animals fended
for themselves on the island and could be driven as herds in
the manner of other livestock. They would provide an ambulant and self-reproducing food supply on the march. Once the
party was on its journey inland there would be no further
dependence on supply by ships. Extremadura, whence De Soto
and most of his men came from, is of old a land of mast-fed
swine, bred long of snout and limb, adept foragers, and accustomed to being driven in herds. De Soto's men knew how

7. U.S. De Soto Comm., Appendix G.

to manage such a breed, which had been brought to Cuba and thrived there, and De Soto had the wit to thus provide the expedition.

The ships sent from Havana to check the Florida coast returned with selection of a port of debarkation and brought captive Indians to be used as guides. The preparations completed, the expedition sailed from Havana on May 18, 1539, came in sight of the intended port on May 25 and examined its shore to find a suitable landing in the bay, where landing began May 30.[8] The bay being large and having several arms, this took several days. By common Spanish practice it was named by church calendar Espiritu Santo Bay, the later Tampa Bay.

Fourteen months had passed since the expedition left Spain, the greater part of the time well spent in Cuba in training personnel, organizing facilities, and stocking provisions.

BEGINNING OF THE MARCH AND
THE FIRST WINTER CAMP (1539–1540)

While unloading, a small horse party was sent scouting, met some Indians who were coming to take a look at the strangers, attacked them, killed two, and lost a horse in the fracas. This was the first contact with natives. De Soto took possession of an Indian town near Tampa Bay, the inhabitants having fled. The chief's house stood on an artificial mound, a temple across town. Having taken their desired quarters the temple and other houses were destroyed, according to the Gentleman of Elvas. Early in June detachments went out to capture Indians. In one encounter six Christians were wounded, one mortally. An attack on another Indian band was halted when one of them identified himself as a Spaniard, left there from the Narváez expedition eleven years earlier. This Juan Ortiz brought proffer of friendship from his chief, Mocoso, whose town was eight leagues distant inland. Ortiz was to serve for several years as interpreter and guide. The unprovoked violence with which De Soto had entered was halted for a short time, but only with regard to the friendly chief. Elsewhere

8. The U.S. Commission placed this north of Bradenton near the mouth of Tampa Bay. The De Soto National Monument was established in 1948 to the west of Bradenton.

there were clashes with Indians, burning of villages, and an occasional native thrown to dogs that were trained to attack, one of which Rangel identified as an Irish hound.

De Soto was in the land of the Timucua Indians where Narváez had preceded him. Narváez had kept close to the coast in his march north from Tampa Bay; De Soto took his course north farther inland. Removal from port to the interior was piecemeal and slow and is of obscure record. In mid-July De Soto left the bay with a strong party, horses, hogs, and dogs for the lake-strewn country of the interior—a land of sinks and depressions formed by solution of limestone beds. Lakes are mentioned, swamps and cornfields (July 19), and named towns. The U.S. Commission reconstructed the route as leading almost due north (Dade City to Ocala to Gainesville). The various reporters, being in different parties, gave different dates and halts. The Gentleman of Elvas, who was not in the governor's party, told of having used up the provisions and resorting to boiling greens and eating the young stalks of maize plants and palmetto cabbages. At the end of July the parties gathered in the province of Ocale (Ocala), where there was abundance of ripe maize in the fields, also of beans. Small dogs (Biedma) were given as presents, the first mention of this delicacy. They remained in this productive and populous province into August (fig. 14).

The journey north was resumed into the fertile country about Gainesville, where there were villages in number, one of which was named Villaharta because of its abundance of maize. Prisoners were taken and there was occasional fighting. Farther on Rangel called attention to a tract of dwarf chestnut trees, in contrast to the tall chestnut trees elsewhere. The U.S. Commission recognized them as the dwarf chinquapin, "found mainly where the Indians periodically burned over the land," still a feature of that section. On August 16 a bridge was built over the River of Discords (Santa Fe River) to get to the village of Caliquen (Elvas). There being promise of ample provisions, the governor and advance party awaited the coming of the main body, which arrived September 4. On leaving, they took the chief and his daughter (according to Rangel), and on September 10 reached a pleasant town of many people, much food, a very large house, and a large open plaza (vicinity of Lake City). From Ocala to Lake City they had turned west of

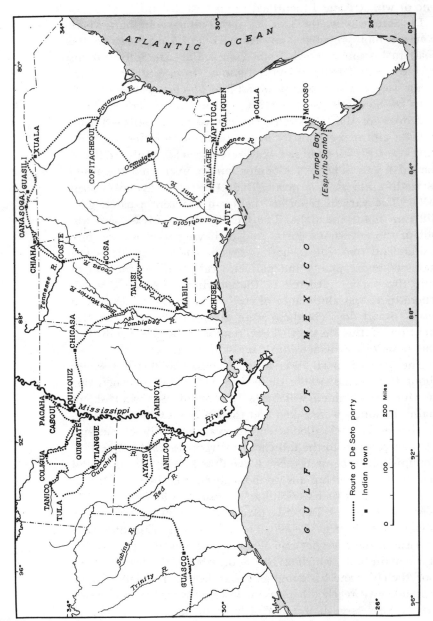

Fig. 14. Route of the De Soto party (after U.S. De Soto Commission).

north, keeping close to the present line of railroad and highway leading north from Tampa, probably a main Indian
trail.

The U.S. Commission located the next leg of the route as
north of west, reaching Napituca (vicinity of the town of Live
Oak) September 15, "a very pleasant village, in a pretty spot,
with plenty of food." Nearby the first sharp fight took place,
the so-called battle of the lakes, in which the Indians attempted to rescue their captive chief. According to Rangel,
three hundred captives were taken and the chain gang procedure was begun, a file of chained porters that was to
be a regular feature of the march. Napituca was left September 23 to cross the River of the Deer by a bridge they made of
pine trees (Suwanee River) and so on through villages, fields,
and woods to reach the end of the Timucua country September 30 at the Aucilla River (the modern spelling of the varying
form used by the reporters).

Beyond the Aucilla River they were in the land of the
Apalachees, a once numerous Muskogean people related to the
Choctaws. The first town reached had been set afire by its
people. Passing through villages and fields, the party got to
the main town of Apalachen October 6 at or near Tallahassee
and took up winter quarters there. The inhabitants had fled;
there were many houses and an abundance of food both in fields
and also stored. "The province of Apalachen is very fertile and
abounds greatly in yield of much maize and beans and squash
and diverse fruits and many deer and great diversity of birds
and fish" (Rangel). The party was based here for five months—
about five hundred Spaniards, a similar number of captives,
and a large herd of horses and of swine. There was no lack of
food at any time. When the journey was resumed in March
1540 as much corn was loaded as could be carried. (Narváez
and his large party had spent a month there in early summer
and found ample supplies.)

The dispossessed Indians prowled about the camp. One
slipped by the sentinels and set fire to the town, burning two
thirds of it with the aid of a high wind (Elvas). Punishment
was no deterrent. "If any had their hands or nose cut off they
made no more of it than did the Roman Scaevola" Rangel
wrote, in tribute to their courage.

De Soto, with Juan Ortiz as interpreter and informant,
planned his next season's campaign. He sent one party to the

gulf to find the harbor at which Narváez had built his boats. Another went back to Tampa Bay to bring up the brigantines that had remained there. The boats came up to Apalachee Bay south of Tallahassee and then were sent on west as far as Pensacola Bay, perhaps to Mobile Bay. De Soto wanted to know more about the gulf coast but had no intention of following it as Narváez had done. Other parties ranged north, finding the country poor and thinly populated.

An Indian who had been captured at the battle of the lakes told stories of his homeland far off toward the rising sun, of its queen living in a great city, and of the tribute she received, including much gold. Perico, as he was nicknamed, showed how the gold was mined and smelted so that his hearers were convinced that he had witnessed what he described. The Spaniards wanted to hear about gold and there was much idle time in the long winter quarters to spin yarns. Wishful thinking became great expectations, and when spring came De Soto set out to find riches as he had done in Peru.

THE MARCH TO COFITACHEQUI
(SPRING OF 1540)

Most of the Indians in forced service, "being naked and in chains," had died during the winter, and the local Apalachees had run away. Everyone therefore was required to provide himself with maize for the journey of sixty leagues through the poor country ahead (the outer coast plain of South Georgia). The horsemen packed the corn on their mounts, those afoot on their backs (Elvas).

The entire body started from Apalachen March 3 and it took two months to get to their objective, Cofitachequi, where the famed queen lived, crossing the State of Georgia from its southwest corner to the Savannah River below Augusta. It was a very rainy spring, streams were out of their banks and a number of them had to be crossed. There were few landmarks or settlements of note. The U.S. Commission, plotting the course, decided somewhat hesitantly on a route north to cross Flint River, continuing northwest of the river, recrossing it, and then striking across country to the southwest bend of the Ocmulgee River, being thus engaged throughout the month of March, often struggling through water and mud. Occasionally villages supplied store of corn.

The Indian Perico served as guide to the Ocmulgee valley, where his knowledge of the route came to an end. The valley had numerous villages, divers food, including many fat dogs, and provided seven hundred or more bearers. They had entered the more fertile inner coast plain, turning north-east (about Hawkinsville on the Ocmulgee?) to cut across a number of rivers flowing southeast, with the loss of many pigs at one crossing. The men were at a loss as to what trail to follow and were short of food, sustaining themselves on wild greens and a small ration of pork. From one village they took fifty bushels of dry corn and thirty more that had been parched. Indians that were picked up as guides were unresponsive; one was burned alive.

April 30 De Soto came to a great river (the Savannah) and sent for canoes to cross to Cofitachequi. Rangel described their ceremonial reception by the queen who was borne on an ornamented, covered litter carried by men of rank. She took off a string of pearls and placed it about the neck of the governor. "A very clean people and of polished manners," dressed in fine skins and furs. Cofitachequi, a capital of the Creek Nation about twenty-five miles downstream from Augusta, entertained the visitors well for the fortnight of their stay. The comfort and plenty in the Creek towns were well appreciated in all the accounts.

The promised treasure for which they had come was only a lot of freshwater pearls found in river mussels and common to rivers of the coastal plain and Mississippi Valley. Here they were worn as necklaces and bracelets and decked the bodies of the deceased, which were stored above ground in "temples." The Spaniards helped themselves liberally to these mortuary gifts, without hindrance, De Soto carrying away a chest full of pearls. Some of the temples were in abandoned towns, said to have been depopulated by a pestilence two years earlier.

Corn of the past year's harvest was stored in large cribs (*barbacoas*) to which the guests helped themselves at will, seven full cribs being emptied in one town. Whatever the natives thought of the strange behavior of the guests there was no clash, and the Spaniards departed in mid-May in peace, but took the queen (or her niece) with them.

FROM THE SAVANNAH TO THE
TENNESSEE RIVER (MAY AND JUNE 1540)

A chest of pearls of inferior quality was the extent of the riches they had come to seek. A year had passed since they had sailed from Havana. They had heard of people rich in gold in mountains inland and had not yet seen so much as a hill. There was word of a farther land of wealth called Chiaha to which they set out in mid-May, going north across the Piedmont of South Carolina. This took a week, during which they met natives of ruder culture, timid and naked, who had but little maize. However, these natives brought in a great many turkeys that were roasted on barbecues, also some small dogs that were good eating and which were raised in their houses (Rangel). This part of the Piedmont was later occupied by Cherokees. Swanton, the best authority, thought that the Cherokees did not live that far south at that time and that these simpler people probably were Cheraws, relatives of the Siouan-speaking Catawbas.

At Xuala (May 22–25) they were at the foot of the Blue Ridge (vicinity of Walhalla, South Carolina). Here they were provided with bearers, maize, dogs, and hampers; Rangel noted also that there were better indications of gold to be found than any they had seen before. Someone may have known something about gold-bearing quartz veins in crystalline rocks. They did not stop to investigate the geology or the sand and gravel in the mountain streams but made the arduous crossing of the Blue Ridge without giving details. During this passage the Lady of Cofitachequi made her escape, as did three slaves, a Cuban Indian, a Berber, and a Negro. The U.S. Commission carried their route to a headwater of the Little Tennessee River at Highlands, North Carolina, downstream to Franklin, and thence west by a still recognizable Indian trail (now Federal Route 64) to the Hiwassee Valley and the old Hiwassee Indian town, Guasili in the De Soto reports, "an old village location in a beautiful plain where Peachtree Creek unites with the Hiwassee" (U.S. Commission). The distance from Xuala to Guasili was about a hundred miles and was traveled in five days—a formidable performance across mountain country and possible only by the existence of a major

Indian trail. Perhaps the elapsed time applied to the advance horse party; but the entire party, pigs and all, did go across the mountains.

At Guasili they were well into Cherokee country and at one of the main Cherokee towns. (It is now the site of a North Carolina prison camp, three miles east of Murphy.) Knowing the taste of the Spaniards for fat roast dog, the chief presented them with three hundred (Elvas), maize, and fresh bearers.

Below Murphy the Hiwassee River has cut a deep passage across the Unicoi Mountains, now blocked by reservoirs. At the time of the Commission there was a path along the gorge considered difficult but passable and by which the exit from the mountains is considered to have been made. The Hiwassee emerges abruptly into the Valley of East Tennessee south of Etowah, whence Conasauga Creek drains south into the Hiwassee (U.S. Highway 411 parallels the base of the mountains). At Canasoga (thus spelled) they were met by twenty Indians bringing baskets of mulberries. On June 3 they came to the Tennessee River, which they followed downstream past the site of Chattanooga, reaching Chiaha (on Burns Island, above the Alabama state line) on June 6.

This was the first crossing of the Appalachian Mountains by Europeans and was made by a large party with a lot of equipment and driving a large herd of swine. It was supplied with provisions along the way by hospitable Indians and was done in the remarkably good time of three weeks from Savannah River to Chiaha. The next penetration by Europeans into the interior United States east of the Mississippi River was by Frenchmen more than a century later.

Before they got to Chiaha they were met by fifteen men bearing maize and word from the chief that twenty full barbacoas of maize awaited them (Elvas). Almost a month was spent in the town, resting and eating. For two weeks they fraternized, Indians and Spaniards swimming and playing games together. Food was plentiful—cribs full of maize, gourds full of nut oil and bear grease, even a pot of bee honey (Elvas). The horses, gaunt from the long mountain travel, were put out to pasture on good grass. This town of the Upper Creek Nation was a pleasant place to be, but it was obvious again that it lacked the treasure for which De Soto had come. Garcilaso told how the chief instructed the governor how to take pearl mussels from the river. Two scouts sent north to a rumored gold country came back bringing only a long haired, well-dressed cow hide (probably a traded buffalo robe).

The good relations ended abruptly. On June 19 the Indians began to run away "for a certain thing the governor asked of them, which was that they should provide women" (Rangel). De Soto put pressure on the chief, requesting him to provide thirty women as slaves (Elvas). The cacique in the end agreed to furnish five hundred porters who would wear collars and chains.[9] Elvas wrote that while the governor pursued Indians who had fled the town and destroyed their large maize fields, he offered not to require their women if he would be provided with porters, as had been done before on demand by all Indians.

THE MARCH SOUTH THROUGH ALABAMA
(JULY TO NOVEMBER 1540)

At the end of June De Soto started south from Chiaha, taking its chief as hostage. He had heard of another great chief named Cosa with whom he expected to find the treasure he was seeking. The party followed the Tennessee River southwest to its great bend (Guntersville) and there turned south overland to the Coosa River (near Childersburg, southeast of Birmingham, according to the U.S. Commission). About the town of Cosa there was "great quantity of maize and beans, both in cribs and in the fields. It was a land of large and numerous settlements and the fields were continuous" (Elvas). The Coosa valley was an important Creek Indian district.

Their reception was a ceremony resembling that on the Savannah River. The chief came to greet the governor, being carried on a litter covered with white cloth and borne by men of rank. Festival turned to duress. The high chief was made prisoner as were his Indians, both men and women. "As was the custom of the soldiers these began to enter the corn cribs" (Rangel), and "not content therewith they broke discipline and entered the houses and took what they could find" (Elvas). "The governor was accustomed to place the chiefs

---

9. The verb *echar* was translated by Swanton as "to leave off." It has the meaning of throwing away, but also of putting on. De Soto traveled with chain gangs that were released when a new lot of captives was available.

under guard and to take them with him until he left their land, expecting the people of the villages to give him guides and porters. On leaving their lands he permitted them and the porters to return to their homes as soon as he came to another seignory. . . . Many Indian men and women were taken and put in chains" (Elvas).

The departure from the town of Cosa was on August 20, taking its high chief along as prisoner. As they went south along the Coosa River they took supplies and natives in village after village without resistance. They continued thus beyond the junction of the Coosa with the Alabama River, past the site of Montgomery to the end of the domain of chief Cosa and of the Upper Creek nation. This was at the village of Talisi on the Alabama River, east of Selma (September 17). Its chief and inhabitants had fled but were induced to return and furnish porters, women, and supplies, the high chief still being held captive. "From that place they sent and released the cacique of Cosa so that he might return to his home, and he left greatly vexed and in tears because the governor would not give up his sister whom they were taking along" (Rangel). The Creek territory was left October 5. No treasure had been found in it.

The land ahead, down the Alabama River, was the province of another great chief, called Tascaloosa, which means "black warrior" in Choctaw. They were entering the land of the Mabila (Mobile) branch of the Choctaws and met the great chief in a village on the Alabama River October 10. The reception was elaborate, the chief seated in a balcony on a mound at the side of a plaza. Rangel described him as tall and of noble bearing, and wearing a feather mantle reaching to his feet. Before him an attendant held a sunshade on which a white cross in a black field resembled the insignia of the Knights of St. John of Rhodes. He remained seated as if he were a king when the governor came up to greet him. At night the chief was detained, in effect placed under arrest. Tascaloosa assigned them four hundred porters and promised a hundred women when they arrived at the town of Mabila. The slow march to Mabila took until the morning of the 18th, the soldiers foraging in the villages on the way.

De Soto, well guarded, entered the town of Mabila where they were received by a dance in the plaza. The dance changed into a battle that lasted all day. The town was burned with much of the Spanish baggage, including the chest and pearls from the Savannah River. Rangel counted 22 Spaniards killed, 148 wounded, 7 horses killed and 28 wounded; at the time of leaving Mabila 102 members of the party that had started from Tampa had died. He estimated that more than three thousand Indians were killed at Mabila, including the son of the chief, the fate of the latter unknown. The Spaniards remained at Mabila until November 14 recovering from their wounds, repairing their equipment, and devastating the country round about.

Mabila lay west of the Alabama River in the narrow strip of land between it and the Tombigbee River, a short distance above the junction of the two rivers that form Mobile River. The U.S. Commission favored a location at or above Choctaw Bluff, formerly Fort Stonewall.

WINTER IN THE
CHICKASAW COUNTRY (1540–1541)

The march south, almost the length of the state of Alabama, may be explained by the stubborn ignorance of De Soto, who held to the idea that where there was a lot of land there were sure to be accumulated riches. He knew nothing of minerals but thought of treasure in the possession of caciques, as he had in Panama. Mobile Bay was within two days' march of Mabila but there was no great chief there, and if he went to the gulf his men might want to go home. He would continue his search of treasure in the interior, return his men to the hard life of marches and bivouacs, plundering as they had been doing, and holding forth the hope that they would come upon a place of large treasure. He may have known the tales of another Mexico to the north that Viceroy Mendoza was then exploring; he had in fact warned the viceroy not to interfere with his own discoveries, and would probe anew the unknown interior, open without limit to him by royal license.

De Soto pushed north from ruined Mabila, more or less along the route of U.S. 43, crossed the Black Warrior River in the vicinity of Demopolis, and passed the last of the Choctaw villages December 9. The land of the Chickasaws lay to the west; their villages were along the upper Tombigbee River, called Chicasa River in the accounts. The river was reached in mid-December (Columbus, Mississippi?) and crossed higher up, the Commission favoring Aberdeen, Mississippi, or above. The first river town they found deserted. They spent Christmas there in a snowstorm; Rangel said just as though they were in Burgos in Old Castile. The winter of 1540–1541 was passed in two Chickasaw towns, tentatively placed about Pontotoc, west of the Tombigbee River. This eastern Chickasaw land was largely savanna in the uplands, hardwoods along the valleys. Elvas considered it as fertile, very populous and having much maize, largely still standing in the fields, and sufficient to supply the party through the winter. He told of a cacique carried on the shoulders of his men, who brought deerskins and little dogs. A few days later a hundred and fifty rabbits were presented.

On March 4, 1541, Indians made an attack at dawn on the town in which the Spaniards were quartered, setting it afire, killing a dozen Christians, more than fifty horses, three hundred pigs, and destroying the greater part of the equipment. The Spanish loss was greater than in the battle of Mabila, the Indians suffering little hurt. Quarters were moved to a nearby village to repair the damage. A forge was set up, bellows made of bearskins, arms retempered, new saddle-trees made, and lances fashioned from good ash wood (Rangel). The Indians waited ten days for a second attack, by which time the Spaniards were ready for successful defense. The departure was delayed until well into spring, starting April 26.

WEST ACROSS THE MISSISSIPPI RIVER
(SUMMER AND FALL OF 1541)

There had been serious losses and no profit in the Chickasaw country of northeast Mississippi. De Soto determined, for reasons unknown, to try the west. The route was almost due west, with some fighting at first; then they crossed the sparsely populated inner coast plain and swamps of the Lower Mississippi Valley to the first sight of the great river on May 8 in the Quizquiz area, a number of villages with large store of maize. These were down river from the higher land at Memphis, on natural river levees. On May 21 the building of four barges began, watched from the other side of the river by two hundred canoes and seven thousand Indians having stoutly woven shields and shooting arrows (Rangel). The demonstration was harmless—the Indians went away before the barges were launched. The river was crossed without incident June 18 during normal June flood as indicated by the driftwood and muddy water noted.

The U.S. Commission had its greatest difficulty placing the events of the next two months. These were spent moving about leisurely between villages in the lowland of northern Arkansas, the great alluvial plain formed and changed by flood of the Mississippi and St. Francis Rivers, consisting of bayous, swamps, and the arcuate ridges of natural levees, which marked former river courses. The levees had well-drained and rich soil, well suited to Indian cultivation and settlement, the bayous had excellent fishing; the Indian population was large, gathered in towns of unusual size, and of advanced skills. The Spanish reporters did not remember clearly how they moved about in this complex pattern of dry land, wet land, and water. In the four hundred years since, the rivers have kept on changing their meandered courses, bayous have filled and new ones formed, and the New Madrid earthquake altered the configuration of some of the land.

Having crossed to the Arkansas side, they took ten days to pass through two major towns, Aquixo and Casqui, to a third, Pacaha. The general direction was north and the pace was unhurried. They were in the alluvial lands between the Mississippi and St. Francis Rivers, entering south of Memphis and going north fifty, perhaps eighty, miles; there is no way to estimate. Crowley's Ridge, loess-covered, high above the lowlands, is west of the St. Francis and runs parallel to that river. It attracted the earliest American settlers, has numerous sites of Indian occupation, and would seem to have been the obvious route of Spanish entry.

Rangel remembered the three towns as the best pueblos they had found in Florida and the best palisaded. Aquixo was the chief town of a tribe, "beautifully situated." Casqui had very good *buhios* (an Arawak name, properly for large, round ceremonial buildings) "and above the entry many skulls of bulls, very fierce" (trophy heads of buffalo, brought from farther west). Pacaha, farthest north, "was very well enclosed, with towers on the walls, and a moat about it." As to its chief, *ranchearonle bravamente,* which translates as giving him a rough going over. The party stayed at Pacaha for a month well into July, in ample supply of food. A detachment was sent north (to the Ozarks?) on a rumor of gold. Biedma, who was with this scouting party, told that they came to Indians living in huts that were taken down and moved whenever they went to a new place to hunt and fish (tepees of plains Indians).

Leaving northeast Arkansas they came on August 5 to a fourth main town, Quiguate on the lower Rio Casqui (St. Francis River), considered the largest of all, with extensive cornfields on fertile river levees (Elvas). Three weeks were spent here.

The tribes encountered in the two and a half months have not been identified. Swanton thought they might have been a northwestern part of the Muskogeans, perhaps related to the Natchez.

Was De Soto still confident that he would find treasure? Why had he gone to the labor of crossing the Mississippi, spent more than two months in towns west of the river, and turned south again? The main body stayed in towns where food was provided from field and stream, while scouting parties probed briefly north and west. It is not clear that there was an objective left other than to move on.

The expedition left Quiguate August 26, headed west for the Coligua River (Arkansas River), reached at Pine Bluff according to the Commission, and followed the river to Little Rock, apparently the location of the town of Coligua. They left the river here on September 6 to turn southwest into the Ouachita Mountains, perhaps by way of Benton and Hot Springs (Tanico: where there was hot water). Having crossed to the drainage of the Ouachita River, they spent October in the Ouachita hills and by the first of November were out in the plains about Camden. Before getting to the hot springs they had a sharp fight with Indians at Tula, the best fighters the Christians had met, who used lances with fire-hardened tips (Rangel). Their nationality is unknown, Swanton assigning those of the Ouachita basin, next entered, to the Caddo group. There were numerous villages on the route south from Little Rock, the Indians making salt at some, and the Spaniards stopping to do likewise.

THE THIRD WINTER QUARTERS (1541–1542)

Winter quarters were taken early in November, occupying the village of Utiangue (at or below Camden) and building a stout stockade about it. They stayed there for four months:

with great supply of maize and beans, nuts, dried plums, and rabbits. The Spaniards until then had lacked the means to kill rabbits. At Utiangue the Indians showed how to do so, which was by
strong snares that yanked them from the ground by a noose of
stout cord around the neck and a piece of cane that prevented
gnawing through the cord. Many were thus taken in the cornfields,
especially when it was freezing or snowing. Because of the snow the
Christians did not get out of their quarters for a month. (Elvas)

The winter was exceptionally severe but was spent in comfort. They did not lack food or firewood, and they had local
Indians who helped and also captives they had brought. Each
Spaniard was allotted space in the village according to the
number of Indians he had.

RETREAT

The winter camp was left on March 6, 1542, to start south
along the Ouachita River. De Soto, it may be inferred, was
giving up his search for treasure. He had found none to the
north, knew that to the west were buffalo country and hunting tribes and that Cabeza de Vaca had met only primitive
Indians when he was in the southwest. He had learned the
hard way that there was no treasure to be found where there
was no working or prizing of precious metals. All that he
gained, and lost, was a chest of freshwater pearls. Elvas said
that the governor was looking for a route to the great river
so as to get to the sea and procure men and horses to replace
his losses. Perhaps this is what his men were told. It would
have meant going to New Spain, which was governed by Mendoza whom he considered his rival for the possession of the
north and who could not be expected to equip him.

Juan Ortiz, who had been their chief interpreter since
Tampa Bay, died after the spring start. He had known the
language and ways of the Timucuas, a southern Muskogean
people. Most of the time the expedition had been in Muskogean lands. After his death they lacked an informed interme-
diary. Elvas judged that what Ortiz explained in four words
took a day to understand from another interpreter and then
was likely to be wrong.

After ten days they got to the province of Ayays and its
town (Columbia, Louisiana, south of Monroe, according to the
Commission), where they were held up for four days by an

unusually late snowstorm. At the end of March they came to the province of Anilco (at Jonesville, Louisiana), where they had difficulty with high water of the Ouachita River. They were about twenty-five miles west of the Mississippi River (at Natchez), in a land of many natural levees along rivers and bayous, richly productive of maize and beans and well populated. Elvas ranked it with Coosa and Apalachen. Parties were sent out to reconnoiter the country east to the Mississippi and attacked one village, in which a hundred Indians were killed and eighty women and children taken prisoner.

De Soto, increasingly ill of a fever, died in the latter part of May, naming Luis de Moscoso, another veteran of Peru, as his successor. His body, weighted with sand, was taken at night to be dropped in the Mississippi River near Natchez.

It was agreed to get out overland to the Spanish settlements in Pánuco and so a start west was made at the beginning of June. Their route has been traced, somewhat uncertainly, to crossing the Red River about or above Shreveport. In eastern Texas they found maize grown in a district called Guasco, sufficient to load their Indian slaves and horses. Here they saw turquoises and cotton mantas from the Pueblo country, though this was not recognized by the visitors. From this land of sedentary farming Caddoan Indians they pushed southwest, perhaps as far as the Brazos River, where they found some natives in poor, small huts. After four months they decided to turn back, making the return to Anilco in two months.

The Anilco settlements had not recovered from the previous visitation, but an unspoiled Aminoya district to the northeast, located on or near the Mississippi above Natchez, was found to have good supplies. It was chosen for the fourth and last winter camp. They began building barges for their departure in the spring of 1543 and appropriated six thousand fanegas of maize from the town (a fanega being about two bushels).

An early rise of the river delayed the departure of the barges until July 2, 1543, with three hundred Spaniards, a score of horses, and a hundred Indian slaves, about five hundred being left behind. As they drifted past Indian villages, canoes came out to attack. The horses were killed en route to reduce the load. They entered the gulf on July 18. Having prepared sails and being guided by a competent pilot, they reached Pánuco September 10, empty-handed and dressed in patches of skin and cloth, four years and four months after they had left Havana.

THE VERDICTS OF GÓMARA AND OVIEDO

López de Gómara, writing his history of the Indies at mid-century, summed up the objectives and acts of De Soto:

He went about for five years hunting mines, thinking it would be like Peru. He made no settlement and thus he died and destroyed those who went with him. Never will conquerors do well unless they settle before they undertake anything else, especially here where the Indians are valiant bowmen and strong.

Oviedo had accompanied Pedrarias to Darién as a senior official, De Soto having gone at the same time as a young soldier of fortune. As Oviedo took down what Rangel told of the De Soto expedition, he was reminded of the brutality and greed with which Panama had been overun and the manner of taking Peru.

This governor [De Soto] was given to the chase (*montería*) and killing of Indians from the time he began soldiering for Governor Pedrarias in the provinces of Castilla del Oro and Nicaragua. Also he was in Peru and present at the imprisonment of the great lord Atahualpa, by which he became rich. He was one of those who came back to Spain owning great wealth, for he brought back to Sevilla and placed in security there more than a hundred thousand gold pesos, which, by contracting to return to the Indies, he thereafter lost, along with his life, continuing the bloodstained practices he had followed earlier.
 This misdirected greed and wrong indoctrination Hernando de Soto taught to those deceived soldiers whom he brought to a land in which he had never been or set foot upon.

Oviedo asked a hidalgo (Rangel?) who had taken part in this expedition

why they demanded those *tamemes* or Indian porters and why they took so many women, and those not the old or ugly ones, and why, having been given what they asked, they detained the chiefs and principals. Never staying or resting anywhere they went, they made neither settlement nor conquest but caused alteration and desolation of the land and loss of liberty of the people, without making Christians or friends of any of the Indians. His answer was, that the tamemes were additional slaves and servants to carry things, the women were taken to serve and satisfy their carnal pleasures, the chiefs were detained to keep their subjects quiet. Neither the governor nor any one else knew where they were headed other than to find a land so rich as to satisfy their desires and to discover the great secrets which the governor said he knew.

Oviedo ended with the epilogue:

Reader, do not cry any less for the conquered Indians than for the Christian conquerors, killers of themselves as they were of others, and heed the results of such government, ill governed, taught in the school of Pedrarias how to waste Castilla del Oro and ruin its Indians, graduated by the death of the natives of Nicaragua, and canonized in Peru by entry into the order of the Pizarros.

No contemporary historian defended De Soto nor did the three participants who gave the principal account. The Inca Garcilaso de la Vega later made the expedition into an epic of Spanish courage.

Oviedo was right in attributing the conduct and objective of De Soto to his experience in Panama and Peru. De Soto landed at Tampa equipped with collars and chains to be used on gangs of captives. His tactics were to attack settlements, or if he was received hospitably, to provoke hostility. He had learned in Panama that seizure of a cacique would ensure compliance of the subjects, and followed the same practice in the north. It worked to a degree, but the Muskogean and Caddoan tribes were a tougher breed, and they were excellent bowmen. To the indignities against a proud people by seizure of their chiefs, chain gangs, and rape of women were added the robbing of stores, occupation or destruction of towns, and devastation of fields. The invading host met its first serious check in the battle at Mabila, where a large number of warriors came from various places to rescue their high chief. They failed, but the resistance by Choctaw forces blunted the Spanish aggressiveness. The attrition of Spanish strength continued with serious results the winter following when Chickasaws made a concerted and damaging attack on the Spanish winter quarters.

De Soto paid no attention to the instructions given him to

establish a colony, as Gómara pointed out. It is apparent that he was only looking for loot as he had in Panama, Nicaragua, and Peru. In those countries the persons of rulers, their houses, and temples yielded large and quick booty; the robbing of graves a steadier and continuing profit. In the stubborn and stupid belief that Indians elsewhere had accumulated such treasures De Soto wandered up and down the coast plain seeking out the towns where important chiefs lived. He knew nothing of mining, crossing the Blue Ridge where gold quartz might have been found in a hurry to get to a great town of which he had heard. He was not misled by legends of treasure as Coronado had been. His restless and senseless search was driven by his obsessive memories.

NOTES ON THE INDIAN ECONOMY

The natives had great skill in hunting and fishing which the Christians lacked, as Elvas acknowledged. In the Carolina Piedmont they were given seven hundred turkeys at one place. In northeast Arkansas they were provided with abundant catches of fish, probably largely taken in bayous and including channel catfish. The only description of the manner of procurement was at the winter quarters in the Ouachita valley where the natives taught the Spaniards how to snare rabbits.

Farming was a major part of Indian living everywhere except in the farther parts of Texas. Moscoso went several hundred miles into Texas on the way to Pánuco before he turned back. The De Soto expedition depended always on the supplies it took from the Indians, dry corn being the mainstay. Moscoso was not stopped by Indians or obstacles of terrain. He got beyond the agricultural settlements in Texas and thereby ran out of provisions.

Indian corn made the four-year campaign possible. Its yields were high; in much of the south two or three crops a year were produced. Some was eaten before maturity as roasting ears; the ripe corn was harvested at leisure, the ears stored in log cribs such as those used later by the white settlers. The grain was prepared as needed by pounding in hollowed logs—in coarser form as grits, still a staple food in the south, or reduced to finer size as corn meal, readily baked as cakes. Indian women were taken to do the cooking, who prepared also beans of several kinds and squash, commonly grown interplanted with maize.

The productivity of Indian agriculture is demonstrated by the Spanish winter quarters. During each of the four winters a host of Christians, captive Indians, horses, and swine remained for four months or longer. In each town the supplies were ample throughout the time of occupation. When they left in spring they took stores of maize with them. The first winter quarters were at Apalachen (Tallahassee) because it was known that ahead was a wide stretch of poor sandy plains. The other three sites were chosen when the approach of winter indicated that it was time to stop. They stopped early and stayed long.

The Indians fields mainly were on alluvial land, along the Savannah, Coosa, Alabama, and Tombigbee rivers and their tributaries, on natural levees of the lower Mississippi Valley (including loess on Crowley's Ridge), and in the Ouachita valley. These fertile, easily tilled, and adequately drained tracts were of high and lasting productivity. This was permanent cultivation and settlement. Centuries before De Soto's time agricultural people planted there and built earth mounds, some of which were noted in the De Soto accounts as features of Indian villages visited. Towns were located at places of permanent attraction because of fertile land and on routes of travel by water and land, at sites occupied in archaeologic time by mound builders. Fields that fed De Soto's men may have been under cultivation since the time when farming began in that area.

The nut trees (*nogales*) noticed east of the Mississippi River were mainly black walnut (*Juglans nigra*), recognized as akin to the Persian walnut of European cultivation. Its preferred habitat in well-drained alluvial lands was also the land most used in Indian farming. Indian agriculture, unlike European practice, did not require that the fields be cleared of trees. Trees that yielded useful fruit were left standing, as may still be seen in parts of Mexico and Central America. The management of Indian fields was by assemblage of divers planted annuals, with preservation of the most desirable trees. Walnut trees, growing well dispersed and deep rooted, did not deprive the annuals of light or nourishment. Elvas noted in the Savannah and Tennessee valleys that nut trees were common in the Indian fields. Biedma observed that nut oil was stored in quantity in the Creek town of Chiaha on the Tennessee River. The Indians of the Eastern Woodlands supplemented their diet by crushing nuts, boiling them, and skimming off the oil, which was stored. This practice here first recorded for the United States was later known as common to the farming tribes of the Eastern Woodlands.

When the De Soto party reached the Mississippi River at Quizquiz it became acquainted with pecan nuts. Biedma said that this was where they "found the first small native nuts, which are much better than those of Castile" (the Persian walnut). West of the Mississippi this was the nut most used. Elvas observed in northeast Arkansas: "In the fields there were many trees of the kind of nuts that aré ground (*molares*). They are shaped like acorns, and in the houses many such were found in storage by the Indians. In other ways the nut trees did not differ from those of Spain or from those we had seen before, except in having smaller leaves." The smooth, oblong fruit resembling an acorn and the narrow leaflets characterize the pecan. These trees also were noted as standing in fields.

Fleshy fruits were appreciated fresh in season, dried for use at other times. The American mulberry (*Morus rubra*) was important for fruit and bast. Elvas gave the first account of its use for bark cloth (spring of 1540):

[The women] wore mantles (mantas), made from the bark of mulberry trees, not the outer bark, but that beneath, and they know how to work and spin and prepare and weave it so as to make very fine mantas which they wear in the fashion of gypsies that at times wander about Spain, some of the mantas are very fine. The mulberry trees are like those of Spain, as large and larger, the leaves softer and better for silkworms, and the fruit better to eat.

He was right as to the use of the inner bark but wrong about its being spun and woven. Bark cloth was made in the southeastern United States by beating the bast into a felted tissue of the desired fineness. The "Queen" of Cofitachequi on the Savannah River was carried in a litter draped in white "with cotton cloth" (Rangel); probably bark cloth was mistaken for cotton, which was not known in the southeast. Mulberries were the earliest tree fruit. Twenty Indians greeted them in the Tennessee Valley the first of June bringing baskets of mulberries, "many and good" (Elvas).

In Alabama the Coosa and Tallapoosa valleys had grapes as good as those of Spain, Elvas thought, Rangel agreeing. Along the river bank the grapevines climbed into the trees;

however, away from the river they were low vines, with large sweet grapes having large seeds (Elvas). The latter are indicated as muscadines (*Vitis rotundifolia*), large seeded and impressive in size of fruit, the superior wild grape of the South. Both it and the small summer grape (*V. aestivalis*) are vigorous woody climbers. The low growing habit is unexplained unless they were cut back.

De Soto's men found the plums (*ciruelas*) as good as those of Spain and thought that some were in fact the cultivated prune of Europe. At their winter quarters in Apalachen they were well supplied with maize, beans, squash, and "dried plums of the country, which are better than those of Spain and grow in the fields without being planted" (Elvas). Referring to the abundance and quality of mulberries, nuts, and plums in the Savannah and Tennessee valleys, Elvas observed that "the trees grow in the *campo* without being planted or cultivated and are as large and vigorous as though they were in orchards that are tilled and irrigated." For the Coosa valley Rangel reported "many plums of the early sort of Sevilla, very good, like those of Spain both as to fruit and trees." Elvas agreeing, "many plums, as well those of Spain as those native to the country." Arrived at Quizquiz on the Mississippi in spring they were given "loaves of a mass of plums made into bricks." At Casqui (on Crowley's Ridge?) in late June there were "many plum trees, with red plums like those of Spain and others of dark color, different and much better, and all the trees as luxuriant as though they were in gardens and open groves" (Elvas). During their third winter, quartered in the Ouachita valley, they were again well supplied with dried plums.

From Florida to Tennessee and Arkansas plums were freely provided, fresh fruit in summer, dried in winter. The fruit grew on sizable trees, as in Spain. Their location is given as "on the campo," an ambivalent term that perhaps might be rendered as open ground outside of the settlements or as fields. Fruit trees of superior quality and growth were found in stands in proximity to settlements.

DOGS AND HOGS

Dogs were presented as food to the De Soto party from Florida to Louisiana. The first notice was at Ocala by Biedma, where "they found some maize, beans, and small dogs, no small refreshment for people who were about to die of hunger." This was a report to officials in Spain and perhaps an apology. They landed with a lot of supplies a month before, had foraged along the way, and were not starving, having with them the large herd of swine. In the spring of 1540, when they were on the Ocmulgee River, midway between Apalachen and the Savannah River, a chief gave them "many small dogs, which the Christians esteemed as though they had been fat lambs" (Elvas). In the Piedmont of South Carolina they were brought a gift of "little dogs which do not bark and which are reared in the houses in order to be eaten" (Rangel). At Guasili in North Carolina, probably a Cherokee town, Biedma, Rangel, and Elvas reported a present of small dogs. According to Elvas, "there the Indians gave tribute of three hundred dogs, seeing that the Christians esteemed them and wanted them to eat, whereas among themselves they are not eaten." At Chicasa, the principal Chickasaw town in Mississippi, they were provided dogs (Biedma). The last record of a present of edible dogs was in the rich maize country across from Natchez.

The breed was small, fat, barkless, and was raised in the houses. These were not hunting or watchdogs. Elvas and Rangel disagreed as to whether they were eaten by the natives. The Indians along the route were informed that they were held a delicacy by the Spaniards and brought them in number as gifts. Dogs of similar description had been eaten by the Spaniards in Española during the famine of 1494. In the conquest of Mexico a long-bodied, short-legged dog, barkless, and reared indoors was consumed by Spaniards almost to its extermination.[10]

Extremadura and adjacent Portugal, whence the majority of De Soto's men came, are noted for long-legged and long-snouted hogs that feed on mast and are moved about under the direction of swineherds. Such range hogs were taken early to the Spanish West Indies islands, where they multiplied exceedingly. Cuba became rapidly and greatly stocked with hogs that fended for themselves but still accepted herding control. De Soto loaded his ships in Havana with hogs to serve as an ambulant supply of meat. They were driven through the long

10. It is probably represented in archaeologic pottery figurines of western Mexico.

march from Tampa to the embarkation on the Mississippi. Many were lost, as in the crossing of streams and by Indian thefts and attacks, three out of four hundred having been reported lost in the Chickasaw attack of March, 1541. After De Soto's death in Louisiana his estate was credited with seven hundred hogs. This was about fifteen months after the Chickasaw attack.[11] The recovery of numbers may be over-estimated, but these hogs had been greatly fecund in the islands and they were in equally or more advantageous situation on the mainland as to mast and foraging on Indian fields.

Indians watched these strange and attractive animals, good to eat, able to travel with the Spaniards and their horses, thriving as they foraged, and responding to control by man. The Indians were accustomed to raising small dogs in their houses; here was a new and greater opportunity to keep a useful domestic animal. That they did so was told by Elvas: While the boats were being built on the Mississippi in the spring of 1543 for the final departure, Indians from a nearby town (Guachoya, Ferriday in Louisiana?) "came many times to bring mantles and fish and pigs reared from some sows lost there the year before."

In its concluding remarks the Commission came to the "presumption that swine were permanently introduced into the Southeast" by the De Soto expedition. The Southeast was a prime ecologic niche for the Spanish range hog by abundance and diversity of food, lack of competition, and adoption into Indian culture. The agile, long-snouted razorback hog of the South is therefore attributed to Spanish ancestry, not to the heavy, short-legged breeds later brought by Dutch and English colonists.

11. U.S. De Soto Comm., p. 260.

Part III

Strategic Importance of
Florida

10

Florida,
Part of New Spain
(1557–1561)

Dominican friars began to assert full human rights of Indians
in 1511. This was in Española, too late to save the island
natives there. Bartolomé de Las Casas found his life's mission
as protector and apostle of the Indians in New Spain, where
he was given the right in 1535 to try peaceful conversion of
Indians in a district that had resisted conquest by Spanish
arms. In two years' time he succeeded in making a Christian
Indian land of the interior of Guatemala, to become known
as the province of Vera Paz. While Dominicans continued
their ministry there, Las Casas returned to Spain to plead the
Indian cause, which resulted in the passage of the New Laws,
the charter of Indian freedom (1542). While thus engaged he
wrote his famous tract on the destruction of the Indies, using
Florida as one example of evil military conquest. He was
ordained Bishop of Chiapas in 1544, a new see, mainly Indian.

Florida he hoped would become another Christian land,
yielding to the gentle ministration of Dominican missionaries.
Fray Luis de Cáncer wrote Las Casas from Guatemala (1545)
offering to go to repair the destruction done by "the four
tyrants who went to Florida and did no good service, but only

evil." [1] The mission in charge of Cáncer left Veracruz in 1549, cautioned by Las Casas to avoid any port entered by a prior Spanish expedition.

Instead, the ship sailed into Tampa Bay, where De Soto and Narváez had landed.[2] Gómara told the result tersely, how Fray Luis went "to subdue that land and convert its people by word alone." Cáncer, four friars, and some sailors went ashore unarmed. Many Floridians came to watch the landing and, without listening to what Fray Luis had to say, killed him and two friars who were with him, Gómara having heard that they were eaten. "There then came to the ship a page who had been with De Soto and told how the friars' scalps with their tonsures (*coronas*) had been placed in the temples." [3] The Timucuas living about Tampa Bay had reason to remember that men who came in ships brought danger. They had cared for a Spanish lad who was lost from the De Soto party, but they wanted no more landings. Dominican friars came again to Florida years later with Menéndez, but with military protection, and not as bearers of the true peace that Las Casas had proposed.

STRATEGIC IMPERATIVE

From whatever point of origin—New Spain, Peru, New Granada—shipping to Spain entered the Straits of Florida from the west, to ride the streaming of the sea out of the Gulf of Mexico, through the Bahama Channel, and on north into the Atlantic. At Cape Canaveral the Gulf Stream has a summer rate of flow of seventy miles a day, fifty miles to the east of the Sea Islands of Georgia and South Carolina. Current-borne, the ships sailed steadily and comfortably into higher latitudes where they might expect to meet westerly winds to carry them to the Azores and Spain. This was the *carrera de las Indias* eastbound. Havana was the last port of call in the New World, the next chance of succor or supply being the Azores.

By 1550 silver mines, richer than had been known anywhere in the world, were in large production. At Vera Cruz the silver from Zacatecas, Guanajuato, and other mines of the north was

1. CDI, vol. 7, pp. 186 ff.
2. Alfonso Trueba, *Expediciónes a la Florida* (Mexico, 1955).
3. Gómara, chap. 45.

loaded on ships. The silver of Peru was taken across the Isthmus of Panama and shipped by way of Yucatán Channel and the Straits of Florida. Large cargo ships were employed, less responsive to helm and sail than the caravels, brigantines, and other small ships of earlier days.

Shipwreck and piracy were the increasing dangers, in particular in the passage around the Peninsula of Florida. At the south a hundred and fifty mile stretch of reefs and banks of the Florida Keys had to be avoided. The Florida east coast has four hundred miles of strand, sandbars, and shoal water. Ships kept their distance from shore but on occasion were caught in a storm and driven ashore, especially by hurricanes in summer and fall.

In 1550 a treasure fleet out of Nombre de Dios and Cartagena was wrecked on the east coast of Florida with the loss of many passengers.[4] González de Barcia's *Chronology of Florida* had numerous entries.[5] In 1551 "the seas were full of French pirates because of the war declared against France; neither the coasts of Spain nor those of the Indies were safe." In 1552 a treasure fleet was gotten ready at Vera Cruz and sailed in 1553, richly laden and carrying more than a thousand people, many being persons of importance. It was caught in a great storm in the Bahama Channel and wrecked on the coast of Florida. Three hundred survivors made it ashore but only a handful got to Pánuco, after great suffering. In 1554 Viceroy Velasco sent a ship from New Spain to see whether part of the treasure could be recovered. Storms and French corsairs continued to take toll of the new wealth of the Spanish Indies.

A port of refuge, rescue, and salvage was needed on the mainland, and it should also be armed for protection against the French. Philip II succeeded his father to the crown of Spain in 1556 and soon conferred with the Council of the Indies as to protective measures. The discussions concerned location of the port, a colony to feed it, and who should administer and pay for the job. New Spain would benefit most and its treasury could well bear the expense. Luis de Velasco the elder had succeeded Mendoza as viceroy of New Spain. De Soto's title to Florida had lapsed with his death. The deci-

---

4. *Infra,* the Escalante account.
5. The *Chronology* is appended to Barcia's edition of Garcilaso de la Vega's *La Florida* (Madrid, 1723), a careful compilation, in part from lost sources.

sion was that the vacant province of Florida be attached to New Spain. At the end of 1557 Velasco was given instructions to proceed with a settlement at Punta de Santa Elena.[6]

Saint Helena Island and Sound, in the Sea Islands of South Carolina (fig. 15 below), carry the name and are at the location to which Velasco was directed. King and Council had studied the sailing charts and fixed on an area where the coast turns to the northeast, well to north of the Florida beaches, and where there are broad and safe sounds.[7]

Velasco was to equip, direct, and pay for the new settlement. Expressing his opinion of the plan, he proposed an amendment: Santa Elena, he wrote, was distant 170 leagues from Havana and 460 from Vera Cruz by a circuitous route. It would be better to begin with a settlement in the northeast of the Gulf of Mexico, on a bay such as Narváez had used when he built the barges for his escape. From here a land route could be laid out across the peninsula to Santa Elena, passing through populous country and only about eighty leagues long. Heavy equipment, such as artillery, could be taken by sea to Santa Elena.[8] The amended plan was informed as to geography. A Gulf port, connected to Santa Elena by a road across the base of the Florida penninsula, would shorten the distance, avoid the hazards of the exposed Atlantic coast, and occupy a land of Indian farmers suited for colonization. Also, being on the Gulf of Mexico, it was beyond the range of corsairs. Velasco went ahead with his amended plan.

This was no repetition of the prior Florida ventures of conquest and treasure hunting. The new colony was to guard Spanish shipping from acts of God and Frenchmen, would use known harbors, engage in growing food, and live in peace with the natives. The Viceroyalty of New Spain took charge of the mainland called Florida and would set up a new manner of administration.

6. The instructions are included in CDU, vol. 18, p. 83 ff.

7. The locality was an early coastal landmark. Oviedo, copying from the padrón that Chaves had revised to 1536, placed Cabo Santa Elena at 33° and Rio Santa Elena adjacent to it at the north. The Ayllón colony had located nearby on the Savannah River in 1526, and knew the place, perhaps by that name. It is one of the oldest place names in the United States. That the name has survived tells of the continued interest in that location.

8. CDU, vol. 18, p. 86.

THE LUNA COLONY

Tristan de Luna y Arellano was named Governor of Florida and sworn in at a ceremony in the Cathedral of Mexico in November 1558. Luna had commanded the main body in the Coronado expedition and had done good service there.[9]

The fleet of eleven ships left Vera Cruz June 11, 1559 with fifteen hundred persons. A number were veterans of De Soto's expedition who had stayed in New Spain, among them Biedma and Rangel. Tlaxcalan Indians from the plateau of Mexico, with wives and families, were recruited as the agricultural base of the colony. These were free men, Christians, and had been friends of the Spaniards from the days of Cortés.[10]

The voyage took about two months by a roundabout course in which they went to Tampa Bay. They were looking for the bay of Achuse which De Soto's barks had visited and which was thought to be a proper location for Velasco's intermediate settlement. To find it they repeated the course of De Soto's barks, the whole fleet going to Tampa and then several hundred miles northwest to land in Mobile Bay. This bay not seeming to fit the account they had of Achuse, a frigate was sent on reconnaissance and returned with word that the right bay was the next one east. The fleet doubled back to Pensacola Bay, arriving there August 15, 1559. The date being the day of Assumption of the Virgin, the bay was named the port of Santa Maria de Achuse or Santa Maria Filipina (in honor of the king).

At Pensacola Bay they had come to a good harbor, large, well protected from the gulf, with a river of fresh water, and dry ground for camping. A Franciscan, Fray Augustín Dávila, wrote of the coolness of the beach in early morning and after sunset, the beach enjoyed to the gentle plash of wavelets.[11]

The unloading of supplies sufficient for a year was begun and two ships were made ready to take the news of the good port to Vera Cruz. Scouting parties were sent inland. Within a week of the landing a hurricane brought disaster. In a letter

9. In the Coronado annals he was usually called Arellano.
10. Tlaxcalan colonies were important in advancing the Spanish frontier north through Mexico.
11. *Fundación de la Provincia de Santiago* (1596), chaps. 65–69, has details of locality and events on Achuse. U.S. De Soto Comm., pp. 163–164.

to the king, Luna told how the great storm came from the north, the wind changing through all directions of the compass and increasing in violence for twenty-four hours. Only one caravel and two other ships remained afloat, the loss including one of the best ships of the Indies. Most of the food and other supplies were lost or water soaked. One party would stay with what had been saved. He would take the rest inland to find sustenance. Help would come from the viceroy. Meanwhile they would manage and begin to carry the Gospel to the natives.[12]

Late in September 1559 the main body started north for the land of Mabila that De Soto had wasted. They came to a town of eighty houses, the people having fled, abandoning their store of maize and beans. The houses had been built on the ruins of a larger town of larger structures, perhaps the one where De Soto had fought the battle of Mabila. They named it Santa Cruz Nanicpatna and took up their winter quarters. According to Dávila, more than a thousand gathered here to spend the winter. Assured that these strangers were friendly the natives returned, listened to the Christian services, and shared food with them while the stores lasted. By spring the hunger was sharp and was relieved but little by young acorns and chestnuts.

Men who had been with De Soto recalled that by going up the Alabama River they would get to the rich Coosa country. They led the way to northern Alabama, on which march all suffered great hunger and ate everything from green berries to harness leather. At the principal Creek town in Coosa they were well received and provided with stored corn.

By the summer of 1560 colonists were dispersed widely through Alabama, largely dependent on native charity. There is no note of conflict nor of how the Tlaxcalans fared. During the summer the married soldiers asked to be sent back and so did the Tlaxcalans. In August Luna sent a ship to take possession of Santa Elena; it got no farther than Yucatán. Disaffected officers took complaints and charges to Mexico. The operation was coming apart, and meanwhile Luna fell sick. In January 1561 he was replaced by Villafañe, who was given orders to leave a garrison (at Pensacola) and proceed to the occupation of Santa Elena. He got there, promptly turned about, and wound up in Santo Domingo. The last of the venture was abandoned by summer of 1561.

12. CDI, vol. 13, pp. 280 ff.

Velasco tried repeatedly to send help but the back of the project was broken at its start by the hurricane and faint-hearted personnel. There was never a chance to settle down, build houses, and grow food. Velasco, knowing that a colony would need to feed itself, sent families of Tlaxcalan farmers and asked the king to send five hundred farmers from Spain. The fertile Coosa valley he thought rightly could be the granary for the colony. This inland base then would also serve Santa Elena. Livestock were to be driven to it from the cattle ranches of northern New Spain, with stations along the route. If the Tlaxcalans proved to be good settlers he would send more Indians. Velasco thought of a Spanish frontier stretching from Zacatecas to the Sea Islands. If Santa Elena was to be the distant eastern port of New Spain it should be connected by an occupied hinterland, with farms and stock ranches along the way. The large plan was based on geographic reality but lacked sufficient means and time.

11

The
French in Florida
(1562–1565)

HUGUENOTS OVERSEAS

While the religious conflict was preparing in France, Gaspard de Coligny, protector of Huguenots, was made Admiral of France with authority over merchant as well as naval shipping (1552). As life became more difficult for French Protestants they looked to freedom overseas. The Reformation had taken strong root in towns of Normandy and those of the Atlantic coast, the ports most experienced in New World trade and raid. A Huguenot colony at Rio de Janeiro was established in 1555; its Fort Coligny was taken by Portuguese arms in 1560. After the Brazilian settlement was lost, the Admiral turned to Florida.[1]

The Spanish colony planned for Santa Elena and launched at Pensacola Bay had failed. The circumstances, which were well known in France, could be turned to advantage by a French settlement that would take hold of the Florida coast while Spain was undecided as to its next action. Coligny thought it time to make his move and he knew where to make it—on the Santa Elena coast.

VOYAGE TO PORT ROYAL
AND REPORT BY RIBAULT

In February 1562 Coligny sent two ships from the Norman port of Havre de Grace (Le Havre) under command of two

1. Trudel, vol. 1, chap. 4 for an excellent perspective.

Protestant captains, Jean Ribault and Goulaine de Laudonnière, the party of a hundred and fifty being mostly Norman
and Protestant. The orders were to follow the coast north from
the cape of Florida (Canaveral). The course was direct, across
the Atlantic to a landfall at 29½°, above Cape Canaveral, and
thence north along the coast.

On May 1 a large river was entered and therefore named
Rivière de Mai (St. Johns River). Here a column of stone was
erected, bearing the arms of France. Continuing north a
succession of sounds off the Georgia coast was entered, each
given the name of a river of France.[2] Ribault identified this
as the land of Chicora, which is correct, the colony of Ayllón
having located about the mouth of the Savannah River. The
coast is described as where "many other rivers and arms of the
sea divide and make many other great islands by which we
may travel from one island to another between land and land.
And it seemeth that we may go and sail without danger
through all the country and enter into the great seas, which
were a wonderful advantage." A fair description of the Sea
Islands.

On May 17 they came to a great sound, three leagues wide,
deep enough for any ships, facing south, having a snug inlet
for small vessels, and an island proper for a fort to guard the
roadstead. They named it Port Royal, a name still retained
for this largest sound of the Sea Islands. Another monument
of stone was set up on the island and a small fort built, named
Charlesfort, at Parris Island on Port Royal Sound, now a base
of the U.S. Marine Corps. The reconnaissance was not carried
farther and there was no mention of the name Santa Elena,
the "point" of which they passed in going into Port Royal
Sound, a few miles from Charlesfort.

A volunteer garrison remained at Charlesfort, the ships
returning to France in July 1562 to find the religious war
underway. The men at the fort waited in vain for the return
of ships. They quarreled, fought, and killed. Some drifted
away to live with Indians. Others built a boat of sorts. Their
wild voyage across the Atlantic degenerated to cannibalism
before they were picked up by an English ship. In June 1564
a Spanish party came to the abandoned Charlesfort, razed it,

2. The account is by Ribault, *The whole and true discoverye of Terra
Florida* (1563). The religious wars having broken out, Ribault had
taken refuge in England and printed his report there, in English.

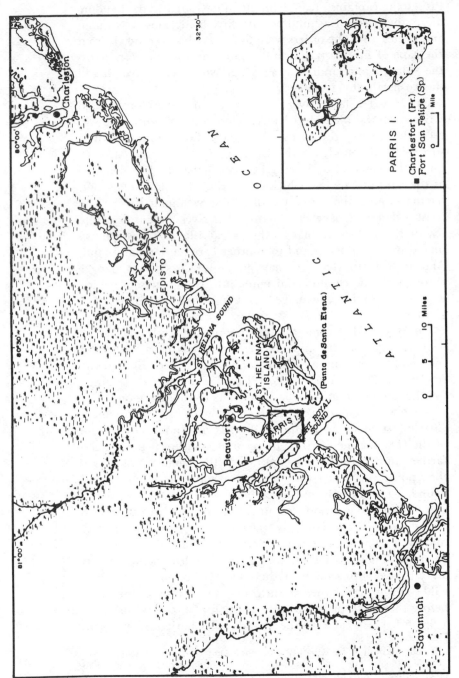

FIG. 15. The Sea Islands in the French-Spanish conflict.

and looked around to see whether any "Lutherans" were still about.

RETURN OF LAUDONNIÈRE TO FLORIDA (1564)

Coligny, occupied by the religious civil war, was unable to take up the Florida enterprise until the spring of 1564, when he sent Laudonnière with three ships and three hundred men. A brief look was taken at the "river of dolphins" (St. Augustine Inlet), which was found inadequate for settlement (fig. 16). A suitable site was found two leagues up the river of May (St. Johns), on a bluff south of the river below Jacksonville, covered with cedars, palms, and laurels, having a view out to to sea, a place so pleasing "that melancholics would be constrained to change their nature." Inland was a great green valley "in which were the most beautiful prairies in all the world and herbage most suited for pasturing livestock." [3]

The building of Fort Caroline began in July.[4] Indians gathered to help and for a while life was idyllic. The alteration began when Laudonnière mixed into a quarrel between two chiefs. Also it was found that the natives were in possession of bars and worked pieces of silver and gold, salvaged from Spanish shipwrecks, which the French mistook for local products. Their source was sought inland, to the annoyance and injury of the natives. The natives stopped bringing voluntary supplies of food, the French having negelected to plant crops. The welcome of 1564 became a state of war between natives and French in 1565.[5]

Laudonnière soon was faced by mutiny, attempts on his life, and the unauthorized departure of men to raid Spanish islands. One party engaged in successful piracy about Jamaica to the alarm of Spanish authorities. Unexpected relief came to Fort Caroline by the visit of John Hawkins, August 3, 1565. The English captain had been on a long voyage of plunder and contraband trade along the Guinea Coast of Africa and in the West Indies and looked in on the French to learn what they were doing in Florida. He traded them a ship and foodstuff for French artillery. Laudonnière was about to set sail

3. Cited in Trudel, pp. 202–203.
4. T. Frederick Davis, *Fla. Hist. Soc.*, vol. 12, pp. 77–83 describes the site.
5. Trudel, p. 204.

for France, abandoning Fort Caroline, when Ribault arrived
with seven large ships (August 27, 1565).

RIBAULT AND THE DISASTER
OF SEPTEMBER 1565

Laudonnière was to build a fort and hold it until the arrival
of Ribault, who would bring families, artisans, servants, and
more soldiers and arms. It was known that a fleet was being
prepared in Spain to move against the French in Florida.
(France and Spain were not at war and a clash away from the
home countries could take place without resulting in war at
home. Such was the expectation here and this is what happened.) Strangely, Ribault was in no hurry to get there. The
fleet left France in mid-June, took its leisurely course by way
of the Canaries and the West Indies, and arrived at Fort
Caroline after ten and a half weeks. The provocation to Philip
as defender of the Catholic faith was emphasized by Coligny's
dispatch of Protestant soldiers and colonists under Protestant
commanders who had been engaged in the religious civil war.

Both sides prepared for the fight—Ribault in command of
the French forces, Pedro Menéndez de Avilés, named Governor and Captain General of Florida, of the Spanish ones.
Menéndez was experienced at fighting French corsairs and
had warned his king that French possession of Florida might
lead to the loss of the islands of the West Indies, which were
mainly populated by Negroes and mulattos whom the French,
who had no slaves, would incite to revolt.[6]

A part of Menéndez' fleet came to St. Augustine Inlet almost
at the same time that Ribault arrived at Fort Caroline, forty
miles to the north. On September 4 Menéndez engaged the
French ships briefly below the fort and then withdrew south
to the inlet of St. Augustine. Ribault, eager for combat, loaded
the able-bodied men of the fort aboard (September 8) and
sailed out to meet the enemy. A great storm began on the
tenth and is reported to have continued for twelve days. While
the French ships were storm scattered at sea Menéndez
marched by land against Fort Caroline, which had been left
almost without defenses and was not on guard during the

6. Bartolomé Barrientos, *Pedro Menéndez de Avilés,* chaps. 8 and 9
(written 1567, first published 1902; University of Florida, 1965, with
English translation).

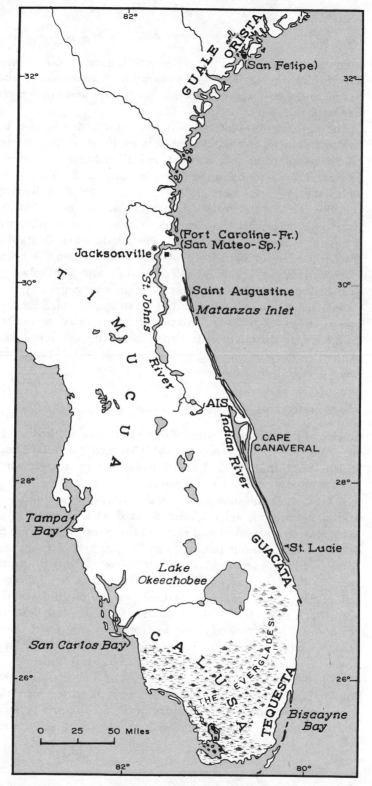

FIG. 16. East coast of Florida during the French-Spanish confrontation.

storm, took it easily, and put the men to the sword, the women and children being held for deportation. Laudonnière, who was ill, and a few others escaped to small ships and made their way back to France.

The fighting ships of Ribault were storm driven one by one to strand on the barrier beaches south of St. Augustine. Menéndez captured the shipwrecked Frenchmen at leisure. The first lot was found at the first inlet south of St. Augustine, which the castaways were trying to cross to get back to Fort Caroline, unaware of its destruction. Two hundred, excepting some who declared that they were Catholics, were marched across the dunes and slaughtered, whence the name Matanzas Inlet (the place of slaughter) to the present. Another lot was taken farther on which included Ribault and a number of principal persons. It was disposed of in the same way, the sixteen spared including a band of musicians. A third lot had taken refuge about Cape Canaveral. Some escaped across Indian River to the safety of Indian villages; the rest were taken captive. Menéndez stayed further killing, there being no more danger from Frenchmen.

EPILOGUE

Stories of the massacre stirred France and grew with the telling. The French government had provoked the retaliation, which was brutal. It had not intended to go to war with Spain and it would not do so now.

A Gascon, Dominique de Gourgues, veteran of Spanish war and prison and a good Catholic, decided on a private war of vengeance. He prepared and manned three vessels in which he left Bordeaux without public notice August 1567, corsairs not being inclined to announce their intentions. Perhaps Gourgues went raiding; it was eight months later that he appeared before St. Augustine. The Spanish garrison, thinking the ships Spanish and homeward bound, fired a salute and received one in acknowledgment as Gourgues continued north into a sound beyond St. Johns River (probably St. Marys River at the boundary between Georgia and Florida). A French lad who had escaped the Fort Caroline massacre was found living with Indians. He described the three forts the Spaniards had built to guard entry to the St. Johns. The local Indians, having become annoyed at the Spaniards, were ready to join the French. French and Indians moved in together and took the forts one by one, in the time of two days. Gourgues hanged the garrisons of all three and sailed back to France, saving his government embarrassment by slipping in as quietly as he had left and going into hiding.

FRENCH OBSERVATIONS OF
COUNTRY AND PEOPLE: RIBAULT

The first report was the one Ribault had intended for Coligny and which was published in English at London (1563). It told of sighting land (above Cape Canaveral), a shore of great length with an infinite number of tall and fair trees, the land being plain without any hills. They sailed on, viewing the coast "with an unspeakable pleasure of the odoriferous smell and beauty."

Natives were first met at the entry of the river May (St. Johns). "We perceived a good number of Indians, inhabitants there, coming along the sands and sea banks somewhat near unto us, without any token of fear or doubt, showing unto us the easiest landing place." The chief sent a girdle of red leather, and they were taken to a clear space on which branches of sweet bay had been spread. The natives were described as well built, tawny, and hawk nosed, the men dressed in short buckskins, cunningly painted, their bodies painted blue, red, and black.

"About their houses they labor and till the ground, sowing their fields with a grain called Mahiz, whereof they make their meal, and in their gardens they plant beans, gourds, cucumbers, citrons, pease and many other simples and roots unknown to us. Their spades and mattock be of wood, so well and fitly made as is possible, which they make with certain stones, oyster shells, and mussels." The plants misnamed gourds, cucumbers, and citrons all were varieties of squash (*Cucurbita pepo*, perhaps also *C. moschata*), the beans and peas were New World *Phaseolus* kinds, the spades the lance-like planting sticks common to Indian agriculture. Mattocks made of wood are the one unusual item.

An Indian town on the river had "houses fitly made and close, of wood set upright and covered with reed, the most part of them after the fashion of a pavilion, but there was one amongst the rest, very great, long and broad, with settles round about made of reeds, firmly couched together, which serve them both for beds and seats; they be of height two feet from the ground, set upon great round pillars painted with red, yellow, and blue, well polished." Pavilions were army tents, usually round, with conical top and vertical wall. The description appears to be of round houses made of vertical posts covered with reeds including a great ceremonial house with a circle of council benches.

Boats were made of single logs and held fifteen to twenty persons, standing up as they used short paddles made after the fashion of a shovel. Fishing was a major occupation. "They take fish in their parks [weirs], made in the water with great reeds so well and cunningly set together, after the fashion of a labyrinth or maze, with so many turns or crooks, as it is impossible to do with more cunning or industry." Freshwater pearls were abundant.

There were many kinds of waterfowl. In Port Royal Sound, "in a little island at the entry of the haven, on the eastnortheast side, there is so great a number of egrets that the bushes be all white and covered with them." Guinea cocks (turkeys) were "in marvelous number."

Game included "wild swine." Being far beyond the range of peccaries, the only American swine, the indication is that hogs lost from De Soto's herd, driven north some twenty years earlier, had increased greatly in the wild. The land route taken by De Soto was about fifty miles west of St. Johns River.

OBSERVATIONS BY LAUDONNIÈRE

Laudonnière's *Histoire notable de la Floride* added observations [7]:

The land is flat, traversed by numerous rivers and humid for that reason, and sandy toward the sea coast. Pines grow there in great number but do not have nutlets in their fruits. There are oaks, walnuts, cherries, mulberries, lentiscs [*Bursera Simaruba?*], and chestnuts, not native as in France (?). There are many cedars, cypresses, laurels, palms, hollies, and wild vines that climb the trees and bear good grapes. There is a sort of medlar [persimmon] the fruit of which is better than that of France. Also there are plum trees that bear a handsome fruit, but not very good, and a small seed we call *graine bleue* [blueberry], very good to eat. Roots grow there,

7. Gaffarel, pp. 349–353.

called *hases* in their language, of which they make bread in time of need.

They sow their maize (*mil*) twice a year, namely in March and June, and do so on the same ground. This grain requires only three months from the time it is sown until it is ready to be harvested. The remaining six months they allow the ground to rest. They also grow good squashes and very good beans. They do not burn the land except when they wish to sow, setting fire to the herbs that grew during the six months. They burn them all. They work the land with a wooden tool shaped like a broad hoe such as is used in France to cultivate vines: they plant two or three grains of maize together. When it is harvested it is all brought together to the public storehouse, where it is given out to each person according to his rank. They plant only what they think necessary for six months' supply and then hardly enough, for in winter they retire to the woods for three or four months, where they make huts of palm leaves for sleeping, and living there by hunting and fishing, taking oysters, deer, turkeys (poules d'Inde) and other animals. [Meat was roasted on coals, or barbecued. The women were great swimmers, etc.]

By early summer of 1565 Fort Caroline was out of food. "We subsisted only on raspberries of a certain kind, round seeded, small and black, and on the roots of small palms (*palmites*) that we gathered along the river banks." The berries may have been the dewberries of the South, a trailing *Rubus.* For the edible "palm roots" the semi-subterranean stalks of coontie (*Zamia,* a Cycad) are suggested, from which Florida Indians prepared a kind of sago.

Ceremony had the attention of Laudonnière. He held the authority of the chief to be great. The Indians, their bodies painted or tattooed, "assemble each morning in the great public hall, where the king takes his seat, higher than the rest," receives formal salutation, and presides over the council.

He then orders that the *cassine* be prepared, which is a drink made from the leaves of a certain tree, which cassine is drunk very hot. He drinks first, then passes it from one to another in the same vessel, which holds a quart by Paris measure. They make so much of this beverage that no one can drink in this assembly who has not proved himself in war. Moreover the beverage has the virtue that as soon as they have drunk they fall into a sweat, which having passed, they are without hunger or thirst for twenty-four hours thereafter.

One of the hollies native to the South, *Ilex cassine*, was used as here described for ceremonial sweating, a less noted ritual than that of the emetic "black drink" made of *Ilex vomitoria*. Laudonnière added a short description of a ball game that was played on a court with a goalpost at the center.

Concerning metals: "Gold and silver is found in quantity among the savages, which as I have understood from them, comes from ships that have been lost on the coast. They trade it among themselves, and what moreover had made me thus believe is that there is more silver on the coast towards the Cape [Canaveral], where ships are lost ordinarily, than to the North. They aver that in the mountains of Appalesse there are mines of copper, which I think are of gold." He was correct in recognizing the silver and gold as salvaged from Spanish ships wrecked on the coast above Cape Canaveral. The mountains inland had begun to be known as Appalachians. The attribution of copper mines to them may be vague Indian knowledge that native copper was found to the northwest, that is, on Lake Superior.

THE LE MOYNE–DE BRY DATA

Theodore De Bry published a collection of travels at Frankfurt at the end of the century in elegantly produced and illustrated folio volumes, the part on French Florida credited to Jacques Le Moyne de Morgues.[8] Le Moyne had escaped from Fort Caroline with Laudonnière, fled to England during the Huguenot persecution, and met De Bry there. His sketches came into De Bry's hands and were engraved at Frankfurt in the romantic style of the time. Unfortunately they were altered to suit the taste of the engraver and lost much of their representational value. Since they are often cited and reproduced, a word of caution is in order.

There are forty-two plates, beginning with the landing in Florida. Ten show the advance up the coast and the building of the fort. Thirty-two portray Indians, their ceremonies and work. These were Timucua, a once important Muskogean people of whom little is known after the sixteenth century.

8. Charles de la Roncière, *La Floride française* reproduced map and plates of a hand-colored copy. I have here reproduced in reduced size plates from a black and white volume of 1591 in the University of California Library at Berkeley.

The plates and accompanying text therefore should be an invaluable record, and have been so considered, like the map that is credited to Le Moyne.[9] Instead, the figures—human, plant, animal, or whatever—are drawn as a European who had not been there might imagine them. Three examples are here reproduced (figs. 17–19).

The landing at Port Royal was shown in Plate V (fig. 17). The trees are of the habit of growth in European parks. The grapes shown are not on vines climbing into trees as the French saw them, but as large bunches on short woody stocks as in European vineyards. Squashes, in the shape of oblong melons, hang suspended in the air, as they cannot do.

Plate XXI (fig. 18) represents Indian field cultivation. A large field is laid out in parallel ridges, as in European plowing. One woman is punching holes with a stick at regular intervals, followed by two women who are dropping seeds from a tray. The holes remain open. A large carrying basket with shoulder straps is modeled from the kind used in European vineyards. At one side men are breaking the ground with heavy recurved hoes of strange design. The engraving was not made from observation of Indian planting practices but agrees with its accompanying text:

The Indians cultivate the ground diligently; the men having learned to make heavy hoes out of the bones of fish, to which wooden handles are attached, dig the ground rather easily, since it is soft. The earth having been broken and leveled, the women sow beans and milium or Mayz, some going ahead who make holes in the ground, thrusting a stick, dropping thus seed of beans and corn. The sowing done they leave the fields; for at that time, fleeing winter, which is rather cold, that region being between West and North, and [winter] lasting about three months from December 24 to March 15, being naked they retire to the woods. When winter is past, they return to their homes to await the ripening of the crop. The harvest done, it is stored for use during the whole year, not sold, and only occasionally bartered.

9. The map of Florida attributed by De Bry to Le Moyne is a poor compilation. The location of Fort Caroline and the course of St. Johns River as shown are wrong, as are distance and position of Charlesfort. In the interior the name Apalatci is inscribed for a town, mountains, and lake, adding "in this lake the natives find grains of silver." The towns of Isabela and Monte Cristi are transferred from the north coast of Haiti to that of Cuba. Isabela had been abandoned at the beginning of the century.

Portus Regalis, sive F.S.Helenæ.

Prom Lupi.

Fig. 17. Théodor de Bry's version of the French landing at Port Royal. *Collectiones peregrimationum in Indiam Orientalem et Indiam Occidentalem*, I, Frankfurt, 1590.

21

F᪲ɪɢ. 18. Indians planting corn as pictured by de Bry, 1590.

FIG. 19. A Timucua village by de Bry, 1590. An imaginary reconstruction by European draftsmen of a palisaded town.

Some of the information is correct, but the writer thought that corn planting was done in the fall as is the case with small grains in Europe and that the planted fields were left unattended. Le Moyne did not write that text nor did he supervise the engraving.

ADDITIONAL OBSERVATIONS

Le Challeux, a carpenter from Dieppe, also escaped the massacre at Fort Caroline and wrote a tract on his experiences.[10] "All their dwellings are round in form, covered above with palm leaves and withstand wind and tempest." He gave the best description of Indian corn: "They have maize in abundance and it grows to a height of seven feet, the stalk as thick as a cane, the grain the size of a pea, and the ear a foot long. Its color is that of fresh wax. The manner of use is mainly by bruising and breaking it to a meal; thereupon they work it into a mass and make their *migan,* which resembles the *risque* in this country [Latin *reseco,* something broken up]; it should be eaten as soon as done because it changes quickly and does not keep." Grapevines were rampant on trees but no wine was made; instead they made a drink called *cassinet* (Ilex), of indifferent taste.

An anonymous letter told of being served "their excellent beverage" and of *esquine* wood, a valuable drug of commercial promise (later known as sassafras). "There is a lot of cedar, red as blood, and there are woods of almost nothing else; also there are many pines and another kind of wood that is very yellow" (bald cypress).[11]

SUMMARY

The contacts were with three Timucua tribes—Saturiva on the lower St. Johns, Utina farther up the river, and Patano to the west. Tribe and chief were of one name. The person and authority of the chief were greatly respected. Tribal councils were held in large ceremonial buildings, circular like the the dwelling houses. Meetings began by drinking a sudorific tea, *cassiné.*

The numerous population lived in villages by farming,

10. Gaffarel, pp. 339–340; text of tract pp. 457–476.
11. Gaffarel, pp. 403–408.

fishing, gathering, and hunting, the last a winter occupation. Maize yielded two crops a year, on the same ground. It was described as having foot-long ears, the seeds of the color of fresh beeswax and the size of peas. Beans and squashes of several kinds were grown. Fish were a major food and were taken in elaborate weirs.

Secondary vegetation is implied in the stand of red cedar (*Juniperus virginiana*), persimmons, sassafras, and berry patches, the result of fire clearings and regrowth in old fields.

12
Spanish Florida
(1565–1597)

LESSONS OF THE MAP

Spanish authorities at midcentury knew the essentials of the physical geography of their domain overseas. The island chain of the West Indies enclosed a mediterranean sea which was entered at the south, usually by the Dominica Passage. Unlike the European Mediterranean, a great sea stream flows out into the Atlantic Ocean from the northeast. The Gulf Stream, pent between the peninsula of Florida and the islands of Cuba and Bahamas, carried their returning ships into the open ocean. Its discovery set the route of passage from New Spain and also from Peru and New Granada (Colombia).

The passage was endangered in the season of hurricanes by the Florida Keys and farther north by the wide shoals and long strands of the Florida east coast, with few and poor inlets. At the north the Sea Islands offered ample and protected sounds. These were known early to Spanish navigation and were the object of the colonization ordered by King and Council to be made at Santa Elena, the name retained for St. Helena Island and Sound. The plan was good; its execution failed because of the misfortune that happened to the Luna expedition.

ALTERNATIVE LOCATIONS FOR A FORT

While Spain considered its next action the French moved into the Santa Elena area in 1562 and built Charlesfort on the greater sound which they named Port Royal. Two years later in June 1564 Laudonnière returned with a body of artisans, soldiers, sailors, and artillery. He looked at St. Augustine Inlet, found it inadequate, and went on to build Fort Caroline on St. Johns River below Jacksonville. The place had been visited on the prior voyage and claimed for France. A hundred fifty miles south of Port Royal, it had the preferred qualities as to port and productive land. Also it was most convenient for attack on Spanish shipping. Fort Caroline was to be the French stronghold, to which Ribault in 1565 brought soldiers and colonists with families, estimated as from six to twelve hundred persons. The location was at the most advantageous site on that coast and was followed by the quick and total destruction of the plans for a French Protestant Florida.

The third location, St. Augustine, was far inferior as Laudonnière had judged, but it was chosen in emergency by Menéndez when he confronted Ribault. Beginning as a landing behind the sandbar of Anastasia Island it was moved to the mainland side of the shallow, narrow inlet in a swampy, sandy plain of pine and palmetto, thinly populated. It was emergency, not choice, that determined its start. The inertia of structures continued it, although with some interruption, to be known as the first European town on soil of the United States.

Having burned Fort Caroline, Menéndez built there the Spanish San Mateo, a triangle of forts, destroyed by the raid of Gourgues in 1568 during Menéndez' absence.

Menéndez complied with the request of King and Council, made in 1566, to establish a base at Santa Elena. He occupied the razed site of Charlesfort on Parris Island and built on it the fort he named San Felipe in honor of the king. The settlement and vicinity continued to be known as Santa Elena.[1]

Menéndez thus put to use the three most eligible harbors of the mainland, convenient to the sailing route that followed the Gulf Stream.

MENÉNDEZ, FOUNDER OF SPANISH FLORIDA

Pedro Menéndez was of an Asturian family in Avilés that was long notable in the navy of Spain. His services in American

1. Mary L. Ross (*Ga. Hist. Quart.* 1925, pp. 352 ff.) identified the site. She has contributed largely to the Spanish history of the Sea Islands in

waters dated from 1554 when he brought back a Spanish fleet from Vera Cruz laden with treasure. In 1557 he escorted a fleet to Cádiz with a cargo valued in millions in treasure, cochineal, sugar, and hides. Mainly he was engaged in patrolling both sides of the Atlantic against pirates, largely French. Coligny had begun to occupy Florida at Port Royal in 1562, followed it with the establishment on St. Johns River of Fort Caroline in 1564, and was preparing to send Ribault with a formidable force in March 1565. King Philip appointed Menéndez Adelantado of Florida to retake his invaded domain.[2]

The counteroffensive by Menéndez was told by the priest López de Mendoza Grajales in a journal, from departure at Cádiz to the execution of the first lot of French castaways on the beach on September 29.[3] Briefly the Mendoza account is as follows: Off Puerto Rico Menéndez disclosed to his men a letter from the king telling that they were being sent against a French fleet of seven ships, seven hundred men, and two hundred women, dispatched May 20 for Florida. Rumor enlarged the number of Frenchmen awaiting them in Florida to two thousand. Florida was sighted August 28 and shortly St. Augustine Inlet, where they were cordially received at an Indian village. Continuing north they found four French men-of-war off the mouth of St. Johns River on September 4 and engaged in a demonstration of insults and shots. Overnight a storm began, the Spanish ships retiring to the shelter of the inlet to the south, where the great house of the cacique was placed at their disposal. During the storm the general decided to march overland with five hundred men against the French fort and did so on September 16. The priest, remaining at the village on St. Augustine Inlet, told how a messenger came September 23 crying *"victoria"* and telling how Fort Caroline had been taken. An Indian brought word that a French ship had been wrecked nearby, the survivors huddled about a fire on the beach, some gathering shellfish to eat. Menéndez set out to pick them up and, by count of the priest who went

that journal and as co-author with Professor Bolton of *The Debatable Land*.

2. Woodbury Lowery, *The Spanish Settlements* (1911, republished 19959) is the standard reference. Barcia's *Cronologia* of 1724 gives detailed year by year account of events. The Barrientos biography of Menéndez, written in 1567, is the major account written at the time.

3. CDI, vol. 3, pp. 441–479.

along to offer last rites, executed a hundred and eleven. End of the account.

Having eliminated the French, Menéndez wrote the king of the great things to be done in Florida. He would plant sugarcane and vineyards, raise herds of livestock, exploit the pine woods for naval stores, and collect pearls from the rivers. He would build a chain of forts across the interior to the mines of Zacatecas in New Spain (the plan of Velasco). He would explore the coast to the north to find a sea passage to China.[4] He hoped to bring greater wealth to Spain than was produced by New Spain or Peru.

Menéndez applied himself with great dedication to organizing his government. He moved from place to place, to Havana and to Santa Elena, across the peninsula, founding stations, bringing men and supplies, visiting native chiefs. The year 1566 was spent in roughing out the grand design of the lands he would win for Spain and the Catholic Church. These, not the acquisition of personal wealth, were his commitment. As Commander of the Order of Santiago, he was the military and civil arm of the crown and the patron and protector of the Christian missionaries.

Having established St. Augustine and San Mateo (replacing Fort Caroline), he went south to Cape Canaveral for a visit to the great lagoon behind it, now known as Indian River. The Ais Indians, mainly fishermen, beachcomers, and hunters, were friendly (Barcia). Menéndez left a garrison of about two hundred there to build another post while he sailed back to Cuba to report his success in disposing of the French. The troops left soon were in trouble with the natives and removed twenty leagues farther south on Indian River to the Guacata tribe, where they built a fort named Santa Lucia, the name retained as St. Lucie at the southern end of Indian River for inlet, canal, and county (see fig. 16 above).

Barcia gave forty folio pages to the events of 1566—the repeated coming and going of Menéndez—the commissions to subordinates, the meetings with Indian chiefs, and in October the chasing of pirates out of the West Indies. In March 1567 he made a third visit to the great cacique Carlos in south Florida, of whom more below, and then returned to Spain to

4. Urdaneta in 1561 told a story that French were said to have found a sea passage at the north, which account was known to Menéndez (CDI, vol. 2, p. 137).

report, having added San Felipe in the Santa Elena area to
St. Augustine and San Mateo (Jacksonville) as fortified bases.
Also he put small garrisons in the south, one on Indian River,
as noted, one a hundred miles farther south among the Tequesta tribe on Biscayne Bay (Miami), one on the west coast
at or near San Carlos Harbor, and one on Tampa Bay
(fig. 16). While in Cuba he secured the services of the first
Jesuits arrived in the Spanish Indies. These priests were on
their way to Peru or Mexico and were diverted by him to
begin instead their mission in Florida.

At the north the Spaniards at St. Augustine and San Mateo,
in the absence of their commander, got into trouble among
themselves and by outrages on the Indians. Indians made an
attack on St. Augustine, shot fire arrows into the thatch roofs
that blew up the powder magazine, and burned a good part
of the fort. Barcia, describing the breakdown of discipline,
wrote that the Spaniards dared leave the forts only in groups
to gather oysters, crawfish, and palm shoots.

Santa Elena on the other hand prospered. The local Indians
and their chief, both known as Orista (hence the current place
name Edisto?) were at outs with the Guale tribe about the
Savannah River, where the Ayllón colony had attempted to
settle. The adelantado made peace between them which lasted,
aided by the Jesuit ministration. The Indians remained
friendly, supplying the Spaniards with food from waters and
fields.

Late in 1566 Menéndez sent Juan Pardo from Santa Elena
to find a land route to the mines of Zacatecas, as he had
promised Philip the year before in accordance with the plan
of Viceroy Velasco. The party reportedly went a hundred and
fifty leagues, built a stockade at the foot of the mountains, and
brought back word that all the chiefs desired to be brothers to
the adelantado. The U.S. De Soto Commission thought that
Pardo might have followed the route taken by De Soto from
Cofitachequi (Augusta) to the Blue Ridge. The direction was
about the same; both parties were rather large, depended on
Indian supplies, and took a main-traveled Indian road.

Spanish interest in the north was in the protection of the
sea lane, further exploration of the coast, a route overland to
the Mexican mines, and especially at Santa Elena, in conversion of the natives. Obviously three bases were not needed;
Santa Elena was considered the most advantageous.

South Florida was another matter, with the dangerous shores on which Spanish ships were lost, the Keys at the south, and the shoals from Cape Canaveral south. A great chief was said to be lord of the south, in possession of Spanish treasure and also of Spaniards who had been wrecked on those shores. This was common knowledge, even to the French. Laudonnière heard at Fort Caroline of two strange men living to the south, had them brought, and found that they were Spaniards who had been wrecked fifteen years before on the Florida Keys. He was told that the Keys belonged to the king of Calos, who had a great deal of gold and silver from Spanish ships and also some Spanish women. Indians confirmed that this king had treasure from ships lost in the strait.

This great chief of South Florida was known to the Spanish as Carlos, the story being that having heard of the great white chief called Carlos, the Emperor, he had adopted that name. The identification of tribe and chief by the same name, usual throughout the east, had its basis in the fact that the principal chiefs were hereditary rulers of large authority and ceremonial deference. The chief of the south was the head of the Calusa tribe, "lord of much sea coast as far as the Martyrs and Canal of Bahama" (Barcia). The name persists in San Carlos Bay, perhaps in Charlotte Harbor.

In February 1566 Menéndez sailed from Havana with five hundred men to make the first of three visits to the cacique Carlos (Calos). He landed in San Carlos Bay, half a league from the town of Carlos. The meeting was with much ceremony, the chief coming with three hundred bowmen, Menéndez with as many men-at-arms. They marched together in parade to the great house of the chief, which had room for two thousand persons. The chief, a young man of about twenty-five, took his place on the high seat, flanked by dignitaries, and presided over the reception. After elaborate civilities Menéndez was given a dozen Spanish castaways, men and women, also silver and gold that had been salvaged from wrecks, and departed. A return visit was made in September to build a "fort" by the side of the town of Carlos, which was said to have in excess of four thousand inhabitants. It was hoped to learn if a river two leagues distant connected with the Laguna de Mayaimi (Lake Okeechobee). (The Caloosahatchee River drains part of the Everglades into San Carlos Bay.)

THE RELATION OF ESCALANTE FONTANEDA

The best informed account of Florida was addressed to the king by Escalante Fontaneda, a castaway from a wreck in 1551 to the time of his release by Menéndez.[5] He lived in South Florida from the age of thirteen, when the ship on which he was being sent from Cartagena (Colombia) to be educated in Spain was wrecked on the Florida Keys. He was thirty at the time of his release.

The Keys were inhabited by Indians of large stature; the men wore breech clouts made of palm leaves, the women skirts of a plant growing on trees (Spanish moss). Their food, as he learned while with them, was fish, turtles, shellfish, and whales, also seals [monk seals], langostas, and conchs (*chapin*). There were many deer on the Keys and on some there were large bears that swam from one key to another. The wood known to physicians [guayacan?] grew there and also there were many fruits. Two villages were named.

To the west are "islands without trees; these islands are of sand and in times past must have been keys (*cayos*) that were worn away by the sea and have remained as sand flats without trees. They are seven leagues in circuit and are called Islas Tortugas, there being many turtles that come at night to lay eggs in the sand. These turtles are of the size of a large shield and have as much meat as a cow, the meat being of several kinds." A fair account of the Dry Tortugas.

Escalante went on to describe the Province of Carlos where he lived much of the time. It extended on the Gulf from the Keys north [to San Carlos Bay] and east to Guacata (St. Lucie, noted above). The name Carlos (Calusa) he understood to mean fierce people, being warlike and artful and lords of fifty pueblos. He named twenty-seven of these, five of them on the freshwater lake of Mayaimi [Okeechobee]. This lake was in the middle of the land and had outlets both east and west to the sea. Fishing on it was excellent, there being eels as thick as a man's arm, huge trout-like fish, muskrats, and tortoises (*galápagos*). Deer and waterfowl were hunted. Bread was made from roots. The people of lake and swamp were vassals of Carlos and paid tribute in food, buckskins, and the like. (Notice of the Everglades and Lake Okeechobee.)

5. CDI, vol. 5, pp. 532–548; also vol. 10, pp. 66–80.

Chief Carlos also controlled two pueblos in the Bahama Islands. (Since these had been stripped of natives more than a generation before for forced labor in Española, the implication is that Florida Indians had moved across the Bahama Channel.) Formerly Cuban Indians had come in quest of the fountain of youth, some of whom "the father of King Carlos took and made a pueblo of them, their descendants thus living to the present time."

Escalante had some knowledge of provinces north and independent of Carlos, from Tocobaga and Moscoso (both Timucua chiefs and tribes about Tampa Bay) to the land of the Apalachees. The Ais of the east coast (Indian River near Cape Canaveral) he had not visited; these people were poor in products of the land "but rich from the sea by reason of the many ships laden with silver and gold that had been lost there." The Ais Indians divided among five caciques more than a million (ducats) in bars of silver, gold, and Mexican jewelry. He enumerated ships that were lost in his time and named persons of wealth and rank who had been on them. "Many Spaniards escaped with their lives by finding Christian companions there ahead of them," who knew the language and custom as did he. Some were killed because they did not sing and dance when ordered to do so. When Escalante explained to the Indians that the refugees failed to comply because they did not understand what they were expected to do they were accepted into the native communities. He ended the relation with the recommendation that a small fort be built to look after shipwrecks.

THE FLORIDA ESTABLISHMENTS TO 1573

Menéndez was called to Spain in the summer of 1567 by the Council of the Indies, which business occupied him there until April 1568 (Barcia). In that time Gourgues destroyed San Mateo and its occupants. It was not rebuilt.

Menéndez returned with ten Jesuits to engage in converting the natives. By 1569 Santa Elena was the largest Spanish post and had one Jesuit mission among the local Orista and another among the Guale toward the Savannah River. There were very few conversions, but relations were satisfactory on the whole (Barcia). Menéndez was appointed General of the Armada of the Indies that year and thereafter saw little of the Florida posts, being kept busy with the convoy of ships across the sea and with patrolling the waters to the south against corsairs.

For 1572 Barcia reported only seven married residents (*vecinos*) at St. Augustine, forty-eight at Santa Elena. López de Velasco had data of 1573 for his geography. He reported that there were only these two forts, "with a garrison of a hundred and fifty and as many more *labradores*, all in diminution because of lack of supplies. There is no other Spanish population, nor do these have any other trade and traffic than some hunting and whatever the labradores may sow and such livestock as they are beginning to have." Three hundred Spaniards, half soldiers, half civilian workers, did a little cultivating and raising of livestock. There were no Spaniards left in the south. The post in the bay of Carlos had been abandoned in 1571 because of a rebellion, for which the chief and a score of the principal men were executed. The post at Tocobaga on Tampa Bay had been lost, its men killed. Tequesta post on Biscayne Bay and a fourth, unnamed, had the same fate.

SPANISH JESUITS TO CHESAPEAKE BAY

Chesapeake Bay was known to Spaniards before 1536, as Bahía de Santa Maria. Oviedo thus recorded it from the Chaves map. It was known as a wide opening in the coastline, its interior unexplored.

Viceroy Luis de Velasco, engaged in the venture on which he sent Luna to occupy Santa Elena, had disturbing information about the coast to the north.[6] An Englishman born in Bristol, at the time living in Yucatán, had been in a fleet (apparently French) that was awaiting Spanish ships, when a storm forced them to take shelter in a very good bay in 37° N. latitude. After a trade in pelts with the Indians they sailed south to 33°, which the Englishman thought was Punta de Santa Elena. Velasco was concerned that the French were moving south to Santa Elena. Menéndez at the time (1560–1561) was in New Spain and was asked by Velasco to make a reconnaissance of the coast north from Santa Elena. It is not of record that this was done.

6. Clifford M. Lewis and Albert J. Loomie, *The Spanish Jesuit Mission in Virginia*, pp. 13–15. Monograph by Jesuit scholars, with appended documents, some published for the first time.

About this time a young Indian from the Chesapeake region, known as Don Luis de Velasco, became the key figure involved in Ajacan, the land of Powhatan to the English of the next century. Accounts of the time disagree as to when and how the Indian came into Spanish hands. He was a protégé of the Viceroy of New Spain, took his name, and was his godson. Velasco having died in 1564, King Philip in March 1565 ordered the Audiencia of New Spain to remand the Indian to the custody of Menéndez who was then in Spain preparing for his combat with the French in Florida.[7]

Also at the same time Menéndez asked the General of the Jesuits, Francisco Borgia, to provide him with missionaries for Florida. The order then making many converts in the Orient, the adelantado urged on the Jesuit General that Florida would serve them as a way station to the Far East: "This land of Florida should be connected with Tartary or China, or there should be an arm of the sea . . . by which one may go to China and Maluco and return to the land of Florida." [8] Before the fight for Florida began with the French Menéndez had planned Spanish possession of Santa Maria (Chesapeake Bay), which he hoped would be the passage to the Orient. He would have Jesuit missionaries gentle the Indians. And he had the Indian Don Luis to show the way and make contact with his people.

After the destruction of French Florida there were many matters that needed attention, such as natives in the southern peninsula who were holding Spanish persons and treasure. Menéndez was called to Spain for a year and then was placed in charge of policing the transatlantic sailing. There was less time for Florida as the demands increased at Havana and Veracruz. The Indian Don Luis was instructed in Spanish ways and Christian observance, reached Spain and may have stayed there for about two years. He enjoyed the attention he received there, in Florida, and in Havana. The Jesuit fathers were toiling in their Florida missions with scant success, thought of the large harvest of souls elsewhere, and began to ask that they be transferred.

Father Segura was sent from Spain as Jesuit vice-provincial in the summer of 1568. After a year's experience of the futility of their efforts in Florida he wrote Father General Borgia (De-

7. *Ibid.,* pp. 15–18, 21.
8. *Ibid.,* p. 21, note 41.

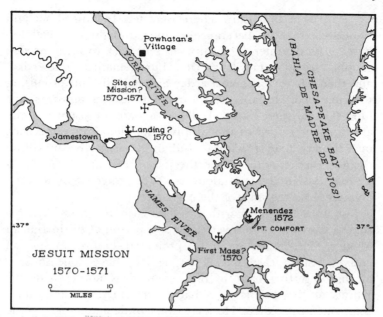

FIG. 20. The Jesuit mission to Powhatan country (in Virginia); after Lewis and Loomie, *The Spanish Jesuit Mission in Virginia, 1570–1572*, Chapel Hill, 1953.

cember 1569) about their removal, "should the opportunity offer to go to China from here, for the Indians have found a route."[9] Don Luis was the one Indian familiar with the coast to the north who might guide them to a sea passage to the Orient.

Menéndez brought Don Luis to Havana to confer with Father Segura about the mission to Ajacan, the homeland of the Indian. Segura and the Indian sailed to Santa Elena, where they collected a party of religious and of young men inclined to enter the society. The ship left Santa Elena August 5, 1570.[10]

The course of the voyage, the landing in the tidal James River, the crossing of the narrow neck of land to York River and the location of the first mission have been reconstructed by Lewis and Loomie (fig. 20).[11]

They were met as they debarked (September 10) in Virginia

9. *Ibid.*, p. 25.
10. *Ibid.*, pp. 26–28.
11. *Ibid.*, pp. 28–41.

by relatives of Don Luis. There were few Indians about and those were in want because of a long drought that had followed a hard winter. The ship was sent back to bring needed supplies from Santa Elena. Don Luis remained a few days and then left for his home, a day and half distant, promising to bring food. He failed to return or to answer messages sent him. The mission party eked out a bare subsistence while awaiting the return of the supply ship. Don Luis came back on February 4, 1571, with an Indian band that began killing the missionaries and finished the job on February 9. A son of a settler at Santa Elena alone escaped, protected by a chief, and later told the store of the massacre.

Don Luis had lived with the Spaniards for years, had become a Christian, and was treated as a person of distinction in Mexico, Florida, and Spain. He promoted the plan of Spanish entry to Chesapeake Bay. That he may have done so as a means of getting back to his people does not explain the killing of the Jesuits who had come unarmed and unaccompanied by soldiers. He was visited while among his people by some of the religious, found "living in sin," and ordered to return to Christian conduct. This, it is suggested, brought on the crisis in his mind that made him regard the missionaries as the enemy.[12] When the relief ship came it was attacked, some of the Indians wearing Jesuit cassocks, and was forced to turn back. The defiance was clear: Christian missionaries were excluded.

Another expedition was prepared at Havana and taken charge of in Florida by Menéndez. It left St. Augustine July 30, 1572, stopped at Santa Elena, and sailed north, Menéndez taking his last leave of the New World, being under orders from the King to return to Spain to take charge of building a fleet of warships. On arriving in the waters of Ajacan (James River) Indians were welcomed aboard. Fighting followed when one group of principals was seized. Menéndez asked for the surrender of Don Luis, failing which he hanged eight of the inferred participants in the killing.

Ajacan was Tidewater Virginia, occupied by the Powhatan Indians. The high chief was thought to be an uncle of Don Luis. Comments on Indian life are scant. Father Rogel: "What I have seen in this land is that there are more people than in

12. *Ibid.*, pp. 47–48. Hallowell and Swanton are cited as to effects among other tribes of such prohibition of native customs.

any part I have seen on the known coast; and it seems to me that they live here better settled (*mas de asiento*) than anywhere else I have been." Father Oré noted corncribs: "There are *garitas* throughout Florida for storage of the maize for their sustenance and these are storerooms set upon four tall and heavy posts, raised above the ground." Father Juan de Carrera added the most specific and curious observation:

In the month of August 1572 . . . we landed in the Bay of Madre de Dios [Santa Maria or Chesapeake] and at this port we found a very beautiful vineyard (*viña*), as well laid out (*concertado*) and ordered as the vineyards in Spain, located in a sandy tract (*arenal*), the stocks of the vines (*cepas*) laden with very fine white grapes, large and ripe, which the Lord had there prepared for us, for which we gave Him great thanks. Also within the vineyard were a great number of trees, plums, cherries, and medlars [persimmons], like those of Spain, laden with ripe fruit, whereof we ate and took for our road.

The best indication that they really saw an Indian vineyard is that the grapes were white, a color selected for by domestication. That a Spaniard should have considered them large suggests that the grapes were scuppernongs, the white domestic variety of the wild muscadines of the South.[13]

DECLINE OF FLORIDA

The adelantado was succeeded by his nephew, Pedro Menéndez Marquez, to carry on as best he could. Florida was a half forgotten backwater. Spain was hard put to it at the time to break the revolt in the Low Countries. The armada for which the elder Menéndez had been called back to Spain was prepared for that campaign. France was torn by religious wars and the number of French corsairs was thereby reduced. The Florida garrisons were rarely supplied by ship. The handful of settlers, mainly about Santa Elena, produced little. After the Ajacan disaster the Jesuits moved to missionary labors in New Spain and elsewhere.

The last quarter of the century was recorded by Barcia: In 1576 there were two hundred men in the presidios of St. Augustine and Santa Elena, the latter having been attacked and set afire by Indians. In 1579 a French pirate (bearing the

13. *Ibid.*, pp. 106 (Rogel), 173 (Oré and de Carrera).

distinguished Florentine name Strozzi), was hanged with his crew at St. Augustine. In 1584 the presidios were reported as being in great want. In 1586 Francis Drake and Martin Frobisher came to destroy Santa Elena, were prevented by weather, and instead burned St. Augustine completely. In 1589 Menéndez Marquez sent a ship north to Chesapeake Bay to find out what the English were up to. (It did not locate the Roanoke Colony.) [14] By 1589 St. Augustine had been rebuilt and the presidio at Santa Elena abandoned. The Council of the Indies decided to send Franciscan missionaries to ease the Indian unrest. These reached Florida in 1594, at a time when "the soldiers did not dare to go out even to hunt or fish because the Indians killed them." Most of the friars went to the more pacific Guale Indians about Savannah. In 1595 "the Franciscans began to cool the indignation of the barbarians," but two years later one friar after another was slain, the governor able only to take reprisal by burning Indian cornfields. As the century ended Spanish Florida consisted of a meager garrison at St. Augustine, surrounded by unfriendly Indians and unable to guard the sea passage.

GLOSS ON SASSAFRAS

Nicolas Monardes, a physician in Sevilla, became known all through western Europe for his books on cures by medicinal plants from the New World. To the first tract of 1569 a second was added in 1571, and these were incorporated into the famous edition of 1574, translated into various languages, in English as *Joyful News Out of the Newe-Founde World* (London, 1596). Monardes gave case histories of many grave illnesses that were completely cured by some particular plant from the New World.

Sassafras was such a plant that had fame as a sovereign remedy for many diseases and as a tonic.[15] Monardes observed that the men who returned from Florida with the adelantado (1567) were in robust health, had good color, and attributed their condition to the use of sassafras, a supply of which they brought with them. Tertian fever (malaria) was then common

14. *Ibid.*, pp. 185–192, with Spanish documentation.
15. This Spanish name appears to have been a mistaken identification with *Saxifrage*. It had been known to the French as *Esquine*, perhaps an Indian name.

in Spain and according to Monardes yielded quickly to drinking sassafras tea. The Spaniards, he said, had learned about the medicine from the French and these from Florida natives. A Frenchman in Sevilla gave him his first acquaintance with sassafras. In the second tract, in the section entitled "things that are brought from our western Indies that serve for the use of medicine," he gave major space to this new medicinal, convenient to use and without risk. The bark, preferably of the root, when boiled to a good color and drunk freely instead of wine cured fevers and other sicknesses and ensured good health.

Monardes prefaced the second tract with a woodcut of the sassafras tree which shows that he had not seen one. The text however was fairly well informed. The tree grew from the size of a sapling to that of a medium pine tree, with a cup-shaped crown. The leaves resembled those of the fig when mature, the young ones those of a pear tree. The roots spread laterally and therefore were easily dug. In places, as about Santa Elena and San Mateo, it formed stands (*montes*). (Sassafras is conspicuous as second growth.) It grew on land that was neither very wet nor very dry. Where it was abundant it scented the air about with an odor resembling cinnamon. (It is a pleasantly aromatic member of the laurel family.)

Monardes introduced sassafras to wide use in Europe medicine. The suppliers however were mainly English colonists of later time. Sassafras tea, pleasant of taste and smell, continued to be a popular drink, with repute as a spring tonic, in the Eastern states. The powdered leaves, as filé, still are important in French cooking in Louisiana.

Part IV

The English Came Late

13
Englishmen Overseas
(1527–1587)

During the reign of Henry VIII many Englishmen were living as merchants in Spain, especially at Sevilla and its outport Sanlúcar de Barrameda, centers of commerce and news of the New World. The Thorne family of Bristol had backed John Cabot when he sailed to find a western passage. Sebastian Cabot moved from English to Spanish services in 1512 and later held the office of Pilot Major at Sevilla, while Robert Thorne represented the family interest in Sevilla. When Sebastian led a Spanish fleet in 1526 to the La Plata estuary for possible passage to the South Sea, Robert Thorne contributed substantially and sent along two Englishmen, "somewhat learned in cosmography," one being Robert Barlow. Thorne explained that the voyage might inform his deputies of a way to the Spice Islands "by the new found land that we have discovered. And that wise we should be nearer the spicery by almost 2000 leagues than the Emperor or king of Portugal are."

Robert Thorne and Robert Barlow returned to England in 1530 and wrote jointly a *Declaration of the Indies* for the information of the king, proposing the short northern route by way of Newfoundland, in effect the project John Cabot had promoted a generation earlier. Thorne died in 1532; Barlow worked on the book until 1540 or 1541. Although the manuscript was available it was not printed until 1932, by the Hakluyt Society.[1]

For the most part the Barlow Geography is a translation of the *Suma de Geographia* of Fernández de Enciso, which was printed in Sevilla in 1519 and reprinted in 1530, the first Spanish treatise of the sort. Enciso was the first governor, de facto, of the Spanish colony of Darién. Barlow did not name his source, a neglect that was not unusual at the time. He added some observations of his own for the La Plata region which he had visited, also a revised proposal for a northwest passage:

the new found land, which was first discovered by merchants of Bristol, where now the Bretons do trade thither every year afishing and is called the bacaliaus [Span. *bacalao*]. It lieth westnorthwest of Galicia and hath many good ports and islands, and northeast of it hath the land of Labrador which is not yet known for it hath not been labored, but it is to be presupposed that there is no riches of gold, spices, nor precious stones, for it standeth far apart from the equinoctial, where the influence of the sun doth nourish and bring forth gold, spices, stones, and pearls. But whereas our English merchants of Bristol did enterprise to discover and discovered that part of the land, if at that season they had followed toward the equinoctial, no doubt but they should have found great riches of gold and pearl as other nations hath done since that time.[2]

In the concluding passage, addressed to the king, Barlow said that of the four parts of the world three had been discovered, Spain sailing all the western and Portugal the eastern seas, Spain having discovered also a great part to the south. There remained to discover only the way of the north, for which England was in the best location. The profit and glory to be gained were far greater than the costs. The unknown northern part of the sea could be sailed in continual light (of summer), a navigation of about three hundred leagues to the pole and the same distance beyond to lands as temperate as England, to Tartary, China, Cathay, Malacca and all the East Indies. And so to "the backside of all the new found land that is discovered by your grace's subjects, until they come into the

1. E. G. R. Taylor (ed.), *A Brief Summe of geographie, by Robert Barlow*.

2. Barlow seems to refer to the Bristol partnership of the beginning of the century from which the name Labrador derived.

south seas on the back side of the Indies occidental. . . . The commodity of the navigation by this way is of so great advantage over the other navigations in shortening of half the way, for the other must sail by great circuits and compasses and these shall sail by straight ways and lines."

Experience by that time indicated that the alternative to Magellan's southern passage must needs be sought in the far north, in effect a great circle route across the North Pole to China. In summer this would be made without darkness of night. No account was taken of a sea frozen the year round.

The idea of a northwest passage was current in England and perhaps had been tried after Sebastian Cabot had gone from England to Spain. One such attempt was recorded in Spanish archives.[3] An English ship, with John Rut as captain, entered the port of Santo Domingo in November 1527. It had three top-mainsails, was well armed, had a pinnace and longboat, and carried a stock of woolen and linen goods that it offered in trade. The story told at Santo Domingo was that it had sailed from England nine months earlier to discover a passage between Newfoundland and Labrador by which to go to Tartary, had got into high, cold latitudes, and lost the pilot and some seamen there. The ship then turned south for refreshment and to find a pilot who would take it back to England. Local witnesses charged that the Englishmen had seized loads of cassava bread and fish and had been stealing clothing, chickens, and eggs. The Spanish authorities were suspicious but took no action against the trespass of a ship from a friendly country.[4]

The most peculiar "Voyage of Master Hore and Divers Other Gentlemen" in 1536 was told in Hakluyt's *Principal Navigations*. Thirty gentlemen and ninety servants sailed from Gravesend on a "voyage of discovery upon the Northwest parts of America":

They came to the Island of Penguin, which is very full of rocks and stone, whereon they went and found it full of great fowls, white

3. CDI, vol. 40, pp. 350–354. Licenciado Zuazo was the examining official.
4. Why would an English ship, in waters frequented at that season by cod fishers of various countries, have made the long voyage to the Caribbean in search of a pilot? From Newfoundland to Española was a much more difficult voyage than the return across the northern sea to England.

and gray, as big as geese, and they saw infinite number of their eggs. They drove a great number of the fowls into their boats upon their sails, and took up many of their eggs; the fowls they flayed and their skins were very like honeycombs, full of holes being flayed off; they dressed and ate them, and found them to be very good and nourishing meat. They saw also store of bears both black and white, of whom they killed some, and took them for no bad food.

The penguin island may have been Funk Island, familiar to cod fishermen for flesh and eggs of the great auk, known by the Welsh name penguin. Polar bears rode the Labrador current south in summer on icebergs and ice floes. That black bears also were taken suggests that the party may have been on an island closer to the Newfoundland shore.

The gentlemen moved to the main island, lost their ship, and starved to the extent that some became cannibals. This in midsummer when berries were ripe and salmon were running in the streams. They got out of the stupid crisis by capturing a French ship that had come into harbor and sailing it home to St. Ives in Cornwall, landing late in October. The "discovery" got no farther than the commercially fished east coast of Newfoundland.

ENGLISH ANTAGONISM TO SPAIN

The relations between England and Spain during the reign of Henry VIII ranged through family union, military alliance, and normal diplomatic relations, somewhat put to a strain by Henry's establishment of the Church of England with himself replacing the pope as its head. When Mary (his daughter by Catherine of Aragon and a good Catholic) became queen, alienation developed quickly and became violent when in 1554 she married Philip, soon to be King of Spain. The restoration of the old faith led to a series of executions beginning in 1555 and then to the unpopular involvement of England on the Spanish side in Flanders and thereby the loss of Calais, the last England possession on the continent. Before the death of Mary in 1558 English sentiment had developed into aggressive nationalism directed against Spain and the Catholic Church.

The sustained and great burst of national energy that was the Elizabethan period opposed the Roman church, subjugated Ireland, harassed Spain to the point of war, and made

England a maritime power. Its champions were rewarded with wealth and honors.

Devon families took a leading part in the Irish wars as well as in trading, privateering, and raiding overseas. Queen Elizabeth rewarded them with grants of lands seized in Ireland, such as the forty thousand acres she gave to her favorite Sir Walter Raleigh. His stepbrother Humphrey Gilbert and other captains from Devon who took part in the desolation of Ireland also were well rewarded with Irish estates. The Devon gentry, largely interrelated, had interests in shipping at Plymouth and other Channel ports. Some held posts in the navy. Loyal to the queen and the new church that had broken with Rome, they led the way in attacks on Spanish shipping and in the making of English sea power.

HAWKINS AND DRAKE

John Hawkins, of a shipowning family in Plymouth, heard in the Canaries of the profits to be made by selling Negro slaves to the West Indies.[5] In 1562 he went to the Sierra Leone coast, captured Portuguese slave ships, and sold the Negroes in the Spanish Indies. Since Portugal was an old friend and ally of England, this was piracy. In 1564 Hawkins was off again to Africa on a larger venture. A Negro town was attacked and a large number of its people taken and sold in Spanish ports of the mainland Caribbean shore. Carrying home great store of precious metal and gems, Hawkins stopped to visit the French Protestants at Fort Caroline in Florida, as noted above. After his return he was given a coat of arms displaying a chained blackamoor.

In 1567 Hawkins sailed with a squadron of six ships, one or two provided by the Queen, with his young kinsman Francis Drake as an officer. Again an African town was taken and burned, Portuguese ships were plundered, and the black cargo was disposed of on the Spanish Main. As he had done before, he claimed duress of storm when he entered Spanish ports and did so when he came to Vera Cruz (September 16, 1568). It chanced that the next day a Spanish fleet of thirteen ships entered the port, bringing the new viceroy. In the fight that followed the English ships were taken, except the two smallest. Hawkins escaped in one, Drake in the other.

5. *DNB* for personal data.

Thereafter Drake became the scourge of the Spanish Indies, hero to England, pirate to Spain because the two countries were not at war and were maintaining diplomatic offices. In 1572 Drake captured Nombre de Dios, the Caribbean port to which the treasure of Peru was carried across the Isthmus of Panama. He crossed the land to have his first sight of the Pacific Ocean, and took so many tons of silver that he was able to carry away only a part.[6]

In 1577 Drake left Plymouth to begin his voyage around the world, the purpose being to harry the Spanish settlements along the unprotected Pacific coast. When he passed the Strait of Magellan and turned north along the coast of Chile, he was reduced to one ship, the *Golden Hind*. At his leisure he followed the coast north to Guatulco on the coast of Oaxaca in New Spain, taking an occasional ship or port for provision or treasure. In the farther course of the famous voyage he reconnoitred the coast of California that Cabrillo had discovered a generation earlier and which had been occasionally seen by a Spanish galleon returning from Manila.

"The fair and good bay" entered by the *Golden Hind* to prepare for the long voyage across the Pacific is held to be the small harbor north of San Francisco called Drakes Bay.[7] The natives flocked to the landing to greet the visitors and engage in an exchange of civilities. They have been identified as Coast Miwoks, living in rude villages. They took fish and fowl in estuaries and streams, and ranged inland to collect seeds, such as acorns, and to hunt. The English made an excursion inland and reported herds of deer ranging up to a thousand, perhaps overestimated. These probably were the tule or California elk (*Cervus*), congregating in good sized herds in the interior valleys. Drake named the land Nova Albion, took formal possession for the Queen, and sailed on to the Moluccas.

The *Golden Hind* returned to Plymouth in September 1580, its captain and crew national heroes. The Spanish ambassador in London demanded redress and punishment for breaking the

6. John Oxenham, who had taken part in this voyage, returned in 1575 to cross the isthmus, was captured, taken to Lima, and hanged as a pirate. In the nineteenth century Charles Kingsley used the event in *Westward Ho*, a romance of English virtues against Spanish cruelty and bigotry.

7. Wagner, *Sir Francis Drake's Voyage*. Francis P. Farquhar and Walter A. Starr, "Drake in California: A Review of the Evidence and the Testimony of the Plate of Brass," *Calif. Hist. Soc. Quart.*, 36 (March 1957), pp. 21–34, on the location of the harbor.

peace, pillage, and injuries. Elizabeth considered a while, and knighted Drake, making it clear that England was ready to challenge Spain.

Drake led another fleet against the Spanish Indies in 1585, Martin Frobisher being vice-admiral. Santo Domingo was taken and partly destroyed, the mainland naval base of Cartagena was pillaged, and on the return St. Augustine was burned.

THE NORTHWEST PASSAGE
PROMOTED AND ATTEMPTED

Learned Englishmen discoursed on the position of the British Isles with regard to the Arctic seas and as to the northern extremities of New and Old World continents. The prospect of a sea passage through America had become dim. It was time to try Arctic waters again for a way to Orient. Cartographers made maps and globes that gave generous room to a circumpolar sea, which it was thought, or hoped, would have open water. Stories were circulating that a ship of this or that nation had thus returned from the South Sea.

Humphrey Gilbert, a Devon gentleman who had gone to school at Eton and Oxford where he learned world geography, became absorbed in the propect of a northwest passage. While on leave from the war in Ireland in 1566 he addressed a petition to the Queen concerning "discovery of a passage by the North to go to Cataia," meaning China. He was sent back to Ireland, to serve with distinction and severity and be knighted in 1570. Between war and politics he found time to elaborate by 1574 the *Discourse of a Discoverie for a New Passage to Cataia* arguing the feasibility of such a route, its advantage of greatly reduced distance, the superior location of England for the northern route, the prior claim of England by the discovery of Cabot, the profit England would gain from the trade, and the opportunity it would give to plant colonies of poor Englishmen along the way. The *Discourse* was drawn up in discussions with a London group that met for that purpose, and was printed in 1576.

Elizabethan England had turned to mastery of the seas. Drake was about to start on his voyage around the world. London enthusiasts of the Northwest passage venture collected funds, secured license, and got Martin Frobisher, one

of their group, to be captain of the expedition, which was
chronicled by George Best in his *True Discourse,* printed in
1578.[8]

Frobisher sailed from the Thames estuary in June 1576 with
two barks of thirty tons and a pinnace of ten. The pinnace
was lost in the first storm, one of the barks shortly defected,
and Frobisher went on with the other and eighteen men.
Landfall was made in Frobisher Bay (then named Frobisher's
Strait) at the southeast of Baffin Island, thought to be mainland Asia, the south side of the bay considered to be the north
coast of America. The Queen afterward named the land
found Meta Incognita, the unknown limits, noncommittal as
to its connection.

There were natives "in small boats of leather," one being
taken. In high summer the land was bright with flowers and
green with grass. They happened upon some black rock
"which by the weight seemed to be some kind of metal." The
natives came ready to trade, from which Stefansson surmised
that the local Eskimos had previous contact with Europeans.
The bark turned back without further exploration. The heavy
stone "was brought to certain Goldfinders in London, to make
assay thereof, who indeed found it to hold gold, and that very
richly" (Best). Other assayers found nothing of value in the
samples but word got around of discovery of gold ore. A company was chartered, called the Cathay Company, to carry on
discovery and develop gold mining in the supposed strait
found by Frobisher.

The hope of more of the same gold ore there to be found, kindled
a greater opinion in the hearts of many to advance the voyage again.
Whereupon, preparation was made for a new voyage against the
year following, and the Captain more specially directed by commission for the searching more of this gold ore than for the searching
any further discovery of the passage [Best].

The Queen provided a ship of two hundred tons and two
small ones. Supposedly experienced "goldfinders" having been
employed, the second expedition took its departure at the
end of May 1577. The place where the heavy stone had been
found yielded nothing. Islands and coast of the bay were

8. In Vilhjalmur Stefánsson, ed., *The Three Voyages of Martin
Frobisher,* in which the Arctic explorer and friend of Eskimos gives a
fully documented and largely annotated study and the original text.

searched and a locality found on the north shore where they thought there was ore. Two hundred tons were loaded before ice began to form and gave notice that it was time to leave, taking along an Eskimo man, woman, and child to be exhibited in England. Best gave a fair description of the treeless country, fauna, and Eskimo habits, their houses partly subterranean, roofed by whale ribs covered with sealskins. He told of two breeds of dogs, the larger kind used to draw sleds, the lesser sort fattened and kept for eating.

The third expedition left Harwich in May 1578 in fifteen ships, carrying a hundred persons who were to settle in Meta Incognita. The instructions were to bring back two thousand tons of the gold ore. They passed through the English Channel and around Cape Clear of Ireland where they "met with a great current from out of the Southwest" and rode this part of the Gulf Stream north. Bearing to west, they came to land in the south of Greenland. Failing to recognize it, Frobisher claimed possession for the Queen and named it West England. The natives were "very like those of Meta Incognita." As they fled in fear of the ships they left a box of nails and "other things artificially wrought, whereby it appeareth that they have trade with some civil people," a note that Europeans were still going to Greenland.

From Greenland they had fair wind with which they sailed west through fog and ice drift. They met many great whales, one of which was struck by a ship, so "that the ship stood still, and stirred neither forward nor backward." On July 2 they came to a headland at the south of Frobisher Bay, the bay in Best's words being "full of walls, mountains and bulwarks of ice," the summer drift of bergs and floes. A ship loaded with lumber for building struck an iceberg and "received such a blow with a rock of ice, that she sank down therewith in sight of the whole fleet." Fog and mist closing in, the ships drifted apart, some getting into "the mistaken strait," perhaps Hudson Strait, which Best surmised as the one they should have taken in the search for the western passage. It was near the end of July when the ships reassembled in Frobisher Bay.

Summer was well advanced before work began. There was no more "ore" where they had collected it the year before. By the time they had located another site they had little more than a month in which to load the ships. Lacking the lumber lost in the ship that had rammed an iceberg, it was out of the question to stay the winter. Frobisher stayed into October 1578, loading rocks as late as he dared. The ore proved worthless.[9] The Company of Cathay was bankrupt and Frobisher returned to action in Ireland and then against Spain.

The mining camp of the third voyage was found in 1861–1862 by Charles Francis Hall at Kodlunarn on the north side of Frobisher Bay. The Eskimo name, meaning "white man's island," still carried the memory of the sixteenth-century episode. Hall found trenches, houses, foundations, bits of glass, tiles, and pottery, and was told folklore about the visitors. In 1927 the Rawson-MacMillan Expedition of the Field Museum of Chicago confirmed the site.[10]

A REPORT OF 1578 ON
THE NEWFOUNDLAND FISHERIES

Knowledge of the Newfoundland fisheries being meager, the elder Richard Hakluyt in 1578 asked a well-informed gentleman of Kent, Anthony Parkhurst, to write about them.[11] Parkhurst had been an officer in Hawkins' 1564 voyage that had visited the French in Florida and returned by way of Newfoundland. He was asked about what he had learned, having been in Newfoundland again for four years past "searching the harbors, creeks, and havens, and also the land much more than ever an Englishman hath done." He did not explain why an English gentleman had gone four times, inferred to have been in the seventies, to observe the cod fishing, the coast, and the land.

During the period of his visits the number of English ships had grown from thirty to fifty but was still smaller than that from France and Spain:

I am informed that there are above 100 sails of Spaniards that come to take cod (who make all wet, and do dry it when they come home), besides 20 or 30 more that come from Biscay to kill whale for train [oil]. These be better appointed for shipping and furniture of munition than any nation saving the Englishmen, who commonly are lords of the harbors where they fish and do use all

9. Appendix 10 in Stefánsson has opinions of geologists as to the black minerals found in Frobisher Bay.

10. Stefánsson, Appendix 9, for the Hall findings and those of the Field Museum.

11. The letter was published by the younger Hakluyt in the *Navigations and Voyages* (in vol. V of the 1927 London edition).

strangers' "help in fishing if need require, according to an old custom of the country, which thing they do willingly, so that you take nothing from them more than a boat [load] or twain of salt, in respect of your protection of them against rovers or other violent intruders, who do often put them from good harbors, ... As touching their tonnage, I think it [Spanish] may be near five or six thousand ton. But of Portugals there are not lightly above 50 sails, and they make all wet in like sort, whose tonnage may amount to three thousand tons and not upwards. Of the French nation and Britons [Bretons] are about one hundred and fifty sails, the most of their shipping is very small, not past forty tons, among which some are great and reasonably well appointed, better than the Portugals and not as the Spaniards, and the burden of them may be some 7000 tons. Their shipping is from all parts of France and Brittany, and the Spaniards from most parts of Spain, the Portugals from Aviero and Viana, and from 2 or 3 ports more. The trade that our nation hath to Iceland maketh that the English are not there in such numbers as other nations."

Thus three hundred and fifty ships were estimated as fishing for cod at that time. The Spanish and Portuguese were said to do all their fishing on the banks ("making wet fish"). A score or more Spanish Basque whale ships engaged in rendering train oil, probably carrying on the operation on shipboard. It would seem that something like twenty thousand persons came annually for cod and whales.

The English, though least numerous, by "old custom" were lords and protectors of the harbors. For a modest fee in salt, willingly given, they took charge of defense against "rovers or other violent intruders." That the authority was by custom suggests it may have derived from the discovery of the fishing grounds by men of Bristol. The fishing was open to all as the landings appear also to have been. The English were in charge of keeping the peace by common consent, not as representatives of a nation state.

Parkhurst knew the coastal waters as teeming with large cod, small fish like smelt (capelins used for bait?), flounder, lobsters, and divers shellfish. Great auks were taken in large numbers, especially on one island (Funk): "At one island named Penguin we may drive them on a plank into our ship as many as shall lade her. These birds are also called Penguins, and cannot fly; there is more meat in one of these than in a goose. French victual themselves always with these birds." (The usage of Cartier's time continued.)

His familiarity with the land extended from the east coast of Newfoundland to Nova Scotia. Roses were as common as brambles in England. Berries of several kinds were in great quantity. There was abundance of birch, alder, and willow. Fir was mainly used for timber, that at Cape Breton and southward growing to sizes large enough for masts of any ship. At one place (in Nova Scotia?) he saw an animal like a camel from a distance and knew by its tracks that it had cloven hooves (cow moose).

THE PLANS OF SIR HUMPHREY GILBERT
AND THEIR RESULTS

Frobisher was on his first voyage to Frobisher Strait in 1576 when Sir Humphrey Gilbert's *Discourse* on the passage to Cathay was printed. In 1577 Frobisher made his second voyage while Gilbert expanded his idea: "how Her Majesty might annoy the King of Spain by fitting out a fleet of war-ships under pretense of a voyage of discovery, and so fall upon the enemy's shipping and destroy his trade in Newfoundland and the West Indies." [12] The two countries were still officially at peace. Drake was starting on his voyage to harass the Spanish on the Pacific coast. Gilbert would also be a war hawk, using the pretense of discovery to destroy Spanish trade in the West Indies and Newfoundland, as Drake had been doing in the West Indies. Newfoundland however was visited only during summer codfishing and whaling, involving only a very small and private element of Spanish shipping. Why then Newfoundland, here appearing for the first time in Gilbert's designs?

In 1578 Frobisher found that the ore in Baffin Island was worthless and Parkhurst, writing of the Newfoundland fisheries, gave a moderate account of the land. In that year Gilbert secured a charter for a term of six years, authorizing him to engage in planting and discovery, limited to "heathen lands not actually possessed of any Christian prince." Gilbert asked for a cover for his designs and got it. The fleet thus dispatched, sailed south in the direction of the tropics, and was met and defeated by a Spanish force off the Cape Verde Islands.

Gilbert took no further action until the term of his charter

12. Quotation from the State Papers, *DNB*.

was about to expire. By its license he was to have a tract of his selection, with a radius of two hundred leagues. The only direction where he might find such, not in actual Spanish or Portuguese possession, was on the Atlantic Coast of North America. He sailed from Plymouth in June 1583 with five ships, the largest turning back after two days. These were no warships with which to annoy the King of Spain nor would they search for the passage to Cathay. "It seemed first very doubtful by what way to shape our course, and to begin our intended discovery, either from the South Northward, or from the North Southward" (Hayes).[13] It was hardly proper to speak of an intended discovery, this North American coast being familiar. The decision was to head directly for New-foundland, "a multitude of ships repairing there for fish, we should be relieved abundantly with many necessities, which after fishing ended, they might well spare" and then "proceed southward and follow still the sun until we arrived at places more temperate to our content." In other words, they would cross the Atlantic as hundreds of fishing ships did each sum-mer, get supplies from some of them, and head south at the end of the fishing season to a temperate coast.

Late in July they came to the Grand Banks, French and Portuguese in "notable trade of fishing upon these banks, where are some sometimes an hundred or more sails." Ice-bergs, "mountains of ice," were drifting in from the north. On July 30 they sighted land, "nothing appeared unto us but hideous rocks and mountains, bare of trees, and void of any green herbs." Turning south, "we had sight of an island named Penguin, of a fowl there breeding in abundance almost incredible, which cannot fly, their wings not able to carry their body, being very large (not much less than a goose) and exceeding fat; which the French now use to take without difficulty upon that Island, and to barrel them up with salt." (Funk Island was a regular place of provision with auks from early years and continued thus to be exploited to their ex-tinction in the nineteenth century.)

The ships had become separated, the forty-ton *Swallow* meanwhile plundering a fishing vessel, the ten-ton pinnace, the *Squirrel*, awaiting outside St. John's Harbor and denied

13. Several relations were collected by Hakluyt (*Navigations and Voy-ages*, vol. VI, pp. 1–78), the one by Edward Hayes most explicit and in-formed. The quotations are taken from it.

entrance by the local England merchants who were in charge
of security. On the arrival of Gilbert and his presentation of
the royal commission the four ships were welcomed into the
harbor.

On August 5 Gilbert assembled the captains and officers of
the thirty ships then in St. John's harbor—English, Spanish,
and Portuguese—read the Queen's commission, took possession for England, and parceled out grounds for drying fish.
The ships present were levied upon for supplies. During the
two weeks in the harbor the "mineral man and refiner," a
Saxon, was sent to make diligent search for metals, the results
of which well satisfied the general, who cautioned that they
be kept secret from the Portuguese, Biscayans, and Frenchmen.

Hayes compiled a relation of the commodities found in
Newfoundland or which might be produced there. The intended colony would depend largely on what had "become the
most famous fishing of the world," taking cod and whales.
Herring, exceeding those of Norway, had not yet been exploited nor had any of other divers and delicate kinds of fish.
The climate was severe and the winters long, but the summers
were warm and grass and herbs grew rapidly. English merchants "carried sheep there for fresh victual and had them
raised exceeding fat in less than three weeks." Peas sown in
May were gathered in August and were served to the general.

The company having been diminished by desertion, death,
and sickness, the general sent the *Swallow* home. On August
20 the *Delight* of 120 tons, the *Golden Hind* of forty, and the
Squirrel of ten tons left St. John's to seek lands to the south,
the general choosing to go in the smallest as "most convenient
to discover upon the coast." The first objective was Sable Island (Isle of Sablon):

Whither we were determined to go upon intelligence we had of a
Portugal, (during our abode in St. John's) who was himself present,
when the Portugals (above thirty years past) did put into the same
Island both Neat [cattle] and Swine to breed, which were since exceedingly multiplied. This seemed unto us very happy tidings, to
have in an Island lying so near unto the main, which we intended
to plant upon, such store of cattle, whereby we might at all times
conveniently be relieved of victual and served of store for breed.

The check on the livestock of Sable Island brought disaster.
The *Delight* went aground on the "flats" of Sable Island with

the loss of a hundred men, including the German miner and the samples of ore. (One boat got to land where there were good trees and salmon fishing [Nova Scotia] and was rescued later by a Basque ship.) The remaining two ships started back to England. The last sight of the ten-ton *Squirrel* was in mid-ocean, "the General sitting abaft with a book in his hand, cried out to us in the *Hind* (so oft as we did approach within hearing). We are as near to heaven by sea as by land."

Sir Humphrey Gilbert did not undertake to find the passage to Cathay for which he had argued in his *Discourse*. He sailed directly to Newfoundland, first to stock up on great auks as was the custom, then to St. John's harbor where, as usual, a number of ships of different nationalities were gathered. Here he took possession by authority of his charter and sent out to discover ore, as Frobisher had done on Baffin Island. He expected to make Newfoundland the first base and a part of the colony he was expecting to establish. Hayes wrote of the general's high spirits persisting after the loss of the *Delight*. "For whereas the General had never before good conceit of these North parts of the world: now his mind was wholly fixed upon the New found land." What he had seen was "enough for us all, and that we needed not to seek any further." The maritime resources were familiar and had been exploited for a good many years. The party saw no Indians nor knew anything of the possibilities of the fur trade. That Gilbert thought to have found in Newfoundland the end of his search means that he believed he had had proof from his Saxon miner of wealth of precious metals.

DISCOVERY OF DAVIS STRAIT

The northwest passage continued to be of special interest to a group of educated Englishmen who were brought up on the classical idea of the universal ocean girdling all continents. They knew at least roughly the position of the major land masses about the globe. They estimated correctly that the shortest distance from Europe to the Orient would be by a polar route. Climates, their classical education had taught them, were arranged as belts of latitude from equatorial heat to polar cold. However, explorers had found that as heat was not great in the tropics, so the summers were warm in high latitudes, as was well known of American coasts, and in some parts the winters were mild, as in Iceland. The long summer days were held to warm the polar regions. It was in summer when ships have continuous light that the polar sea would be crossed. Icebergs and floes would be encountered but were frozen fresh water. The salt ocean, it was thought, did not freeze.

Merchants and moneyed gentry of Devon and London joined forces in 1583 to back the search for a sea passage through Arctic latitudes, with John Davis of Dartmouth, a skilled and schooled navigator, to lead the exploration. His three voyages in 1585, 1586, and 1587 held to that objective.[14]

In the voyage of 1585, made in two barks of fifty and thirty-five tons, the first land sighted was the barren coast of south-eastern Greenland. The ships turned south to round the cape (Farewell) and then went north along the west coast, named Land of Desolation by Davis. At 64° "they came to many fair sounds and green inlets and many green and pleasant isles and were greeted warmly by natives who came up to them in canoes." (This had been the Western Settlement in Norse time; today it is Godthaab district.) The great fjord was named Gilbert Sound after his friend Adrian, brother of Humphrey Gilbert. They continued north almost to the Arctic Circle, where they found an abundance of driftwood, many seals, and stunted birches and willows. (This was the southern part of Nordrsetr of Norse days, to which the Vikings had gone in summer to collect timbers of driftwood and to hunt seals.) On August 1 they stood northwest, bearing away from the land, and after five days came to a high land. (They had crossed Davis Strait to Cumberland Peninsula on Baffin Island.) Here there were low-growing withes and flowers that resembled primroses, also white bears of monstrous bigness. To the south they entered many leagues into a great bay (Cumberland Sound). Dogs were heard howling on shore; "when we came to land the dogs came presently to our boat, very gently," prick-eared, bushy tailed, wolf-like. There were two sleds, one of wood, the other all of whalebone. An oven-like structure held a miniature canoe, an image of wood, a bird carved of

14. The accounts published by Hakluyt, *Principal Navigations*. Davis wrote a major treatise on navigation, *The Seaman's Secrets*, first printed in 1594, which went through eight editions. His *The Worldes Hydrographical Description*, published in 1595, reviewed his voyages. Hakluyt Society (Vol. 59, 1880), edited by Captain, later Admiral, Albert Markham. Sir Clements Markham, *The Life of John Davis*, 1889.

bone, and the like (good Eskimo items). The season being advanced and having determined that they were in an enclosed bay, they sailed home.

The second voyage (1586) was by four ships from Dartmouth, two taking the direct course to the Eskimo settlements (about Godthaab). The fortnight spent there in July is reported in detail as to country, fauna, and Eskimo customs and subsistence, and a vocabulary of forty words. The welcome was repeated, but became annoyance as the natives, prizing iron, turned to pilfering and prying nails out of the boats. Continuing the voyage they fell upon a mighty quantity of ice, in contrast to the summer before. At the beginning of August they got into a good harbor (Sukkertoppen at 65°, according to both Markhams), the weather hot, with a plague of mosquitoes. The large ship was sent home from here, Davis leaving the Greenland coast August 12 to cross again the strait that was to bear his name. The crossing was made in two days to the Baffin shore, not many miles north of where he had been the year before.

For the next fortnight they sailed south from 67° to 57° and came to a very fair harbor 56° on August 28. They were then midway of the Labrador coast, with "very fair woods on both sides," great store of fowl and of cod. They continued south on September 1 in good weather, stopping at 54°30' to try fishing; "the hook was no sooner overboard but presently a fish was taken," the largest and fattest cod anyone had seen. On September 4 "we anchored in a very good road among great store of Isles, the country low land and very full of fair woods. To the north of this place eight leagues we had a perfect hope of the passage, finding a mighty great sea passing between two lands west" (Hamilton Inlet). The wind however being dead against them and the season advanced, they prepared to sail home. Two days farther south along the coast, a ship's party ashore was attacked; "the brutish people of this country lay secretly lurking in the woods, and upon the sudden assaulted our men." Davis had seen a good deal of Eskimos; these were a different people, perhaps Algonquian Naskapis, later known as occupying southern Labrador. The ship returned to England at the beginning of October.

Davis addressed a letter on his return to William Sanderson, saying "I have now experience of much of the Northwest part of the world, and have brought the passage to that likelihood, as I am assured it must be in one of four places, or else not at all." Davis Strait and Hamilton Sound would have been two. In any case there would be certain profit, as in sealskins and other skins.

The third voyage started from Dartmouth on May 19, 1587, and reached Gilbert Sound (Godthaab) June 16. From June 21 to 30 they followed the Greenland coast north to 72°15′ (vicinity of Upernivik), the most northerly point reached. The June 30 entry reads: "For these last 4 days the weather hath been extreme hot and very calm, the Sun being 5 degrees above the horizon at midnight." Thus far the sea was open. They turned west (across Baffin Bay) and after two days encountered "a mighty bank of ice" through which they were unable to find an opening. On July 19 they had sight of the mountainous peninsula of Baffin Island, finding that they were in the strait previously visited, and then entered the gulf to the south (Cumberland Sound). The islands at its entry Davis named the Earl of Cumberland's Isles; the name Cumberland has since been extended to both sound and peninsula. July 31 (62°) and August 1 (61°) they crossed the entry of a "gulf of second passage" (Hudson Strait), "a great bank of ice driven out of that gulf." The day before "an island of ice was carried by the force of the current as fast as our bark could sail." Pack ice had blocked their way at the north; as they sailed south along the Canadian shore they rode the Labrador current across Hudson Strait, freighted with icebergs in July.

On August 1 they came to the promontory at the north end of Labrador. On August 13 they were at 54° among many isles (vicinity of Hamilton Inlet again), and on the 15th "being in the latitude of 52 degrees 12 minutes and 16 leagues from the shore, we shaped our course for England." They were then out at sea east of the Strait of Belle Isle in waters frequented by cod fishermen and whalers, and shortly encountered a whaling ship. August 17: "This day upon the Bank we met a Biscayne bound either for the Grand Bay [Gulf of St. Lawrence west of the Strait of Belle Isle] or the passage [!]. He chased us." By another account, of John Janes, "we met a ship at sea, and as far as we could judge it was a Biscayne; we thought she went a fishing for whales; for in 52 degrees or thereabout we saw very many."

Davis did not go again to North American waters but continued to believe in the northwest passage. In his *Worldes*

Hydrographical Description (1595) he argued not only that the polar sea was navigable but that the inhabitants of polar lands "have a wonderful excellency and an exceeding prerogative above all nations of the earth, for they are in perpetual light and never know what darkness meaneth, by the benefit of twilight and full moons."

14
The
Roanoke Colony
(1584–1590)

Walter Raleigh, stepbrother of Humphrey Gilbert, was high
in the Queen's favors, with large estates in England and Ireland and the income of rich offices. He too was given a patent
like that of his brother, to plant a colony in lands that were
not in the possession of any Christian prince. Raleigh provided
the largest ship to Gilbert's expedition, which however for unknown reasons turned back at the start of the voyage. After
Gilbert's death Raleigh sent a party to reconnoiter the coast
midway between Newfoundland and Spanish Florida, followed
by a series of voyages that were intended to establish an
English colony to bear the name Virginia. What they found
and described provides the earliest English observations of the
nature of that country and its people.[1]

RECONNAISSANCE OF 1584

Two barks sailed in April 1584—Amadas and Barlow captains;
Simon Ferdinando, an Azorian, pilot; the route the usual one

1. The five voyages were published by Hakluyt, *Principal Navigations*
(vol. VI, pp. 121–226 of the 1927 London edition). Professor David Quinn
has collected and annotated the documents in a memoir of a thousand
pages, *The Roanoke Voyages (1584–1590)* (Hakluyt Society, 2d Ser., volumes
104 and 105, London, 1958).

by way of the Canaries and West Indies. Barlow reported to Raleigh that on July 4 "we arrived upon the coast which we supposed to be a continent and firm land, and we sailed along the same a hundred and twenty English miles, before we could find any entrance or river issuing into the sea. The first that appeared unto us we entered, though not without some difficulty." Having sighted the coast in southern North Carolina they followed it north beyond Cape Hatteras, keeping a safe distance away from the Outer Banks, the chain of sandbars that extends for two hundred miles, screening Pamlico and Albemarle sounds from the ocean. The inlets across the banks are subject to change by storm and drift of sand. The one they found was to the north of Cape Hatteras, north of present Oregon Inlet, and almost opposite Roanoke Island.[2] This passage, deep enough only for ships of least size, was known as Port Ferdinando or Hatarask Harbour, long since blocked by drift of sand. The description of the land began:

The land very sandy and low towards the water side, but so full of grapes, as the very beating and surge of the sea overflowed them, [grapes] climbing towards the tops of high cedars that I think in all the world the like abundance not to be found. . . . We passed from the sea side towards the tops of those hills next adjoining, being but of mean height [dunes], and from thence we beheld the Sea on both sides to the North and to the South, finding no end any of both ways. The land lay stretching itself to the West, which after we found to be but an island of twenty leagues long and not above six miles broad. Under the banks or hill whereon we stood, we beheld the valleys replenished with goodly cedar trees, and having discharged our harquebus shot, a flock of Cranes (the most part white) arose under us, with such a cry redoubled by many echoes as if an army of men had shouted all together. This land had many goodly woods . . . the highest and reddest Cedars of the world [also pines, cypress, sassafras and other trees].

The cranes by their description were whooping crane, the only ones of such plumage and cry. Red cedar and cypress perhaps were first misnamed here in English, as they still are, for *Juniperus* and *Taxodium*. The name sassafras is Spanish and implies knowledge of Spanish Florida. As was usual with

2. David Sick, *The Outer Banks of North Carolina 1594-1957* (Chapel Hill, 1958), an account by a resident on the nature and changes of the banks.

early European visitors to North America, the sight of grapevines climbing trees had admiring notice. The description
given as though of the Outer Banks applies to Roanoke Island
and surroundings.

On the third day the first natives were seen, approaching in
a small boat. One of them "never making any show of fear or
doubt" was taken aboard and given food and presents. Returning to his dugout "he fell to fishing, and in less than
half an hour he had laden his boat as deep as it could swim,
with which he came again to the point of the land and there
he divided his fish into two parts, appointing one part to the
ship and the other to the pinnace; after he had (as much as
he might) requited the former benefits received, he departed
out of our sight." The next day they were visited by a chief
and forty or more men, "very handsome and goodly people,
and in their behavior as mannerly and civil as any of Europe."

Throughout the six weeks' visit the natives were hospitable.
"We were entertained with all love and kindness, and with as
much bounty (after their manner) as they could possibly de-
vise. . . . We found the people most gentle, loving, and faith-
ful, void of all guile and treason, and such as lived after the
manner of the golden rule." With some nearby tribes they
were friends, with others foes.

Their hosts had a village on "an Island which they called
Roanoake, distant from the harbour by which we entered
seven leagues; and at the north end thereof there was a village
of nine houses, built of cedar, and fortified round about with
sharp trees to keep out their enemies, and the entrance into it
made like a turn pike [stile] very artificially." The palisaded
village may have been of multifamily houses, the one in which
they were entertained by the "Queen" described as having five
rooms. Here the guests were well served with food and drink
from "earthen pots, very large, white and sweet" and dishes
made of "wooden platters of sweet timber." The drink was
water sodden with spices, one of which was sassafras.

Food was brought daily to the visitors, "bucks, conies, fish,
divers kinds of fruits, melons, walnuts, cucumbers, gourds,
pease, and divers roots, and fruits very excellent good, and
corn of their country, which is very white, fair and well tasted,
and grows three times in five months." Corn planted in May
was ripe in July, that planted in June ripe in August, that
of July in September. "They cast the corn into the ground,

breaking a little of the soft turf with a wooden mattock or pickaxe." Beans were "very fine, of divers colors, and wonderful plenty." This was the maize-bean-squash complex of Indian farmers of the Eastern Woodlands.

Travel about the tidewater sounds was by dugout boats. "Their manner of making their boats is this: they burn down some great tree or take such as are wind fallen and putting myrrh and rosin upon one side thereof they set fire into it, and when it hath burned it hollow, they cut out the coal with their shells, and wherever they would burn it deeper or wider they lay on their gums which burneth away the timber, and by this means they fashion very fine boats, and such as will transport twenty men. Their oars are like scoops, and many times they set with long poles as the depth serveth," that is, poling in shallow water, paddling in deep water.

The women wore bracelets of pearls and pendants of copper (these, perhaps from Lake Superior). The English traded for "chamois, buffe, and deer skins," chamois being soft dressed buckskin, buffe probably buffalo hides, perhaps by long distance Indian trade. Bison were common west of the Appalachians but were known also in the Atlantic coast plain at somewhat later time.

The Indians had some iron tools, made from spikes and nails of a ship wrecked twenty years before.

Roanoke Island lies in the passage between Albemarle and Pamlico sounds and was the base from which the visitors learned about country and people. They had come to the most southernly Algonquian tribes, living on arms of the two great sounds that were drowned river systems flooded by the sea during post-glacial rise, and sheltered from storms at sea by the Outer Banks. It was good country for fishing, hunting, and some farming, and the Englishmen enjoyed the hospitality of people living by practicing the simple virtues. Farther south a different and hostile people were named as living on the River Neus (Neuse), probably Catawbas of Siouan speech, whom they would have found to be hospitable. On their return they took along two youths from Roanoke, Manteo and Wachese, to be trained as interpreters.[3]

Barlow's report was written, as Professor Quinn has pointed out, to aid Raleigh in promoting his colony. Overuse of adjective aside, it was perceptive observation.

3. The two modern towns of the island bear their names.

FIRST ATTEMPT AT SETTLEMENT
(1585–1586)

Sir Richard Grenville, another gentleman mariner and pirate of Southwest England, brought seven ships and six hundred men to Roanoke in 1585. He took the usual route by way of the Canaries and Dominica and landed in Puerto Rico and Española to raid and trade. Also he took thence plants of sugarcane and bananas for cultivation in the colony-to-be. A stop was made at the Caicos Islands for salt and to hunt seals (the long-gone monk seal). The mainland coast was reached south of Cape Fear and followed to the inlet of Wococon in the Outer Banks, where some ships ran aground in the shoals.[4]

While the ships were being refloated Grenville took boats into Pamlico Sound for exploration, getting to Secotan, principal settlement of the Secotan Algonquian tribe, in the freshwater estuary of Pamlico River (fig. 21). Having been well entertained here, he went on to destroy another town and burn cornfields in reprisal for the loss of a silver cup, thereby beginning the Indian troubles. The fleet moved north on July 27 to the inlet of Hatarask or Port Ferdinando, as it had been named the year before. Grenville took more than a hundred men to Roanoke Island to begin building a fort and then sailed home with the rest, capturing a Spanish treasure ship on the way home.

Ralph Lane, a veteran of the Irish wars, was left in charge at Roanoke. A letter to Hakluyt (September 1585) praised the prospect:

We have discovered the main to be the goodliest soil under the cope [vault] of heaven, so abounding with sweet trees, that bring such sundry and most pleasant gums, grapes of such greatness, yet wild, as France, Spain nor Italy hath no greater, so many sorts of Apothecary drugs, such several kinds of flax, and one kind like silk, the same gathered of a grass as common there as grass is here. And now within these few days we have found here a Guinea wheat, whose ear yieldeth corn for bread, 400 upon one ear, and the cane maketh very good and perfect sugar. . . . [The country is] very well peopled and towned, though savagely, and the climate so

4. Quinn, *The Roanoke Voyages,* p. 184, placed the inlet, since closed, across Ocracoke Island, southwest of Hatteras. Sick located it farther south as the present Ocracoke Inlet.

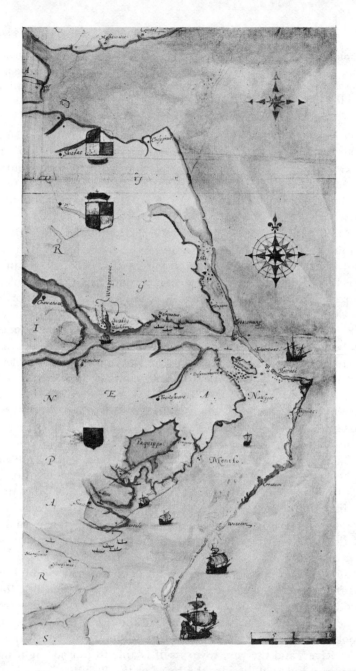

FIG. 21. Water color map of Albemarle and Pamlico sounds by John White. *The American Drawings of John White, 1577–1590*, edited by Hulton and Quinn, 1964. (Reproduced by courtesy of the Trustees of the British Museum.)

wholesome that we have not had one sick since we touched land
here. To conclude, if Virginia had but horses and kine in some
reasonable proportion, I dare assure myself, being inhabited with
English, no realm in Christendom were comparable to it.[5]

The advertisement was large exaggeration. The sandy and
marshy coast plain was not highly attractive for English or
other agriculture or for livestock. Indian corn in time would
become the important breadstuff for European settlers but not
a source of sugar. There was no flax. His silk grass probably
was *Yucca*.

After his return to England in 1586 Lane gave Raleigh a
rambling account of the ten months the party had remained
and explored.[6] It had become apparent that Roanoke Island
was accessible only by shallow inlet through the Outer Banks,
impassable to most ships. An exploration had been made north
to Chesapeake Bay to the vicinity of Norfolk, using a shallow
and hazardous channel, probably through Currituck Sound
and Dismal Swamp. "The territory and soil of the Chesepians
(being distant fifteen miles from the [sea] shore) was for ples-
antness of seat, for temperature of climate, for fertility of
soil, and for the commodity of the Sea, besides multitudes of
bears (being excellent good victual), with great woods of
sassafras and walnut trees, is not to be excelled by any other."
The relocation on Chesapeake Bay was not carried out.

The fort at the north end of Roanoke Island looked out on
Albemarle Sound, arms of which reach far into the coast
plain. Along the northern shore of the main sound was the
Indian "state" of Weapemeoc, six Indian towns named as
being of its jurisdiction. To the northwest was the long estuary
of the Chowan River. "To the northwest the farthest place of
our discovery was to Chawanook distant from Roanoke about
130 miles. Our passage thither lies through a broad sound, but
all fresh water, and the channel of a great depth, navigable for
good shipping, but out of channel full of shoals." There were
goodly cornfields on high land beside the tidal river. "Chawanook itself is the greatest province and Seignorie lying upon
that River, and the very town itself is able to put 700 fighting
men into the field, besides the force of the Province."

The middle estuary of Albemarle Sound, Roanoke River,

5. Hakluyt, *Principal Navigations*, vol. VI, p. 140.
6. *Ibid.*, pp. 141–162.

was most notable and famous. Its people were known as Morotocs (also Algonquians). Beyond them to the west were the Mangoaks, a different sort, having a strange mineral called *wassador*, of the color of copper but more soft and pale. "Of this metal the Mangoaks have so great store, by report of all the savages adjoining, that they beautify their houses with great plates of the same." The metal was said to be secured by bowls washed in rapid water. By some accounts this metal country lay far beyond that of the Mangoaks. The story related to a people in the interior where there was bedrock and swift water, perhaps the Tuscaroras of the Piedmont. Raleigh, like his brother Gilbert, was hoping to find gold and had also sent a German, supposed to be an expert in metals. The English had seen copper ornaments among the people on the coast. They thought perhaps this wassador of the west was gold. They imagined its recovery by panning and beating into great plates.

In the spring of 1586 Lane took a party up the Morotoc (Roanoke) River to discover the land of metal. As they crossed the land of the Morotocs "who had ever dealt kindly with us" they found that these "had retired themselves with their Crenepoes [women] and their corn within the main [land]: insomuch as having passed three days' voyage up the River we could not meet a man nor find a grain of corn in any of their Towns." They were out of food, suffered an Indian attack, and went back to Roanoke Island.

The time of hospitality was at an end. The English lived on what the Indians produced. They helped themselves to corn in the fields and in storage and to fish from Indian weirs. Lane complained that a conspiracy had spread from one Indian town to another until only the chief of Roanoke Island remained a friend, and even he was disposed "with all his Savages to have run away from us and to have left his ground in the Island unsowed, which if he had done, there had been no possibility in common reason (but by the immediate hand of God) that we could have been preserved from starving out of hand. For at that time we had no weirs for fish, neither had our men skill of the making of them, neither had we one grain of corn for seed to put into the ground." The chief was persuaded to set up weirs and to plant a quantity of ground sufficient for the whole company, "which put us in marvelous comfort, if we could pass from April until the beginning of

July [which was to have been the beginning of their harvest] that then a new supply out of England or else our own store would well enough maintain us." Meanwhile men were assigned to dig roots and take oysters. Others were sent south to Croatan, an island of the Outer Banks south of Cape Hatteras, to sustain themselves there and "keep watch, if any shipping came upon the coast."

On June 8 word was sent from Croatan that a great fleet of twenty-three sails had been sighted. Drake, returning with the loot and ransom of the Spanish Main, stopped by to see how the colony was doing.[7] He offered supplies or passage to England. Everyone chose to go home.

Shortly after the settlement on Roanoke Island had been abandoned Grenville came with the awaited supplies from England. He left fifteen men to guard the fort and went on to hunt Spanish prizes.

A BRIEFE AND TRUE REPORT . . .

Raleigh sent his tutor of Oxford days, Thomas Hariot, on the expedition of 1585, to be "a member of the colony, and there employed in discovering." Hariot prepared a prospectus of the country and its people for Raleigh, completed in February 1587, addressed to "the Adventurers, Favourers, and Welwillers" of the enterprise, and entitled *A briefe and true report of the new found land of Virginia: of the commodities there found and to be raised, as well merchantable as others.*[8] It gave advice to those who would plant in Virginia, "that you may generally know and learn what the country is; and thereupon how your dealing therein, if it proceeds, may return you profit and gain."

As to merchantable commodities, he began with items that would serve the English textile business. Like Lane, he thought silk grass (*Yucca*) a valuable fiber. The cultivation of silk, flax, and hemp was recommended. Of native dyes sumac yielded a black dye. As mordant he thought alum abundantly available. The planting of woad should be tried.

---

7. Professor Quinn noted that Drake brought three hundred Indians and a hundred Negroes for labor at Roanoke. They were not thus employed.

8. It was printed in 1588 and republished by Hakluyt.

Naval stores of pitch, tar, rosin, and turpentine could be made from such pines as grew on Roanoke Island. Red cedar was "a very sweet wood and fine timber" for making cabinets. Sassafras was "of most rare virtues in physic for the cure of many diseases" (the Spanish name was familiar in England before the translation of Monardes). Holly, maple, witchhazel, beech, and two kinds of walnut were of interest and recognized by English names.

Planting sugarcane and citrus fruits should be successful because Virginia was in the latitude of Mediterranean countries. Like other Europeans he was impressed by the wild grapes. "There are two kinds of grapes that the soil doth yield naturally; the one is small and sour of the ordinary bigness of ours in England; the other far greater and of himself luscious sweet. When they are planted and husbanded as they ought, a principal commodity of wine by them may be raised." (The latter probably referred to the muscadine grape, *Vitis rotundifolia,* native to those parts.)

Furs and skins would be available by trade. There were pearls in the rivers. From the interior there were reports of metals.

As to plants cultivated by the Indians, there was the Indian corn called maize in the West Indies, by the English Guinea wheat or Turkey wheat. (It had become known to Englishmen as a Negro staple on the African Guinea Coast.) Its grain was of the size of "ordinary English pease and not much different in form and shape, but of divers colors: some white, some red, some yellow, and some blue. All of them yielded a very white and sweet flour; being used according to his kind it maketh a very good bread." It was a grain of high yield, differing by kind as to time of maturing.

It is a grain of marvelous great increase: of a thousand, fifteen hundred, and some two thousand fold. There are three sorts, of which two are ripe in eleven and twelve weeks at the most, sometimes in ten after the time they are set, and are then of a height in a stalk about six or seven feet. The other sort is ripe in fourteen, and is about ten foot high: of the stalks some bear four heads, some three, some one, and some two; every head containing five, six, or seven hundred grains, within a few more or less. Of these grains, besides bread, the inhabitants make victual, either by parching them, or seething them whole until they be broken, or boiling the flour with water into a pap.

To the maize-beans-squash complex of Indian cultivation Hariot added two more plants, grown as food for their seeds: (1) "There is also another great herb, in form of a Marigold, about six feet in height, the head with the flower is a span in breadth. Some take it to be *Planta solis.* Of the seeds thereof they make both a kind of bread and broth." This was the cultivated sunflower, which was grown largely by Indians of the Eastern Woodlands. (2) A tall herb was grown for seed of which a thick broth and a good pottage were made. Ashes of its leaves supplied salt, and it was thought that the natives had no other salt. "We ourselves used the leaves also for pot herbs." Some thought the plant to be orach or what the Dutch called Melden. Both names apply to *Atriplex hortensis,* an ancient potherb of European gardens, tall growing, of the Chenopodiaceae—the Goosefoot family—to which spinach also belongs. Habit, leaf shape, and taste as cooked greens suggested to the visitors that the cultivated plant was orach or related to the latter. The Roanoke Indians grew it for the food value of its seeds. The English recognition of it as a Chenopod is correct. These bear a great number of small seeds in a terminal spike. One species, *Chenopodium nuttalli,* was an important cultigen in central Mexico for its ripe seeds, immature panicles, and cooked greens and is still grown by Indians there. The southern complex of cultivated annuals in Virginia I think included also a *Chenopodium* and sunflower.

Hariot described the manner of Indian planting as all seeds being "set or sowed, sometimes in grounds apart and severally by themselves, but for the most part together in one ground mixtly," the usual practice in all parts of Indian America. The loose, sandy ground was worked by wooden implements resembling mattocks or hoes with long handles, the trash heaped into piles and burned.

Then their setting or sowing is after this manner. First for their corn, beginning in one corner of the plot, with a pecker they make a hole, wherein they put four grains, with that care that they touch not one another (about an inch asunder) and cover them with the mold again: and so through out the whole plot, making such holes and using them after such manners; but with this regard, that they be made in ranks, every rank differing from other half a fathom or yard, and the holes also in every rank as much. By this means there is a yard spare ground between every hole: where according to discretion here and there, they set as many beans and pease; in divers places also among them seeds of Macocquer [squash], Melden, and Planta solis.

The ground being thus set . . . doth there yield in crop or off-come of corn, beans, and pease, at the least two hundred London bushels, besides the Macocquer, Melden, and Planta solis; when as in England forty bushels of our Wheat yielded out of such an acre is thought to be much.

Tobacco was grown in separate plots. It was used ceremonially, the English discovering that smoking it in pipes dissipated humors and kept them in good health. (This was the potent yellow-flowered *Nicotiana rustica,* a cultigen of Andean origin.)

A half-dozen roots were referred to by native names, for the most part as dug in wet ground, and none mentioned as cultivated. Chestnuts, acorns, and walnuts were collected in quantity and stored for use in winter. In addition to plums and cherries Hariot described the persimmon by the name medlar and used the name prickly pear for cactus (*Opuntia compressa*) growing in open, sandy places.

In the third part Hariot considered "such other things as are behooveful for those which shall plant and inhabit to know of." The natives were "not to be feared, but that they shall have cause both to fear and love us, that shall inhabit with them." The tribal organization under chiefs or weroances was described, as were ceremonies and religion.

Their towns are but small, near the Sea coast but few, some containing but ten or twelve houses; some 20, the greatest that we have seen hath been but of 30 houses; if they be walled, it is only done with barks of trees made fast to stakes, or else with poles only fixed upright, and close one by another.

Their houses are made of small poles, made fast at the tops in round form after the manner as is used in many arbors in our gardens of England, in most towns covered with barks from the tops of the houses down to the ground. The length of them is commonly double to the breadth, in some places they are but 12 and 16 yards long and in others some we have seen of four and twenty.

(Houses were of the form of Quonset huts, roof and walls forming an inverted U, most occupied by several families. They were shown in sketches by John White of the towns of Pomeioc and Secotan, which White and Hariot visited in 1585.

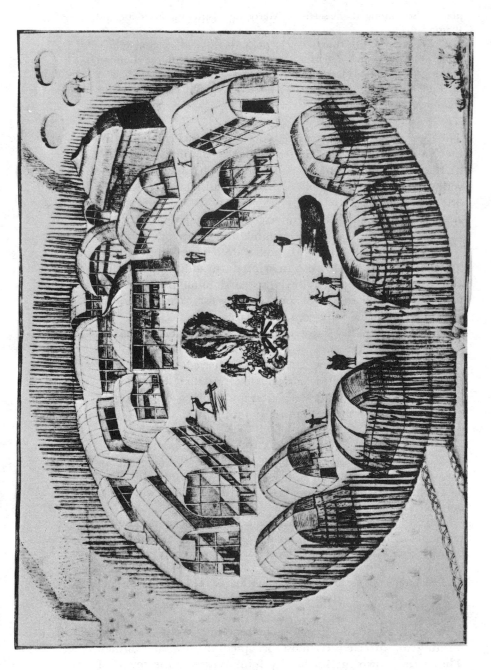

Their ripe corne.

Their greene corne.

Corne newly sprong.

Their sitting at meate.

prayer

The house wherin the Tombe of their Herounds standeth.

SECOTON

A Ceremony in their prayers w strange iestures and songs dansing about posts carued on the topps lyke mens faces.

FIG. 23. John White's water color of the Indian village of Secotan. (Reproduced by courtesy of the Trustees of the British Museum.)

His sketch of Secotan, the principal town on Pamlico River shows sleeping benches along the walls and outside of the village three cornfields representing plantings at three different times.[9])

At the conclusion of his report Hariot said that most of their time had been spent near the sea coast but that at times they went farther inland:

> where we found the soil to be fatter, the trees greater and to grow thinner, the ground more firm and deeper mould, more and larger champaigns, fine grasses. . . . In some places rocky and far more high and hilly ground, more plenty of their fruits, more abundance of beasts, the more inhabited of people, and of greater policy and larger dominions, with greater towns and houses.

He had therefore some knowledge of the Piedmont, its fertility and greater population.

THE SECOND COLONY AND ITS LOSS

In July 1587 the new lot of settlers came to Roanoke Island, ninety-one men, seventeen women, and nine children, John White being governor. They found the bones of one of the guards Grenville had left, deer grazing in the fort, and "melons" growing on the ruins. The expectation had been that they would pick up Grenville's garrison and then move north to found the City of Raleigh on Chesapeake Bay. When the ships returned to England at the end of August John White went along, at the insistence of the colonists, in order to bring further supplies. A lot of would-be settlers who knew nothing of the country, some with wives and children, were left at Roanoke on their own after several weeks spent in visits about the sounds, including one to the friendly Indians of Croatan Island in the Outer Banks. There was no start at planting or of building. The innocents were left on Roanoke Island; their governor who had experience of the country sailed home for supplies and left them to face an indefinite time in ignorance and inevitable need.

9. Figures 22 and 23. White, a water colorist of ability, made many sketches during the Lane expedition, in part of the things Hariot wrote about. Copies of his pictures were engraved as illustrations in De Bry's *America* (1590) with large romantic license by the publisher. A collection of White originals and copies belonging to the British Museum has been published in two fine folio volumes.

The next spring, in April 1588, Raleigh thought to send aid for his Virginia colonists by two ships from Bideford in Devon, taking supplies and some additional colonists. The captain however was interested in capturing prizes. After taking a Scottish, a Breton, and a Dutch ship, he tangled with French ships out of La Rochelle, was trounced, and limped back to Bideford.[10]

Action against the Spanish Armada occupied English ships and seamen in 1588. In March 1590 White had a chance to get to the colony he had left a year and a half before. Three ships, setting out on a privateering voyage, would take him as passenger and agreed to touch on the Virginia coast.[11] After nearly five months spent hunting prizes the ships came to anchor off the Hatteras Banks August 15, seeing "a great smoke rise on Roanoke Isle." They found the stockade vacant, the word CROATAN carved on one of the posts, but did not go to that island of friendly Indians. There had been a mishap at the inlet, the weather turned stormy, victuals were scarce, freshwater casks had been lost. It was decided to go south, "continue in the Indies all the Winter following, with hope to make two rich voyages of one, and at our return to visit our countrymen at Virginia" (White). They started south. A storm blew them so that they "ran upon the wind perforce" and instead of the West Indies they came to the Azores in mid-September, where they found English men-of-war and their prizes, Sir John Hawkins being once again on a raid to the Spanish Main. The ships with John White aboard took their "leave of the Admiral and the whole fleet" after a week and went home to Plymouth.

There was no further search for the lost Roanoke Colony. John Lawson, visiting the Outer Banks in the early eighteenth century, heard Hatteras Indians tell of white ancestors.

10. Quinn in Hakluyt Soc. Vol. 105, pp. 553–556.
11. Hakluyt, *Principal Navigations*, vol. VI, pp. 212 ff.

Part V

The Century Reviewed:
European Interests, Knowledge of Land
and Life, and Impacts on
Native Peoples

15
A Century of
Vain Attempts

Les Vaines Tentatives was the title used by Marcel Trudel
for the sixteenth century in his *Histoire de la Nouvelle France*.
It is as appropriate for what was done by the governments of
Spain, Portugal, and England. At the end of the century
Spain had a small ragtag garrison at St. Augustine, a short-
lived settlement on the Rio Grande, and France had a hand-
ful who were marooned on Sable Island. There were no other
Europeans in extratropical North America.

THE NEWFOUNDLAND FISHERIES,
CONTINUING PRIVATE ENTERPRISE

Cod fishermen came to the waters off Newfoundland well
before the beginning of the century, and throughout it returned each spring to spend the summer taking cod. The
numbers increased to hundreds of ships and thousands of
fishermen each year. They came from the Bristol Channel,
Brittany, Normandy, French, and Spanish ports on the Bay
of Biscay, and from northern Portugal. Basque whalers in
number hunted right whales. The coastal waters about Newfoundland, the Gulf of St. Lawrence, the shores from Cape
Breton south to Maine, and the banks of the sea yielded a
yearly and large harvest shared by men of different nations.
They used the commodity of harbors to prepare their catch

and repair their gear and boats and thereby came into contact with natives and began to trade also for furs. In some harbors, as at St. John's, Newfoundland, ships of all nationalities mingled. Other harbors were frequented by those of one homeland and speech.

The cod fishers and whalers were not the advance guard of national possession. They shared the largess and freedom of the seas, little concerned with the political relations of their governments. Late in the century Sir Humphrey Gilbert came to declare to the assembled shipmasters at St. John's that he was taking possession of the land for England by authority of the Queen. He sailed on to be lost at sea. Nothing was changed among the fishermen in the accustomed regulation of their affairs.

SEARCH FOR A WESTERN PASSAGE
A NATIONAL CONCERN

As the outline of large bodies of land to the west took form they were at first held to be eastward extensions of Asia, as Columbus and John Cabot thought. A new southern continent was recognized by the beginning of the century, its far extent into high southern latitudes made known when the ship that deserted Magellan in Patagonia returned to Spain early in 1521.

Meanwhile surmise and knowledge of a continent to the north began to be added, first appearing on maps derived from Portuguese sources. Thus the first adumbration of the peninsula of Florida and, far to the north, of the land of Corte Real and that of Labrador. In 1507 the cosmographers at St. Dié published their new world map that inferred a continent between Europe and Asia, giving credit for its recognition to Amerigo Vespucci. The world ocean, according to this map, connected the (unnamed Atlantic and Pacific) seas to the north of 50° north latitude.

Discovery of a new world began as demonstration of the spherical earth. The objective was a sea route to the rich kingdoms of the Far East, which it was thought could be reached by sailing west as well as by going around Africa to the east. Thereby western lands were found of such extent as to be known as mainland, the cosmographers at St. Dié introducing the designation of a western and new continent.

The question was whether there was a sea passage through it or whether it would be necessary to sail around its northern or southern extremity. There was no doubt of the world ocean, a continuous sea surrounding all land bodies. The problem of a western passage engaged attention through the century and beyond.

By 1520 Spanish exploration had made certain that there was no strait leading west from the Caribbean Sea or the Gulf of Mexico. After the conquest of Mexico Spain found a satisfactory alternative route to the Orient by transport overland from Vera Cruz to a port on the Pacific coast, later to become a regular service by the Manila galleons. In 1525 Spain sent Gómez to reconnoiter the coast from Florida north, with negative results. Its last search for a sea passage resulted in the Jesuit mission to Chesapeake Bay in 1570–1571.

France sent Verrazzano in 1524 north along the Atlantic Coast to look for a passage, and again Cartier in 1534 into the Gulf of St. Lawrence for the same purpose. In his second voyage in 1535 Cartier went up the St. Lawrence River to the Lachine rapids above Montreal, so named as barring the passage to China.

England was late in seeking its particular route to the Orient, except for the early ventures of John and perhaps of Sebastian Cabot. Gentlemen formed groups to discuss and propose a northwest passage that would give England the shortest and most secure way. Meetings of sixteenth-century theoretical geographers drew up programs and published tracts, Sir Humphrey Gilbert being a leading spokesman. By this time, well into the Elizabethan period, Spanish success in discovery of ores of precious metals had aroused English interest in doing likewise, but even more so in predation on Spanish shipping and ports. Frobisher, the first to sail in search of a northwest passage, was diverted into hunting ore in Baffin Island. His supposed success resulted in the formation of the Cathay Company, which had no interest in Cathay but was a mining speculation. When Gilbert put aside pen and sword at last to sail on discovery, it was to the familiar shores of Newfoundland, where he sent a supposedly knowledgeable prospector to look for ore bodies. John Davis made three voyages that held to the objective of finding passage by polar route to the Orient. He supported the theory of the open Arctic Sea and got into and beyond the strait that bears his name, but not as far as Vikings from Greenland had done five centuries earlier.

Wars were the business of kings and a main drain on the revenues of states. Prince Henry, by using his private fortune and that of his order, led Portugal into overseas commerce and exploration and thereby into maritime colonies that were a new source of revenue. In 1501 the brothers Corte Real, seeking a western passage to the Orient, sent back a cargo of Indians of both sexes from Newfoundland. These pleased the king as promising a source of slaves in addition to those brought from Africa. It was not followed up because of Portuguese success on the African route.

Columbus thought of the islands he discovered as providing income by export of slaves, and he engaged in shipping them from Española to Spain, to the indignation of Queen Isabela. King Ferdinand favored their capture in the "useless islands" for labor in the gold placers of Española, Puerto Rico, and Cuba. To this end Ponce de León went in 1513 on the discovery of Florida. Ayllón, a member of the Audiencia of Santo Domingo, the governing body of the Spanish Indies, was a partner in a 1521 slaving venture to Chicora on the coast of South Carolina. Thereby he acquired the Indian youth who was to lead him to disaster. Gómez, sent by the Spanish Crown to find a western passage, recovered part of the costs by bringing captives, probably taken in Newfoundland. This was against the law, Peter Martyr complained, but it was being done.

Slave or other forced Indian labor was used largely in placer mining, which was the washing of native gold from stream sands and gravels. This practice began in Española and shortly extended to the Darién area of Panama. Here it became known that an easier source of treasure was jewelry, much of it gold alloy, in the possession of the natives, in the houses of chiefs, in ceremonial structures, and stored in graves. Spaniards here made their first entry into a land of advanced metallurgy of gold and copper. Trade, levy, and especially looting the accumulated native treasures of centuries became the preoccupation of Spanish fortune hunters. To the north a culture prizing precious metals was met in Yucatán and then found to be enormously rich, especially in silver objects in the highlands of Mexico. Cortés sent a fabulous Aztec treasure to the king-emperor. From New Spain to Peru the first decades of Spanish occupation were primarily concerned with appropriating the gold and silver artifacts of the high cultures and melting them for their monetary value. These riches, not mines, held the attention of the so-called conquistadores who were generally ignorant of the nature of ores and their reduction.[1]

Viceroy Mendoza of New Spain sent Fray Marcos to check on tales of another Mexico to the north, by which was meant a land of great cities and treasure. The friar came back with the hoped for news of a land of wondrous wealth, Cibola, Maratta, and others. The large expedition of which Coronado was given charge found Cibola to be the Zuñi pueblos, similar Hopi ones, and many more in the valley of the Rio Grande and beyond, all of them mud-walled tenements of frugal farmers who had no precious metals. Disappointed and angry, the Spaniards listened to a treasure tale that located opulent cities and treasure at Quivira, far inland across the Great Plains. Coronado thus came to the villages of the Wichita Indians in central Kansas, the deepest entry of Europeans into interior North America for more than a century to come. The lower Colorado Valley was explored from the sea by Alarcón with the intent thus to bring supplies to Cibola; the projected link resulted in discovery of the Grand Canyon by a party Coronado had sent west across the Colorado Plateau. A good deal was learned of the geography of the American Southwest, but all negative as to the existence of a treasure-prizing native society.

At the same time De Soto began his longer treasure hunt to the east. He was not misled, as Coronado had been, by tales of treasure in the undefined territory of Florida. He had returned to Spain from Peru very rich in loot, but unsatisfied in ambition. His predecessors' experience with the land and people of Florida was disregarded. Where others had failed he would succeed, saying that where there was a lot of land there would be riches, by which he meant the kind of treasure

1. In 1535 Cartier, innocent of any knowledge of minerals, reported that he had found diamonds, gold leaf, and so on along the St. Lawrence River. The conquistadores were no better informed and not as curious.

he had looted in Peru and Central America. The contract with the Crown made clear his expectations. The Crown was to get a fifth of the gold, silver, and gems taken in trade or battle, half of whatever was found in temples or graves. The instruction that he should select a hundred leagues of coast and build towns was wholly disregarded. For four years his party roved up and down the coast plain, inland to Tennessee and Arkansas, in a stupid hunt for treasure in Indian towns, the only success a chest of freshwater pearls taken from cadavers in the vicinity of Augusta, Georgia. His intent was evident when he brought fetters for use on chain gangs. De Soto left a trail of devastation and outrage that was still unrepaired when Luna came twenty years later.

The Coronado expedition was from New Spain by participants who had been led to expect a repetition of Cortés' fortune. They went hard by the turquoise mines of New Mexico without notice. They found no ore bodies, nor is it likely that they would have recognized them.

De Soto heard of gold in the mountains but did not slow his march across the Blue Ridge, where there was gold-bearing quartz. The men he brought from Spain knew nothing of prospecting for ores. A different breed, largely Basque miners, meanwhile were searching in central Mexico, found silver ore there, and by midcentury opened the great mines that changed the history of Spain, together with parallel discoveries in Peru.

CARRERA DE LAS INDIAS

The clockwise course of navigation to and from the Spanish Indies was followed from the time of Columbus—west with the trade winds, home with the westerlies. Spanish occupation did not extend beyond the island of Haiti until 1509. Ships returning to Spain left Caribbean waters through the Mona or Windward Passage, pointing north into the Atlantic and heading well out of tropical latitudes. Thus the Sargasso Sea and the Bermuda Islands became known on the return to the Azores and southern Spain. Occasionally a ship passed through the Bahama Islands and sighted the south Florida coast. The Juan de la Cosa map of 1500 showed Cuba to be an island and also a strait beyond.

Between 1509 and 1519 the Greater Antilles and the Isthmus of Darién were occupied and grievously exploited. The outline of the Gulf of Mexico became known from Yucatán to Vera Cruz and Pánuco and the conquest of Mexico was well under way. Antonio de Alaminos piloted ships into western waters from the 1513 voyage of Ponce de León to Florida to the landing of Cortés at Vera Cruz in 1519. He had greatest experience of the outpouring sea stream from the Gulf of Mexico through the Straits of Florida and the Bahama Channel. His return from Vera Cruz in 1519 established definitively this route as "the life line of the Indies." Havana was built to protect and supply the home-bound shipping.

French corsairs harassed Spanish ships, for a time mainly off Iberian shores and about the Azores. By midcentury, when silver from Mexico and Peru was shipped in large amount, they raided American waters, prowling about the outlet of the Gulf Stream. Storms, especially hurricanes, wrecked ships laden with valuable cargo on the keys of south Florida and on the shoals and strands of its east coast. Philip II and the Council of the Indies determined that a port of refuge, salvage, and defense was needed on the mainland and so designated the St. Helena area of the Sea Islands and charged the Viceroy of New Spain with the task.

The plan was proper. The Sea Islands, north of the shoal east coast of Florida, have deep and protected sounds, convenient to ships riding the Gulf Stream. Velasco made a reasonable modification of the plan. Instead of the long circuit of the Florida peninsula he would establish a colony at the northeast of the Gulf of Mexico, open a land route from it to St. Helena across the base of the peninsula, and send the artillery by sea to the projected fort in the Sea Islands. It was the better plan but was ruined by the hurricane that sank Luna's ships and equipment in Pensacola Bay in 1560.

While Spanish authorities deliberated what to do, Coligny, Admiral of France, made his move against the Spanish sea lane. The French colony at Rio de Janeiro had fallen to the Portuguese, therefore he would confront Spain with a French-Protestant Florida. His first step was a provisional fort in 1562 on Port Royal Sound, the locality that was known as Santa Elena to the Spanish. Two years later Fort Caroline was built on the St. Johns River, at the present location of Jacksonville, the site of greatest advantage in all that coast. In the third move (1565) Ribault was sent with colonists and

arms to take firm hold of French Florida. The challenge of
Spain was met by a hurricane and the bold strategy of
Menéndez that destroyed French Florida.

In the crisis Menéndez had begun fortification on St. Augustine Inlet, an inferior harbor in a poor and thinly populated region. It was maintained as a minor Spanish fort of
little importance.

In the latter part of the century Englishmen were the
main predators on Spanish shipping. While the two countries
maintained diplomatic relations and formally were at peace,
English captains took Spanish prizes and raided Spanish ports;
Drake, for example, burned St. Augustine as a diversion.

NATIVE RELATIONS WITH EUROPEANS

By papal authority Spain and Portugal entered on the possession of non-Christian parts of the world, the beginning of
overseas colonial empires. The acquisition was joined and
challenged by France and then by England.

Spain accepted the obligation to bring Christianity to native peoples. This obligation was wholly disregarded by Ponce
de León, Narváez, De Soto, and virtually so by Coronado.
Ayllón took Dominican friars on his attempted colony of
Chicora and they seem to have kept peace between Spaniards
and natives until Ayllón died. Luna brought Christian Tlaxcalan Indians and Franciscan friars to Alabama, and his party
was given aid by the local Indians at all times. Its promise of
being a good association of Spaniards, Mexican Indians, and
Muskogean natives failed for extraneous reasons. Menéndez
brought Dominicans, Jesuits, and Franciscans with small success, perhaps mainly because the missionary efforts were ne-
gated by the conduct of the soldiers. The improved conditions
of the Indians in New Spain after 1542, resulting from the
New Laws for their protection, had no effect to the north.
In part the failure of Spanish Florida was due to what Barcia
called "the indignation of the barbarians," which was reaction
to military excesses and also to missionary efforts to change
the Indian society and religion. The apostasy of the two young
Indians, Francisco Chicora and "Don Luis de Velasco," showed
the tension of imposed transformation of culture.

The French got along quite well with the Canada Indians,
somewhat less so in Florida. Barlow in the first account of

Roanoke praised the Indians as living by the golden rule. Lane, on the second English stay, noted their growing mistrust and avoidance of the English. When the guest became a squatter and began to make demands, good will gave way to resentment.

ATTEMPTS AT SETTLEMENT

Trading stations such as were being established around Africa were not undertaken. There was no class of native traders except those who went from Mexico to the Pueblo country, primarily for turquoise. Indians around the Gulf of St. Lawrence and south, perhaps to Maine, had newly learned that winter peltry was in demand by ships that came in summer. Cod fishermen and perhaps whalers became fur traders on the side. When Cartier came to Chaleur Bay in midsummer Micmacs awaited him with a stock of furs. They had learned to trap beyond their own needs for a ship-side market. Verrazzano had a similar experience on the coast of Maine. Cartier tried to found a French colony, but it was not until the next century that France looked to the fur trade, supplied by Indians, for the support of New France.

The first settlement by Europeans was in 1521—a group of Portuguese families taken by Fagundes to Nova Scotia, probably to the Bay of Fundy. Fagundes had made prior exploration of the coasts of Nova Scotia and Maine and was given license by the King of Portugal to colonize there at his own expense and, of all things, to build a soap factory. The pattern was that of the seignories by which the Azores and Madeira had been occupied and Brazil shortly would be. The colonists planted crops, raised livestock, and fished. When last heard of they were well satisfied with the fertile land and liked their Indian neighbors. The Indians, practicing little if any farming, would not have been disturbed by the Portuguese settlement. The manner of its loss is not known.

France tried to found a colony in 1541–1543 in the St. Lawrence Valley above the Indian village of Stadacona (Quebec). There was good land here and some crops were grown in 1541. An ample breeding stock was brought—cattle, horses, goats, and sheep. The long winter brought scurvy, want, and discouragement to the French and disaffection of the natives. Cartier and his men abandoned the place in the spring of

1542 and left for France. Roberval brought another group that included women, did no planting, and had a bad winter in 1542–1543, again suffering scurvy, and returned to France. Equipment, seed, and livestock had been amply provided. The Indians supplied fish and other food.

Some of the French colonists were volunteers, others deportees; few knew anything of growing crops or of fishing. None knew that winter would be so long or so cold. According to the classical doctrine of climatic zones the St. Lawrence Valley, being in the same latitude as La Rochelle, should have the same climate. That it did not was attributed to the forests, whereas in France the open ground of fields and pastures was warmed by the sun. If the St. Lawrence Valley was cleared it was expected to enjoy the same climate as northern France. This was scant comfort to those who had not imagined such winters, nor wanted to be husbandmen. The announced mineral wealth was erroneous. The barrels of gold and silver and bushels of gems did not materialize. Canada would await the next century for the coming of the *habitants* who stayed and made a viable society.

The second half of the century was a poor time for new colonies. Colonies needed immigrants, industrious and usually poor, underprivileged persons looking for a chance. Spain had lack of people, not population pressure. The silver mines were producing as mines never had done, business was booming in Spain and the Indies, and the Indians of New Spain were in a decline that shortly was a disaster. Velasco's plan of joining Florida to New Spain by settlements of farmers, stock ranches, and posts needed people from Spain and from Mexico, people that weren't available. Menéndez planned sugar plantations and dreamed of another passage to China. Strategic necessity was overriding but permitted only a little to be undertaken. There was not enough military personnel and only a handful of settlers.

France shipped Protestants to Florida to fight Spain. They are credited with having introduced sassafras to European medicine and they gave good reports of Florida. When Ribault left France to do battle with Menéndez, what purpose did the families he brought serve? Spanish or French, Florida made sense as a game of war but very little as a colony. Menéndez, for examp'., wanted to plant sugar cane in Florida when none was being grown in Cuba, of which he was governor.

The English came last. They knew the success the Spaniards had at mining and smelting ores but little of what such ores were other than that they were dark and heavy. Frobisher found dark heavy rocks in a bay in Baffin Island. As the result the Cathay Company was formed, proposing to mine precious metals and settle poor Englishmen along the route to China. When Humphrey Gilbert, chief advocate of a northwest passage, set out with letters patent to discover and settle he went instead to the fishing coast of Newfoundland, sent a Saxon miner inland to prospect for ore, and said that he held the secret of a rich discovery. Raleigh sent a German miner with the second Roanoke expedition, of which its captain Ralph Lane reported a story of a strange soft copper-colored metal recovered by panning in rapid water and beaten into great plates. Lane tried to get to this interior land but got only as far as the Virginia Piedmont. Raleigh also tried to emulate the Spanish success.

Hariot, a participant of the second Roanoke voyage, wrote a tract for Raleigh that was to promote the Virginia colony. Its first part dealt with "merchantable commodities," both produced there and suited for introduction. Native commodities were silk grass (*Yucca*), sassafras, cedar (profitable to export for cabinet work), oil (of walnuts, acorns, and bear fat), sweet gums, dyes (of sumac, etc.), pitch, tar, resin, and turpentine. Animal products were furs (of otters), deer skins dressed after the manner of chamois, pearls (of freshwater mussels). Copper was reported as available in the interior, also iron, which the infinite store of the firewood would make a good merchantable commodity. "Planted and husbanded as they ought" the native grapes would be a "principal commodity of wines."

Hemp and flax Hariot thought should be introduced and woad, the latter then grown plentifully in the Azores "which are in the same climate. So likewise of madder." The climatic parallel was applied farther:

We carried thither Sugar canes to plant, which being not so well preserved as was requisite, and besides the time of year being past for their setting when we arrived, we could not make that proof of them as we desired. Notwithstanding, seeing that they grow in the same climate, in the south part of Spain, and in Barbary, our hope in reason may yet continue. So likewise for Oranges and Lemons. There may be planted also Quinces. Whereby may be grown in reasonable time, if the action be diligently prosecuted, no small commodities in Sugar, Suckets, and Marmelades.

The English promotional literature had slight basis in fact. Given enough attention, support, and time, some of these items could have been exploited commercially, by industry and good mangement. The English colonists lacked the needed skills, were abandoned to their own poor devices, and disappeared, with the word Croatoan their only message.

All European ventures of the century failed with the exception of the cod and whale fisheries, and these had nothing to do with territorial possession by any power.

16

Nature and Natives
as Seen by Europeans

PHYSICAL GEOGRAPHY

The Atlantic coast was fairly well described in the visits of the century. French exploration began with Verrazzano who noted well the change from sandy coast plain to bedrock at New York Harbor, continuing to Narragansett Bay. Cartier had a good eye for the topography of gulf, river, and valley of St. Lawrence, the exposed bedrock of the Laurentian side of the gulf "like the land God gave Cain," the great fjord of the Saguenay, the horizontal strata of Anticosti Island, the panorama seen from Mount Royal. To the English descriptions of the sounds and banks of North Carolina, John White added a well-delineated map. John Davis observed pack ice and drift of icebergs, terrain and life in Greenland, Baffin Island, and Labrador.

Spanish expeditions inland gave recognizable features of the southern Appalachians, the Tennessee Valley, northeast Arkansas, central Kansas, Taos in New Mexico, and the Grand Canyon of the Colorado. There are only minor uncertainties as to the routes taken. In the East, rivers, lakes, and swamps were significant markers of topography. In the western interior, the plains, their marginal escarpments and box canyons, fresh water or lack of water or presence of saline water, the sighting and crossing of mountain ranges recorded where the parties passed. The recollections as to how Coronado crossed the high plains, as level as the surface of a sea, how they rested in the floor of canyons of its Cap Rock Escarpment and went on to the rolling plains of Kansas are clear and true.

On the Pacific Coast the Cabrillo party described Santa Barbara Channel and Islands and the cliffed foot of the Santa Lucia Mountains that seemed as though they might fall on the ships.

VEGETATION

The northern seafarers took note of bare rock surfaces of the Laurentian land from Baffin Island to the Gulf of St. Lawrence, of stunted shrubs and burst of summer bloom on Baffin Island wherever there was sufficient soil and drainage. To the south, in particular along Nova Scotia, conifers were of interest as ship timbers.

When Europeans came to eastern North America the vegetation was familiar in its major elements. Oaks were recognized as such, as were beech, maple, ash, poplar, and willow. Conifers other than pines were uncertainly named, as indeed they still are in English, French, and Spanish. *Juniperus virginiana,* common to the eastern United States, was and is called red cedar; the northern arbor-vitae, *Thuja,* white cedar. *Taxodium* became cypress to the English, *cedro* or *sabino* to the Spanish, and so on.

The humid east had great diversity and number of nut trees growing on the better soils. In Europe only the Persian walnut and the chestnut were known, both introduced and cultivated. Here there were wild plums and cherries of different kinds, size, and quality, whereas in Europe except for sloe or blackthorn such fruits were few in kind and found only in cultivation. In Europe grapes grew in carefully tended vineyards; over here wild grapevines of several species climbed the hardwood trees from the St. Lawrence Valley to Florida and throughout the Mississippi Valley. Grapes everywhere had the attention of the explorers who thought that they would require only cultivation to flourish as well and provide as good wines as in Europe.

The western limits of the Eastern Hardwoods were reached by the De Soto party in eastern Texas. Coronado got to them in central Kansas, coming from the opposite direction. The woodlands were far richer in diversity of flora than in any part of Europe. Except in wet lands they were open woods, not dense forests. The De Soto expedition, consisting of many people, a large horse herd, and many swine, passed through ten states without difficulty of movement, except occasionally swamp and high water. It found sufficient forage for its many animals along the way.

Within the open woods there were treeless or nearly treeless upland tracts, called savannas by the Spanish, champaigns by the French and English, or prairies. Verrazzano thus described a *campagne* in Rhode Island as beautiful land extending for twenty-five leagues without impediment of trees, somewhat of an exaggeration. Prairies and open woods in the humid east may be explained by long continued Indian practices of setting fires.

The natives of the Eastern Woodlands lived in permanent villages about which the vegetation had been largely altered by the wear and use of people. Such outskirts were occupied by plants that took advantage of human disturbance or were disseminated as human waste, an assemblage that had an ecologic niche found today in roadsides and old fields. Birds, people, bears, raccoons, and other animals distributed the seeds that formed a secondary vegetation at the margins of woodlands.

The visitors to our southern states took note of such differences. The staghorn sumac (*Rhus typhina*), bird distributed and still common on roadsides and old fields, was recognized by the Spaniards as *zumaque*, the Arab name for a Mediterranean species of *Rhus* used in dyeing and tanning. The name passed into English usage, Hariot calling it shoemake. The eastern juniper, *cedro* in Spanish and red cedar to the English, was observed as forming groves. (This again is the result of seeding by birds in open lands.) Sassafras is one of the commonest elements of old fields and roadsides. It had special and continued attention, beginning with Florida, because of its fame as a panacea and tonic that gave it a profitable market in Europe.

Fleshy wild fruits that were important as Indian foods were gathered in the South from such secondary openings adjacent to villages. The most used berries in the South were the trailing dewberry, the vines of which form a ground cover. The persimmon (an Algonquian name said to mean dried fruit), was dried for winter use by Indians thoughout the South. A delicacy to raccoons and opossums, these animals established it largely about woods margins. Europeans knew nothing like it and gave it their name for *Mespilus* (medlar in English) which, like the persimmon, is eaten after frost. Other fruits common to openings at the margin of woods were plums and cherries, of shrubby habit usually, also the red mulberry.

In the semiarid Southwest the flora was first noted by the Cabeza de Vaca party, the great thickets of *Opuntia* cactus south of San Antonio, mesquite in the Pecos drainage, piñon pines (*Pinus cembroides*) in the mountains of New Mexico, the latter described as having thin shells in contrast to the piñon pines of Spain (*P. pinea*). It was largely by vegetation that Hallenbeck traced the Cabeza de Vaca route across Texas and New Mexico. The Coronado expedition added floristic data on southeast Arizona, the Colorado Plateau, the grassy expanse of the Staked Plains, and the humid prairies and woodlands in Kansas.

FISH, FLESH, AND FOWL

Ships in northern waters supplied themselves with abundant and divers animal food. Around Newfoundland and the Gulf of St. Lawrence the cod fishers set the practice. Penguin Island (Funk and perhaps other islands) off the northeast coast of Newfoundland was a great rookery, noted for its huge population of great auks. The flightless birds were herded into boats, clubbed, and the carcasses salted down. Fishing crews did thus, as did Cartier and Gilbert and others at later times, to the extermination of the great auk in the nineteenth century. Cartier, having prior knowledge of similar island rookeries in the Gulf of St. Lawrence, went directly to the Bird Islands and the Magdalen Islands to take great auks, gannets, eggs, in particular of eider ducks, and to hunt walrus. This gulf gave the French their first knowledge of the walrus, then inhabiting various places about its shores and described as "fish in the shape of horses, which go on land at night and into the sea by day," also of the white porpoises or belugas in Saguenay fjord and about Île aux Coudres, in both places at the border of salt and fresh water. Near the latter island there was noted "an inestimable number of large turtles," an item that remains unexplained.

On the Dry Tortugas and off southern Florida Spaniards harvested turtles, their eggs, monk seals, and bird eggs as they did elsewhere about the Gulf of Mexico and the Caribbean.

Except in the Southwest the European land parties mostly moved along water—fresh, salt, or brackish, stream, bayou, lagoon, sound, estuary, marsh, and swamp. The St. Lawrence, the Mississippi and its tributaries and backwaters, the Alabama, Coosa, Tombigbee, and Savannah rivers, the sounds of Albemarle, Pamlico, and the Sea Islands, Galveston and Matagorda bays, the Santa Barbara Channel, all provided large and divers food. Salmon and shad in the north, eels and catfish in the Mississippi and other gulf rivers were major fare. Oyster beds were harvested in shallow bays of the Atlantic and Gulf coast, as were freshwater mussels in the rivers. Water fowl passed in seasonal migration, overwintered in southern waters, and many were permanent residents.

Indians, fishing and in lesser degree hunting and trapping, supplied the French on the St. Lawrence, the English at Roanoke, French and Spanish in Florida, De Soto's men in the Mississippi waters, and the Cabrillo party in Santa Barbara Channel. The visitors knew little of such skills. Hariot told that the English did not know how to build weirs and helped themselves to those of the Indians, which were artfully constructed. Weirs were in use even by the primitive natives of the Texas coast, who also speared from dugouts. Trapping in weirs, spearing, and netting were noted as principal means of fishing.

The common big game of the Eastern Woodlands were the Virginia white-tailed deer and the black bear. The latter were hunted especially for their store of fat, bear grease being used in food and as ointment. Omnivorous in habit, bears fed on fruits, roots, buds, larvae, birds' eggs, fished and hunted and ranged from dry land to swamp and open water. The white-tailed deer largely are browsers, feeding on brush and herbs, then as now finding their best range in the second growth of abandoned fields and of burned tracts rather than in forest or open prairie. The Indians were not living in a forest primeval but in a vegetation long and largely modified by fire and tillage, providing a habitat favorable to deer. Deer were hunted mainly in winter, not only for meat, but especially for the buckskin that provided clothing and footwear.

The brushy secondary vegetation, largely formed by human

action, also favored the increase of rabbits, quail, and other
small game. During the snowy winter, when De Soto's party
was encamped in the Ouachita Valley, Indians taught the
Spaniards how to snare rabbits in their runways. While De
Soto was crossing the oak woodlands of the Carolina Piedmont
Indians brought a present of a great lot of wild turkeys. The
Eastern Hardwoods were the principal range of the wild
bronze turkey.

The Coronado party found buffalo herds in vast numbers
on the Great Plains between the Pecos River and the Cap
Rock Escarpment in Texas, and smaller herds as far as central
Kansas. On the high plains they met bands of Plains Indians
who lived by following the herds, dogs pulling pole travois on
which skin tepees and belongings were packed. From the east
Wichitas, Pawnees, and Teyas (Texas), sedentary villagers and
farmers sent hunting parties out on the buffalo plains. From
the west Pueblo Indians and others from farther south in
New Mexico went across the Pecos River to hunt buffalo. The
buffalo plains had largess for all, which was shared by all,
unlike their later violent history.

In semiarid southern New Mexico and southeast Arizona the
Cabeza de Vaca party was well supplied by Indians with jack-
rabbits. Melchor Díaz, while making the reconnaissance for
Coronado, saw a great abundance of wild "goats" in the grasslands of the Arizona-Sonora border. (These were pronghorn
antelopes.) He heard of an animal in the Pueblo country that
he thought might be the same but was told that it was different (bighorn sheep). Díaz may also have taken first notice of
the large mule deer, ranging from there west to California.

The Cabrillo expedition described herds of antelope in
California, and that of Drake saw herds of elk inland in
northern California.

INDIAN CROPS

There were two agricultural complexes, related but distinct
by environment and tradition. Both derived from Mexico
and Central America, or in terms of ethnology, from Mesoamerican culture. Both depended on the cultivation of annuals
grown primarily for their seeds and in all or nearly all cases
introduced from the south as cultigens, that is, plants that had
been bred by man and modified to serve his purposes. In both

complexes the dominant crops were maize, beans, and squash (cultigen forms of *Cucurbita,* including pumpkins by English name). In both, the usual mode of planting was to set several kinds in the same prepared spot, which commonly was mounded, and was separated by a space from the next spot, ordinarily not in continuous rows, and never broadcast.

In the Eastern Woodlands farming was carried on from Florida to the St. Lawrence. Information for New England and the Maritime Provinces mostly is of later date. The agricultural settlements were of most imposing size and quality in Arkansas and Louisiana; small ones were found by De Soto's men as far west as the Brazos River in Texas. Coronado reached the eastern Indian farming country in central Kansas and passed through a western outlier of it in the canyon of Palo Duro in north Texas.

The Indian farmers of the East known to Spaniards were Muskogean tribes in the Southeast, mainly Caddoans west of the Mississippi, and some others (perhaps Cherokee) east beyond the Savannah River and in the Tennessee Valley. The English knew the farming practices of Algonquian tribes in North Carolina, the French those of Iroquois in the St. Lawrence Valley. All farmed in similar manner.

The three staples—maize, beans and squash—were grown throughout; the South having the advantage of a long growing season permitting planting more than one crop annually. Tobacco (*Nicotiana rustica*) was described by Cartier as cultivated in the St. Lawrence Valley and by Hariot in Roanoke. This domesticate of the Andes had been carried into Mexico and thence north to the polar limit of farming on the St. Lawrence. Unlike the other plants, it was of necessity grown in plots reserved to it.

Hariot described the cultivated annual sunflower, grown for its oily seeds. It was a secondary Indian crop throughout eastern North America. Often considered as having been domesticated there, I think it, too, is likely to have been introduced from Mexico.

Hariot also gave a good description of the cultivation of a plant from the seed of which they made a pottage, the plant being called Melden in Dutch. I take it to have been a cultivated *Chenopodium.* Such a cultigen was important in central Mexico and is still grown there. It is suggested that it may have been introduced from there to the Eastern Wood-

lands along with the other domesticates. It is also suggested
that the cereal other than maize, of which the Indian Chicora
told Peter Martyr, was this *Chenopodium*. The priest, who
knew no tall plant with large heads of very small seeds other
than millet, guessed it to be the latter.

In the semiarid American Southwest Spanish explorers got
near to the interior limits of Indian agriculture. Cabeza de
Vaca's party saw meager planting along the Rio Grande
above El Paso. Coronado's men visited the intensively tilled
Pueblo lands of the upper Rio Grande and Pecos valleys and
the detached settlements of the Zuñis, Hopis, and Acoma.
Melchor Díaz was first to note the agricultural Pimas in southeastern Arizona and the Yumans, planting their crops on the
flood plain of the lower Colorado River. Maize, beans, and
squash were the staples, the kinds differing from those of the
East. Cotton, unknown in the East, was an important crop of
Rio Grande pueblos and, to the surprise of the Spaniards, in
the Hopi country of extraordinarily short growing season.
It was also reported among Yumans. Sunflower, grain
amaranth, and tobacco were not mentioned, though grown.
Rattles were made from *Lagenaria* gourds (as later documented
by archaeology), an ancient cultigen brought early from afar.
The Spanish visitors were impressed by the quality of Pueblo
agriculture. There were no fruit trees nor knowledge of such.

INCIPIENT HORTICULTURE

In the East the observers were interested in the abundance and
quality of fruits, first of all the grapes, which they had not
known growing wild and which they regarded as needing only
to be cared for to equal those of Europe.

Europe has one species of grapes (*Vitis*); North America
is rich in kinds "of indefinite specific limits." [1] Bailey thus
grouped the vineyard varieties grown in the eastern United
States "in terms of their supposed original species, which are
of the Labrusca, Aestivalis, and Rotundifolia groups." The
Labrusca, or fox grape, and the Aestivalis, or summer grape,
are native from New England south at least to Georgia, Rotundifolia, or muscadine, from southern Delaware to Florida
and Louisiana. All three species have cultivated varieties
(sports or hybrids), some known as propagated since colonial

1. L. H. Bailey, *Manual of Cultivated Plants.*

days. Usually attributed to selection or discovery by American horticulturists, their amelioration by man began, I think, with Indian attention. Bailey's comment of ill-defined species or of large variation (whether by crossing or mutation), applies to these wild grapes of the Eastern Woodlands and did not remain unnoticed by natives.

Verrazzano landed on the peninsula, now given the acronym Delmarva, and observed that ground about vines was kept cleared so that they would do well—that is, care was taken of particular vines of appreciated quality. In Alabama the De Soto party enjoyed summer grapes "as good as those of Spanish vines." Away from river banks they found low vines of large and sweet grapes. Both muscadine and summer grapes being very vigorous climbers, the suggestion is that they were cut back. That there was cultivation and selection of grapes is claimed in a Jesuit account of the Powhatan country. It described a vineyard there as being as well laid out as those in Spain, the cepas (vinestock, low-cut trunk of the vine) laden with very fine large white grapes. The grapes being large and white, scuppernongs are indicated, the horticultural variety of the muscadine grape. A white sport of the large fruited purple muscadines might occur in nature, but not a stand of them. There are no white, amber, or greenish varieties of wild grapes. Scuppernongs, borne a few on a cluster, are of the size of the largest European table grapes.

The Indian towns of the southeastern United States were permanent, in some cases occupying the sites of ancient moundbuilders. The waste of stone fruits was discarded about the settlements and the fruits carried in would have been somewhat selected for better taste and larger size. Unlike Europe, the Eastern Woodlands have a divers lot of wild plums and, even more so than our grapes, they are uncertainly demarked as to species. *Prunus americana, P. nigra, P. angustifolia, P. hortulana,* and *P. munsoniana* may or may not all be valid species. The taxonomic distinctions are less than assured. Blooming time favors cross-pollination. They are now found mainly on roadsides, woods margins, along gullies, and in abandoned fields, elements of secondary growth by human disturbance, and the fruit is likely to be small and of indifferent or sharp taste. They are mostly of bushy habit, not forming a single or dominant trunk, and often thorny.

The most often mentioned and most appreciated fruits on

the De Soto expedition were plums, from Tallahassee to the Savannah, Tennessee, and Coosa valleys and across the Mississippi to Arkansas. They grew on trees and they were described as plums "like those of Castile," "plums of Castile," and "plums better than in Castile." They were enjoyed fresh in summer and were dried by the Indians for winter use. When Coronado and his men came to the settlements of the Texas Indians in Palo Duro Canyon, and again to the Wichitas of Kansas, they found plums and plum trees "like those of Castile." The Jesuit description of the vineyard in Virginia said that within it were a great number of plum trees. The comparison was with plums of Spain, of good eating out of hand or sun dried, that is, prunes. The repeated comment was of resemblance to European fruit, of tree habit, of excellent quality, and of mass drying for winter use.

The native plums of the southeastern United States, according to Liberty Bailey, are of four uncertainly distinguished species, *Prunus americana*, *P. angustifolia* (Chickasaw plum), *P. munsoniana* (Wild Goose plum), and *P. hortulana* (a species set up by Bailey), the last the only one described as an "upright tree, not sprouting from the root or forming thickets," by its name indicated as a garden or orchard form. Our wild plums, small-fruited, shrubby and thicket-forming, a fringe along the edge of woods or roadsides, are not the kinds described and praised by the visitors of the sixteenth century and later.

When American farmers replaced the Indian communities, native plum trees were commonly planted and were an important element in the home orchard. How they secured these superior kinds is almost unknown, sometimes attributed to a legendary person. One of the best known horticultural varieties, the Wild Goose plum, is said to have been found in the crop of a wild goose by a hunter in Tennessee.[2] There were many such named varieties, especially from the former Chickasaw and Caddo country. The likelier inference is that American settlers who occupied Indian lands kept plum trees they found there, selected by Indians for quality and size of fruit and upright tree habit.

As walnuts were a major source of oil to the Indians east

2. I was told that story in my youth and wondered what wild geese were doing eating plums in Tennessee in July, swallowing these large fruits.

of the Mississippi River, so were pecans to the west. Pecans were found throughout the Indian communities of the Mississippi River Lowlands from northeast Arkansas to southern Louisiana.

By priority of scientific name the pecan is called *Carya illinoensis,* because botanists first described it in Illinois. It was first known to Europeans by the survivors of the Narváez expedition going with Indians from the Texas coast to gather pecans in the river bottoms of the Colorado of Texas and the Brazos. Later Spaniards, coming north from Mexico, named a river farther south in Texas the Nueces because of these nut trees. The pecan is native to well-drained valleys of the coast plain of Texas and Louisiana. De Soto's men did not find it east of the Mississippi. Its northern natural limit is uncertain. In Missouri pecan groves existed, and in part still do on Mississippi and Missouri river bottoms. They were known as found in groves at the beginning of American settlement. Unlike walnuts and other hickories they are not and reportedly were not mingled in the woodlands but, insofar as I know, only in occasional groves on large river bottoms (also in Illinois), suggesting that they may have been brought north by Indian farmers. Pecans were important in the Indian economy of northeast Arkansas, whether in natural habitat or by introduction I do not know. In natural habitat the choosiest of our nut trees, it was limited to well-drained alluvial lands. By Spanish testimony it was not found east of the Mississippi River, but was important to the lowland Indian farmers to the west. This limit suggests that the trees were not only protected but that they were carried by man. In Texas river bottoms, however, they were abundant in the wild woods.

NATIVE CULTURES AND THEIR ENVIRONMENTS: NON-AGRICULTURAL PEOPLE

The simplest cultures encountered were those of Newfoundland and of coastal Texas. The Beothuks of Newfoundland are some of the least known Indians of North America. Much of what we know is through the Corte Real voyages at the beginning of the century.[3] Edward Hayes, reporting the Gilbert Voyage of 1583, wrote "In the South parts we found no inhabitants, which by all likelihood have abandoned those

3. Summarized in my *Northern Mists.*

coasts, being so much frequented by Christians: But in the
North are savages altogether harmless." By that time these
timid and probably ancient Indian people had withdrawn
from the coasts of Newfoundland to the harsher environment
inland.

Of the Indians of the Texas coast plain the Cabeza de
Vaca party gave the only knowledge until Le Salle came near
the end of the next century. The Spanish castaways, untutored
in the demands of primitive survival in a meager environment,
found the hardships extreme. In good part this was because
the natives required them to take part in their labors and,
being its most unskilled members, they were assigned the more
menial tasks of the group. The seasonal changes in food supply
imposed periodic movements between coast and interior, times
of plenty and times of want. Whatever was edible was gathered. There were times when there was little to be found and
also there were times when there was large supply of oysters
and of roots in estuaries, of cactus fruits and pecans inland.
The Indians were adept at fishing and hunting, the Spaniards
had no competence at either. The land was sparsely peopled,
a good deal of the coast plain being poor, sandy land and to
the west increasingly arid. However, there were also fertile
and ample alluvial valleys and other tracts of fertile soils.
The absence of agriculture, therefore, is an anomaly that is
not explained by an adverse environment. Together with adjacent northeastern Mexico, the Texas coast plain is a major
exception to the general rule that land suited to Indian crops
was thus used.

Coastal California also lacked agriculture, although its natives were well acquainted with the Indian farmers of the
lower Colorado Valley. Indian crops are summer crops and
California is a land of summer drought, but this was hardly a
major barrier. Maize, beans, and squash could have been
grown on the Santa Barbara coast but were not. The inhabitants of the lower Colorado valley made pottery; those of the
California coast did not. The coastal people did not follow
these practices, held to mean cultural advance, because they
did not care to make pottery or to grow crops, not because
of ignorance. The people of the Santa Barbara Channel in
particular impressed the Cabrillo party with the quality of
their society as well as by their good livelihood. They had
abundant food from the sea and on land. They were talented

at working wood and stone. The visitors counted more than fifty villages, some of them impressive in form and size. Life was not only easy, it was spirited and good.

Far to the north on the Atlantic coast the specialized hunting culture of Eskimos was known and described as to skin boats, dog sleds, houses, and dress. Here man was the end of the marine food chain and used structural materials provided by the sea. Seals were the primary staple. On Frobisher Bay a strange note was added that the natives kept a second, small breed of dogs to be eaten.

The other hunting culture observed was that of the buffalo hunters of the high plains. These people, perhaps Apaches, followed the herds as mobile predators, deriving almost their entire subsistence thus, as was well described in the Coronado accounts. This way of life was made convenient by the use of dog travois. Dog travois here and dog sleds with the Eskimo were the means by which both hunting cultures functioned. Neither group trained dogs for hunting, nor did any other people of North America.

FARMING PEOPLES—WEST AND EAST

The tribes of the Lower Colorado Valley, probably all Yumans, depended on summer flooding of the alluvial land and on summer thunderstorms for their crops, which were tolerant of high temperatures and rapid maturing. The tepary bean (*Phaseolus acutifolius,* var. *latifolius*), for example, sets seeds in desert heat and with brief supply of water. The villages of the Lower Colorado were estimated as having twenty-two thousand people by Oñate during his visit in 1605, which number Kniffen found acceptable.[4] The land available for planting was of limited extent but of high productivity.

The flat-roofed Pima houses described by Melchor Díaz in the San Pedro Valley of southeast Arizona represented a smaller and more marginal tillage in semiarid country, the valley floor, not as yet trenched by an arroyo, providing land sufficiently moistened by summer rain to grow fair crops.

In the high interior the Pueblo villages on the Colorado Plateau were at altitudes above six thousand feet for Zuñi and Hopi, from five thousand on the middle Rio Grande to seven

4. Fred Kniffen, "Primitive Cultural Landscape of the Colorado Delta," *Univ. Calif. Pubs. Geog.*, vol. 5, No. 2 (1931).

at Taos and Pecos. In the Pueblo country the rains begin late in summer and frost comes early. Crops are grown here by unusual care and industry of dry farming and by extending the season through vernalization, planting seed weeks before rains begin. Maize, beans, squash, and sunflowers are of specially adapted races. In places water was spread over fields by canals and dams. Such special skills were not noted by the earlier Spaniards, who did see, however, that these people were most industrious farmers and that their pueblos were large and many, with limited amount of cultivated land. The Pueblo people were full-time farmers during the growing season; they had little meat and scarcely any fish. Parties went East into the buffalo plains, chiefly to procure hides. Full-length clothing was worn by men and women, mainly of cotton grown in the Rio Grande Valley. Cotton was also grown by the Hopi, who produced it under a shorter growing season than in any other part of the New World.

The Spaniards, disappointed at finding that the supposed treasure cities of Cibola consisted of multistory houses of mud and stone, still were impressed by the number and size of the pueblos. Zuñi was a cluster of six or seven pueblos, Hopi of seven; Acoma, seated on its great rock, had excellent fields near by. A group of twelve pueblos was entered in the Rio Grande Valley in the district about Albuquerque. Scores more were seen up the valley as far as Taos, the latter said to have eighteen quarters (*barrios*) and fifteen thousand people. Others lived in the headwaters of the Pecos, that of Cicuye at the gateway to the high plains the most populous and prosperous.[5]

The humid Eastern Woodlands were fairly well known as far north as Chesapeake Bay, to the Tennessee River about Chattanooga, to Crowley's Ridge in northeast Arkansas, and to the Ouachita Mountains. The growing season throughout was six months or longer, normally with well-distributed rain adequate for all crops. Many rivers, large and small, deposited their sediment in flood plains of good fertility and largely of

5. F. W. Hodge, *Fray Alonso de Bernaldes' Revised Memorial of 1634* (Albuquerque, 1945). There were a lot of people, all accounts agreed, living in good order and busy, of which the Spaniards approved. Their numbers may have been exaggerated, as has been usually inferred, but they are not incredible. Even the large number given for Taos may be plausible for an aggregation of linked communities in the northern part of the Rio Grande Valley.

good natural drainage. The "bottom lands" of rivers and creeks were those preferred for planting by the Indians and later by the white settlers who replaced them.[6] They were fertile and of a texture that was easy to dig. If flooded briefly, the Indian corn withstood the immersion. After longer flooding the growing season often permitted replanting.

The Indian settlements were along streams, or, in Florida, also about lakes. De Soto's march was from river to river, from one town to another, in each case where there was a body of good alluvial land. At some towns there were artificial mounds, made by an earlier people, attesting to the enduring attraction of the site for the permanent cultivation of fields, some from remote times. This was no shifting cultivation, no procedure of slash, burn, plant, and abandon.

Yield was high and labor requirement low. Hariot exaggerated both in praising the Indian agriculture about Roanoke, which was not one of the more fertile regions. He inferred that Indian crop yield was about five-fold that of an English field, and that twenty-four hours of labor would raise most of the food of one person for most of a year. On good alluvium or loess, having a long growing season, one acre in mixed planting of maize, beans, and squash, perhaps with sunflower or *Chenopodium* added, would indeed sustain a person for a year. The plants were all heavy producers of seeds of high nutritive value. All also provided food in immature state as well as when ripe. Except for the St. Lawrence Valley, nearly all the Eastern Woodlands then known had a growing season that permitted more than one harvest. The plants of southern, largely Mexican, origin had been bred by centuries of selection to adaptation to various climates. When European settlers came the superiority of the Indian plants soon brought their adoption by the white colonists. In the South and on the western frontier Indian corn replaced wheat as breadstuff of the American settlers. The productiveness of Indian farming is shown by the comfort in which De Soto's large party of men and animals spent each of their long winter quarters, in Florida, Mississippi, Arkansas, and Louisiana, staying four

6. "First bottom" is the normal flood plain, "second" includes stream terraces and other parts of the thalweg, usually above flood level. The English of Roanoke used creek in the English sense of an inlet of the sea. When English settlements spread inland, from Pennsylvania south, creek became the designation of any stream that was considered smaller than a river.

months and longer in one Indian town, and living well on stored food.

Farming in the Eastern Hardwoods was well supplemented by wild foods—acorns and chestnuts, walnuts in the east, pecans to the west, grapes and plums, mulberries, persimmons, and so on. Food was at hand for man, beast, and fowl in diversity and abundance unknown to Europe. The open woods and their margins were prime habitat of white-tailed deer, black bear, cottontail rabbit, turkey, and other game. "In winter great store of swans and geese," Hariot wrote. The flyways of the Mississippi and along the Atlantic coast were crowded by migrant waterfowl at the onset and end of northern winter. There were oyster beds at the margin of salt water, mussels in the rivers. Runs of anadromous fish supplied weirs built by Indians. "For four months of the year, February, March, April, and May, there are plenty of sturgeons, and also in the same months of herrings" (Hariot), the latter being shad. In bayous and tributaries of the Mississippi catfish, drum, bass, eels, and other fish were taken in weirs, netted, and speared. On the St. Lawrence, both fresh and salt, aquatic life may have provided a greater part of Indian food than did woods or fields.

All the accounts, Spanish, French, and English, agree that the eastern Indians lived well and at ease in a generous land which they used competently and without spoiling it. They lived in permanent villages or towns, in part palisaded, Hochelaga at Montreal being the most elaborate example. Multifamily dwellings seem to have been prevalent. House frames were of timbers, cover of thatch or bark. The Iroquois of the St. Lawrence and the Algonquians of Carolina and Virginia built long houses of Quonset type (figs. 22 and 23), Caddoan tribes west of the Mississippi large domed round houses. Round houses were also found among the Muskogean tribes.

17
European Influences

TRADE

The Pueblos were at the northern periphery of Mesoamerican trade. When the Spaniards came to Mexico they found market places stocked with a great diversity of goods. Cortés and Bernal Díaz wrote their astonishment at seeing the variety and quantity of commodities offered. Professional merchants brought luxury items from distant parts—out of the north the turquoise that was prized throughout Mesoamerica and mainly procured from mines in New Mexico. An Indian merchant thus gave Nuño de Guzmán his first notice of a northern country to become known as New Mexico. The Road to Cibola, as I have called it, was a well-traveled route of commerce between central Mexico, Culiacán, Sonora, Cibola as the Zuñi pueblos were called, and the pueblos of the Rio Grande and Pecos.

Elsewhere there was no record of practice or routes of commerce. Goods that passed from one native people to another were noted as ceremonial exchanges or a giving of gifts such as wampum, copper ornaments, and gourd rattles. The gathering of tribes to share the tuna harvest south of San Antonio was an occasion for some exchange of items, but hardly the beginning of a system of commerce.

The Indian fur trade that later was to be the economic base of French Canada began with the cod fishery, the only profitable European enterprise of the century. It was private enterprise unsupported by governments. Cod fishermen encamped ashore met Indians and found them wearing well-dressed pelts. An offer of a pointed or edged piece of metal, bright cloth, or glass beads might be accepted in exchange for a fur. The codders returned in another year with trade goods. The Indians began to trap more furs than they needed for their own use to acquire things previously unknown to them.

The spread of the new trade about the northeastern shores had only occasional notice. Basque trading ships brought word of the Fagundes colony, thought to have been located on the Bay of Fundy. When Verrazzano visited Narragansett Bay in 1524 he found the natives uninterested in European goods, but when he reached the *mala gente* (on the Maine coast?) he found them to be sharp traders knowing what they wanted of metal ware. He had crossed on his way north, it is inferred, to shores visited by trading ships. Cartier, coming into Chaleur Bay in the summer of 1534, was met by Indians trooping to the shore with loads of furs. This was at the west of the Gulf of St. Lawrence, five hundred miles in from the Atlantic coast, and it was at the time of midsummer heat. These Indians had come to associate sails with Europeans who desired peltry and they were ready and waiting. There is occasional later mention of merchant ships, as at St. John's, their business not stated.

When French settlement of Acadia began, early in the next century, the mainland Indians were already addicted to alcohol, according to Denys, an early historian of Acadia. The implication is that cod fisherman engaged in the fur trade introduced the natives to strong drink, before then unknown in northern America.

SLAVE TRADE

The Corte Real voyage of 1501 brought a cargo of Indians—men, women, and children—from Newfoundland, thought to be Beothuks. The King of Portugal was pleased at the prospect of an additional source of slaves, Portugal having found a major source of profit in the African slave trade. The expectation, however, was not realized. In 1525 Gómez, at the end of his search for a western passage, took a lot of Indians taken in Newfoundland waters to sell in Spain. These probably were Algonquians of New England or Nova Scotia. When Gilbert visited Newfoundland in 1583 Hayes reported that there were no natives left in the southern part of the island, these timid people having retired to the safety of the interior.

Spanish interest in Florida began with Ponce de León in 1513. The Bahama Islands having been depopulated to supply labor in Española and Puerto Rico, he went from the latter island to hunt slaves in Florida, and was driven out. In 1521 two ships were sent from the north coast of Española to the Chicora coast of South Carolina, where the natives were invited to visit on board and then made off with, one ship being lost at sea, the other losing part of its human cargo.

INDIAN INTERMEDIARIES OF
EUROPEAN CULTURE

The Spanish Crown and some of its officials accepted in all seriousness the obligation to bring the Christian faith to heathen lands. Vázquez de Ayllón, judge of the Audiencia of Santo Domingo, at the time the governing body overseas, was a partner in the slaving venture to Chicora and received a young Indian as part of his return. The Indian, known as Francisco Chicora, captivated and dominated his master. Ayllón took him to Spain where he enjoyed attention at court and gave Peter Martyr large and fanciful account of his land and people. Ayllón decided that he would found a Christian colony in the land Chicora had described. Member of the Order of St. James, he was given government of the northern mainland to take Dominicans as missionaries, restore Francisco and other Indians to their homeland, and settle Spaniards. Shortly after they landed on the mainland Francisco and his fellow Indians ran away, not to be heard of again.

The defection of Chicora was repeated later in Virginia. A young Indian from the north was brought to Luis de Velasco, Viceroy of New Spain. He lived in the viceroy's household and became a Christian, and was later known by the name of the viceroy as Don Luis de Velasco. He was treated with respectful attention during his stays in Spain and in Havana. Don Luis became companion and confidant of Menéndez de Avilés and largely was responsible for the plan to establish a mission and way station in his homeland on Chesapeake Bay. He led the Jesuit fathers there and took leave of them, promising to bring back supplies and his people for Christian instruction. When he did return it was to kill the Christians.

Both Indians had been adopted into Spanish society, had been treated as important persons, and professed themselves zealous Christians. Both led a Spanish party to their native land. Chicora ran away, Don Luis came back to massacre the fathers.

Spanish Dominicans, Jesuits, and Franciscans—missionaries from southern Florida to the Sea Islands—all failed; some were martyred. They did not come to represent the force of Spanish arms; where such violence was used there is no evidence that they approved of it. They brought a new religion that would have displaced the old ways. The native cultures rejected radical reordering of life. The natives remained unconverted or, like Francisco and Don Luis, simulated the adoption of an alien faith and conduct.

The French did not undertake to proselytize the natives in either Canada or Florida, in part perhaps because, being largely Protestant, they avoided the religious tensions of France. Cartier took two sons of the chief of Stadacona from his first voyage to be trained as interpreters. They returned with Cartier, unbaptized, and were good intermediaries. Occasionally Indians visited France later on ships in the Newfoundland trade.[1]

The first English visit to Roanoke took back two Indian youths to learn English speech and customs. They returned home the next year with the party that intended to make a settlement. It is to be inferred that they gave Hariot a good deal of the specific information which he put into his report, particularly as to religious beliefs and government and things he did not see. Also that when he "made declaration of the contents of the Bible," which he thought was well received by the natives, he must have done so through such interpreters.

EUROPEANS AS GUESTS, SETTLERS, AND PREDATORS

Europeans were received everywhere with hospitality, except where the natives had reason to fear ill. Ponce de León and later De Soto alerted the Indians to the Florida Gulf coast to

1. Trudel, *Histoire de la Nouvelle-France*, vol. I, p. 215.

the danger that came by ships. Verrazzanno's *mala gente* were people who had become wary of traders. The Zuñi who tried to keep Coronado out of the pueblo knew that men such as these who came out of the south with strange arms and on horseback had been engaged in hunting people in southern Sonora. Zuñis living along the great north-south trade route and taking part in that trade cannot have remained ignorant of years of devastation by Guzmán's men in Sinaloa and Sonora.

European settlement as such raised no objections. Ayllón moved his colonists to the Savannah River among the Guale without starting trouble. Cartier was assisted by Dohnacona's people when he built his fortified camp nearby. This sort of cooperation again took place when the French built Fort Caroline in Florida. The two lost colonies, the Portuguese in Nova Scotia and the English on Roanoke, were at peace with their neighbors when last heard of. There is no evidence that they were destroyed by natives; an Indian tradition held that the English colony was absorbed into an Indian tribe.

The two large and long expeditions of De Soto and Coronado were predatory by intent and conduct. The Tiguex pueblos on the Rio Grande were badly hurt during the first winter spent there by the Coronado party. On the other hand, the excursion to Quivira was without violence, and was freely supplied with Indian provisions and guides.[2]

De Soto used the tactics of terror he had learned in Panama and Peru, which Oviedo summarized in a bitter epitaph. The desolation was still apparent twenty years later when the Luna party found ruined towns, abandoned fields, and hunger.

The herd of swine that De Soto brought from Cuba to be driven from the landing at Tampa Bay to the embarkation on the Mississippi River was an incidental legacy to the natives. The Gentleman of Elvas told that at the point of departure on the Mississippi below Natchez they were brought pigs that Indian women had raised. Twenty-five years after De Soto marched north from Tampa the French reported wild hogs as a game animal of Florida. The long-legged range hog of Extremadura became the razorback of the South.

2. Melchor Díaz, when sent to the Lower Colorado, engaged in hunting Indians as he had been accustomed to do when he was alcalde at Culiacán.

INTRODUCTION OF DISEASE

The coming of Europeans was followed by mass sickness among the natives, sometimes noted as an outbreak of fever. Because smallpox and measles were well known and not mentioned, the epidemics that affected the Indians may have been mainly respiratory infections brought by the visitors.

The castaways of the Narváez expedition spent the winter in Indian camps about Galveston Bay. They arrived in bad shape. The winter was hard and they suffered sickness and death and during the winter half the local Indian population was reported to have died. In the fall of 1535 the four survivors crossed the Tularosa Basin of New Mexico, accompanied by a host of Indians who had gathered from distant and different parts. An outbreak of sickness halted the march; more than three hundred being stricken and many dying.

Cartier built his winter quarters of 1535 near the Indian town Stadacona in order to have convenient communication with the friendly natives. In December there was a great sickness at Stadacona, with more than fifty Indians dying. Shortly thereafter scurvy developed among the French; Cartier mistook this as contagion from the sick Indians and therefore put a stop to contact between the two peoples. By thus cutting off the supply of fresh meat and fish which the Indians had been bringing, the French suffered increased scurvy. The mass sickening of the Indians had come with the onset of winter, when they were congregated within the village, and subject to the spread of a new contagion.

When De Soto visited the Creek towns about the middle Savannah River he found some of them abandoned because of an earlier pestilence. Their mortuary temples and corncribs were intact, so the Spaniards helped themselves to pearls from the cadavers and maize from the cribs. The Ayllón colony had been located a hundred miles down river among another Creek tribe and when it broke up some Spaniards drifted inland. The great pestilence up country from the Ayllón colony indicates its source in the latter.

Thomas Hariot attributed to Providence the high Indian mortality about Roanoke that he witnessed:

There was no town where we had any subtile device practiced against us, we leaving it unpunished or not revenged (because we sought by all means possible to win them by gentleness) but that within a few days after our departure from every such town, the people began to die very fast, and many in short space, in some towns about twenty, in some forty, and in one six score, which in truth was very many in respect to their numbers. This happened in no place that we could learn but where we had been where they used such practice against us, and after such time. The disease also was so strange, that they neither knew what it was, nor how to cure it, the like by report of the oldest men in the country never happened before, time out of mind. . . . All the space of their sickness, there was no man of ours known to die, or that was specially sick.

By Spanish, French, and English reports their coming to Indian towns or camps was followed by sickness and death of natives. Twenty years after De Soto the Alabama country, which he had found a land of abundance and of populous towns, lacked people and food. In addition to its practice of outrage, the expedition of De Soto is indicated as most likely to have introduced diseases over a large area, resulting in sharply reduced population.

The observers provided accounts of the nature of the country and its people at the coming of Europeans and told of resulting disturbances. These were not expeditions "into the wilds of North America" as the Congressional resolution of 1937 declared but first experiences of lands occupied and modified by Indian peoples of different cultures. The European parties went by Indian trails, commonly with Indian guides, from one settlement to another, and usually depended on food grown, collected, fished, or hunted by natives.

Throughout the Eastern Woodlands the observers were impressed by the number, size, and good order of the settlements, and by the appearance and civility of the people. These Indians were not seen as untutored savages but as people living in a society of appreciated values. In the West the Pueblo tribes were described as peaceful farmers applying industry and skill to a land severely limited by a short growing season and low rainfall. On the Pacific coast the people of Santa Barbara Channel were appreciated as enjoying an idyllic life. The obverse picture of a miserable life is found mainly in the accounts of the Cabeza de Vaca party while in Texas, somewhat biased by the abasement of hidalgos to the status of servants of primitive collectors.

Occasionally an Indian tribe was said to be an enemy of another, but there was no record of serious hostility such as warring for possession of territory. In Texas bands from different parts shared in the harvest of pecans in the river bottoms and tunas in the great cactus thickets. The buffalo plains were hunted by mobile plains hunters and as well by Pueblo people from the west and Caddoans from the east. Iroquois canoe parties went from their homes in the St. Lawrence Valley to fish and hunt freely along the north of the Gulf of St. Lawrence as far as the Strait of Belle Isle.

When Champlain came to the St. Lawrence Valley in the next century the Iroquois had been replaced by Algonquians and there was deadly enmity between them. In the Southeast of the United States a large relocation of tribes was under way, including advance of Cherokees, as the studies of Swanton have shown. European activities in the sixteenth century may have set the stage for the turbulent century that followed.

List of Works Frequently Cited

ALBA: *Mapas españoles de América*, portfolio in fascimile (Madrid, 1951), under the auspices of the Duke of Alba and Berwick.

BACCHIANI ON VERAZZANO: Alessandro Bacchiani, "Giovanni da Verazzano e le sue scoperte nell'America settentrionale (1524) secondo l'inedito codice sincrono Céllere di Roma," *Bollettino della Reale Società Geografica Italiana*, vol. XLVI (1909).

BAILEY: Liberty Hyde Bailey, *Manual of cultivated plants most commonly grown in the continental United States and Canada*, Rev. ed., (New York, 1949).

BARCIA: Andrés González de Barcia Carballido y Zúñiga, *Ensayo cronologico para la historia general de la Florida* (1723). Republished in Gainsville, Fla. in 1951 with translation and introduction by Anthony Kerrigan.

BIGGAR, PRECURSORS: Henry Percival Biggar, ed., *The Precursors of Jacques Cartier, 1497–1534* (Ottawa, 1911).

BIGGAR, VOYAGES: H. P. Biggar, ed., *The Voyages of Jacques Cartier*, Pubs. Public Archives of Canada, No. 11 (Ottawa, 1924), sources with critical notes and with maps.

BOLTON: Herbert Eugene Bolton, *Coronado on the turquoise trail, knight of the pueblos and plains* (Albuquerque, 1949).

DE BRY: Théodor de Bry. *Collectiones peregrinationum in Indiam Orientalem et Indiam Occidentalem* (Frankfurt, 1590), 9 vols.

CDI: *Colección de documentos inéditos relativos al descubrimiento, conquista, y organización de las antiguas posesiones españolas de América y Oceania* (Madrid, 1864–1884), 42 vols.

CDU: The succeeding series of the same title but ending . . . *posesiones españolas de ultramar* (Madrid, 1885–1932), 25 vols. Two-volume index to both series by Ernst Schafer, *Indice de documentos inéditos de Indias* (Madrid, 1946–1947).

DNB: *The Dictionary of National Biography*, edited by Sir Leslie

306 Works Frequently Cited

Stephen and Sir Sidney Lee, was first published in 1885–1901, in 66 volumes. I have used the 1921–1922 London edition, a reprint of the 22 volume corrected edition of 1908–1909.

ELVAS: A gentleman of Elvas, *Relação verdadeira dos trabalhos que o governador d. Fernando de Souto e certos fidalgos portugueses passaram no descobrimento da provincia da Flórida agora novamente*, originally published at Evora, 1557. I have used the Lisbon, 1940 edition edited by Frederico Gavazzo Perry Vidal.

GAFFAREL: Paul Louis Jacques Gaffarel, *Histoire de la Floride française* (Paris, 1875). Of Laudonnière's letters: the first *L'histoire notable de la Floride*, is reproduced entire, with parts of the second and third, following the edition of 1586; the fourth letter is omitted.

GÓMARA: Francisco López de Gómara, *La historia general de las Indias* (Anvera, 1554), also contained in Vedia's *Historiadores*, vol. I.

GUÉNIN: Eugène Guénin, *Ango et ses pilotes, d'après des documents inèdits, tirés de archives de France, de Portugal et d'Espagne* (Paris, 1901).

HABERT: Jacques Habert, *La vie et les voyages de Jean de Verrazane* (Montreal, 1964).

HAKLUYT, *Navigations*: Richard Hakluyt, *The principal navigations, voyages, traffiques & discoveries of the English nation*, published in part (the voyages to America and the West Indies) in 1582 and in its final, completed form in 1589. I have used the London edition of 1927–1928, in 8 volumes.

HAKLUYT, *Voyages: The voyages, traffiques & discoveries of foreign voyages*, the concluding part of Hakluyt's *Navigations* (vols. IX and X of the London, 1927–1928 edition), contains voyages by foreign, as distinct from English, writers.

HALLENBECK: Cleve Hallenbeck, *Alvar Núñez Cabeza de Vaca; the journey and route of the first European to cross the continent of North America, 1534–1536* (Glendale, Calif., 1940).

HAMMOND AND REY: George Peter Hammond and Agapito Rey, eds., *Narratives of the Coronado expedition, 1540–1542* (Albuquerque, 1940).

HERRERA: Antonio de Herrera y Tordesillas, *Historia general de los hechos de los castellanos, en las islas, y tierra-firme de el Mar Océano* (1601–1615), 4 vols.

HULTON AND QUINN: Paul Hope Hulton and David Beers Quinn, *The American Drawings of John White, 1577–1590* (London, 1964), 2 vols.

JULIEN: Charles André Julien, *Les voyages de découverte et les premiers establissements (XV–XVI siècles)* (Paris, 1948), a history of the expansion of French colonization.

KRETSCHMER: Konrad Kretschmer, *Die Entdeckung Amerikas in ihrer Bedeutung für die Geschichte des Weltbildes* (Berlin, 1892), with atlas.

LEWIS AND LOOMIE: Clifford Merle Lewis and Albert J. Loomie, *The Spanish Jesuit Mission in Virginia, 1570–1572* (Chapel Hill,

1953), with documents, a narrative summary of them, and their translations.

LOWERY: Woodbury Lowery, *The Spanish settlements within the present limits of the United States, 1513–1561* (New York, 1911).

NAVARRETE: Martín Fernández de Navarrete, *Colección de los viages y descubrimientos que hicieron por mar los Españoles desde fines del siglo XV* (Madrid, 1825–1837), 3 vols.

OVIEDO: Gonzalo Fernández de Oviedo y Valdés, *Historia general y natural de las Indias;* had a partial publication in 1535 and 1547, but was not printed in complete form until 1851–1855 in Madrid.

PETER MARTYR: Pietro Martire d'Angleria published *De Orbe Novo* beginning in 1511 as Latin reports on the New World that he continued to 1525. I have found the Spanish translation by Joaquin Torres Asensio (Madrid, 1892 and republished in Buenos Aires, 1944) most satisfactory, checking occasionally with the Latin. A creditable edition has also been published by Edmundo O'Gorman (Mexico City, 1964)

PORT. MON. CART.: *Portugaliae Monumenta Cartographica*, Armando Cortesão and Avelino Teixeira da Mota (Lisbon, 1960), 6 vols. A monumental collection of maps done by Portuguese Cartographers, superbly reproduced and published by the Government of Portugal. The text by Armando Cortesão is a masterly study of cartographers, their works and their location in libraries.

QUINN: David Beers Quinn, ed., *The Roanoke Voyages, 1584–1590* (London, 1955), collected documents related to the English voyages to North America under the patent granted to Walter Raleigh in 1584, published by the Hakluyt Society.

RIBAULT: Jean Ribault, *The whole and true discoverye of Terra Florida,* facsimile reprint of the London edition of 1563 (DeLand, Fla., 1927).

DE LA RONCIÈRE: Charles Germain Marie Bourel de la Roncière, *La Floride française, scènes de la vie indigènes, peintes en 1564 [par Jacques Le Moyne de Morgues]* (Paris, 1928), with atlas of hand-colored reproductions of Morgues' plates.

SANTA CRUZ: Alonso de Santa Cruz, Cosmógrafo Mayor, *Die Karten von Amerika in dem Islario general,* ca. 1541, published with maps by Franz R. v. Wieser (Innsbruck, 1908).

STEFANSSON: Vilhjalmur Stefansson, ed., *The three voyages of Martin Frobisher in search of a passage to Cathay and India by the north-west, A. D. 1576–8,* edited from the original text of George Best (London, 1938), with maps.

SWANTON: John Reed Swanton, *The Indians of the South-eastern United States* (Washington, 1946).

TAYLOR: Eva G. R. Taylor, ed., *A brief summe of geographie, by Roger Barlow,* a translation of Martín Fernández de Enciso's *Suma de geographia,* printed in London in 1932 for the Hakluyt Society.

TRUDEL: Marcel Trudel, *Histoire de la Nouvelle-France,* volume I, *Les vaines tentatives, 1524–1603* (Montreal, 1963), of superior merit, including its historical geography.

U.S. DE SOTO COMM.: U.S. De Soto Commission, *Final Report of the United States De Soto Expedition Commission* (Washington, 1939), Seventy-sixth Congress, 1st session, House Doc. 71.

VEDIA: Enrique de Vedia, ed., *Historiadores primitivos de Indias* (Madrid, 1852–1853), 2 vols. Included in volume I are Gómara's *Historia general de las Indias* and *Naufragios* by Cabeza de Vaca.

VELASCO: Juan López de Velasco, *Geografía y descripción universal de las Indias, recopilada . . . desde el año de 1571 al de 1574,* first published in 1894 by the Sociedad Geográfica de Madrid.

VIGNERAS: L. A. Vigneras, "New Light on the 1497 Cabot Voyage to America," *Hispanic American Historical Review,* XXXVI, no. 4 (November, 1956).

WAGNER: *Cabrillo:* Henry Raup Wagner, *Juan Rodríguez, discoverer of the coast of California* (San Francisco, 1941).

WAGNER, Cartography: H. R. Wagner, *The cartography of the northwest coast of America to the year 1800* (Berkley, 1937).

WAGNER, Drake: H. R. Wagner, *Sir Francis Drake's voyage around the world; its aims and achievements* (San Francisco, 1926).

WAGNER, Spanish voyages: H. R. Wagner, *Spanish voyages to the northwest coast of America in the sixteenth century* (San Francisco, 1929).

WALDSEEMÜLLER: Waldseemüller's two world maps are reproduced in *Die älteste Karte mit dem Namen Amerika aus dem Jahre 1507* with an introduction by Josef Fischer and Franz von Wieser (Innsbruck, 1903).

WILLIAMSON: James Alexander Williamson, *The Cabot voyages and Bristol discovery under Henry VII,* published for the Hakluyt Society (Cambridge, Eng., 1962), with maps.

WINSHIP: George Parker Winship, *The Coronado Expedition, 1540–1542,* 14th Annual Report of the U.S. Bureau of American Ethnology, 1892–1893 (Washington, 1896).

Index

309